Frontier Military Series
XXXVI

ROAD *to* WAR

The 1871 Yellowstone Surveys

Edited by
M. John Lubetkin

THE ARTHUR H. CLARK COMPANY
An imprint of the University of Oklahoma Press
Norman, Oklahoma
2016

Also by M. John Lubetkin

Jay Cooke's Gamble: The Northern Pacific Railroad, the Sioux, and the Panic of 1873
Custer and the 1873 Yellowstone Survey: A Documentary History
Custer's Gold
Union College's Class of 1868: The Unique Experiences of Some "Average" Americans
Before Custer: Surveying the Yellowstone, 1872

Library of Congress Cataloging-in-Publication Data

Names: Lubetkin, M. John, editor.
Title: Road to war : the 1871 Yellowstone surveys / edited by M. John Lubetkin.
Other titles: Eighteen seventy one Yellowstone surveys | 1871 Yellowstone surveys
Description: Norman, Oklahoma : The Arthur H. Clark Company, [2016] | Includes bibliographical references and index.
Identifiers: LCCN 2016012938 | ISBN 978-0-87062-429-2 (hardcover : alk. paper)
Subjects: LCSH: Yellowstone National Park—Description and travel. | Geological surveys —Yellowstone National Park. | Northern Pacific Railroad Company—History | Irvine, Javan B. (Javan Bradley), 1831–1904—Correspondence. | Yellowstone National Park—History—19th century—Sources.
Classification: LCC F722 .R625 2016 | DDC 978.7/52—dc23
LC record available at http://lccn.loc.gov/2016012938

Road to War: The 1871 Yellowstone Surveys
is Volume 36 in the Frontier Military Series.

The paper in this book meets the guidelines for permanence and durability
of the Committee on Production Guidelines for Book Longevity
of the Council on Library Resources, Inc. ∞

1 2 3 4 5 6 7 8 9 10

To

William Andrew Lubetkin

A Northern Pacific Railroad

Those enterprising and popular capitalists, Messrs. JAY COOKE & CO., have determined to direct the construction of a railroad to connect Lake Superior with Puget Sound. The undertaking is a great, laudable and feasible one—one that will prove remunerative to the projectors and beneficial to the country. Messrs. COOKE & CO. are now preparing the means needed for the successful prosecution of this great enterprise. That this firm will make the undertaking a success cannot be doubted.

PHILADELPHIA INQUIRER

JUNE 6, 1869

Contents

Appendices

Illustrations

Figures

Maps

Tables

Introduction

The Sioux Indian wars, an on-again, off-again affair between 1853 and 1877, ultimately represented the last "independence" for the largest remaining body of Indians attempting to follow their traditional way of life. By the 1870s a handful of Sioux grandfathers could remember their grandfathers telling them about the arrival of horses and, in turn, that *their* grandfathers had been young boys when muskets first became available from New France (Canada). In little more than 150 years, people representing a culture devoid of metallurgy found themselves facing an aggressive race that traveled year-round over land and water by steam-powered equipment.[1] This race was armed with rifled cannon, repeating revolvers and rifles, primitive machine guns, and a telegraph that carried messages as fast as today.[2] Worse, these men had developed significant immunity to or defenses from many of the same microbes (especially smallpox) that, in less than four centuries, killed millions of Native residents in every corner of North and Central America.

The roots of this volume extend back to the late summer of 1831, which saw the initial run of regularly scheduled railroad service between Albany and Schenectady, New York, by the state-chartered Mohawk & Hudson Railroad. The railroad's purpose was strictly economic, to save time lost in the forty miles of Albany-Schenectady water travel (including more than two dozen locks) that could take days to traverse. The initial track did not actually connect the two cities; 1831 engineering could not surmount the grades along the Hudson at Albany or where Schenectady met the Mohawk. In fact, the railroad's sole purpose was to serve travelers,

[1]In short, without metallurgy it was a Stone Age culture.

[2]The transmission speed is the same. What is very different is the uploading and retrieval process.

for then the transfer of freight was never considered. For many years the state would not permit this, only later allowing freight to be carried in winter when the Erie Canal froze. Not until the early 1840s would rail vs. canal competition for freight be permitted.

On September 25, 1831, diarist and former New York City mayor Philip Hone wrote after riding the DeWitt Clinton, "We returned [to Albany on] the American locomotive, twelve and a half miles in thirty-seven minutes, which is at the rate of twenty miles an hour,—quite fast enough in all conscience, and exceedingly pleasant."[3] Compared to physically bruising, often harrowing trips by stage, travel over railed road—stage coach carriages mounted on wheels—was a joy whether pulled by locomotives or horses

Writing just six months later on his way from New York to Washington, D.C., Hone reached New Castle, Delaware, where "we were transferred to the railroad. . . . [It] is just finished, and is an excellent substitute for the bad roads which travelers had formerly to encounter. . . . The cars are new, very handsome, and commodious, and are drawn at present by horses."[4]

For the next fifteen years Hone reported on the development of transportation across the central and northern portions of the United States. He recorded new trackage, engineering permitting reasonable speeds around curves, new bridges, larger capacity engines, and more and larger passenger cars per train. Each year saw the reduction in time and inconvenience between cities. At first gradually and then with a rush, railroads pushed canal traffic aside, first taking their passengers away and then most of their freight. In fact, the growth of railroads was staggering, none of it arithmetically greater than in the eight years after the Civil War when the nation's railroad capacity doubled from some 35,000 miles of track to more than 70,000 (see table on page 83).

Less than thirty-eight years after Hone's DeWitt Clinton ride, on May 10, 1869, champagne toasts were given and church bells rang across the

---

[3] *The Diary of Philip Hone,* September 25, 1831. Wikipedia gives an opening date of September 24, while the *Encyclopedia of North American Railroads* states that it was August 10, 1831. Hone's diary seems to indicate that his travel was no later than the second day of formal operations. Two other trains carrying passengers had run earlier: in Baltimore (Baltimore and Ohio Railroad) on the Tom Thumb (September 18, 1830), and December in Charleston, South Carolina. However, these were more tests versus regularly scheduled operations.

[4] *The Diary of Philip Hone,* March 14, 1832.

nation because the Union Pacific and the Central Pacific railroads had met northwest of Salt Lake City. The newly completed transcontinental railroad now linked the oceans with daily, multidirectional passenger and freight service. The tide of settlement had been so rapid that, in 1869, a handful of people could still remember the seemingly miraculous return of Lewis and Clark from their transcontinental trek sixty-three years earlier.

For Lewis and Clark, careful planning, discipline, and exceptionally good luck had seen to their survival.[5] For almost two and a half years, they had survived an often inhospitable climate and narrowly avoided sustained Indian fighting. Included in Lewis and Clark's report was the identification of what they regarded as a nasty, warlike tribe, the Sioux. In the decades to come, across the Great Plains and west to the Pacific, scores of other tribes would be met and decimated by disease and in battle. Nevertheless, the widely spread Sioux and their Northern Cheyenne and Arapaho allies, despite being pushed from much of their Dakota and Nebraska hunting grounds, remained a force to be considered in post–Civil War planning.

Regarding the Sioux and their allies, the military, government, and clergy were unanimous in their view that these American natives deserved no independent future. Yet how this would play out within the boundaries of professed Christian beliefs was unclear. Fortunately for the Indian, the final decisions would be left to Ulysses S. Grant, who had opposed the Mexican War, as well as being against the annexation of Cuba and western Canada. Ironically, the general who had defeated Robert E. Lee in 1865 was shy, socially reticent, and had a decidedly nonbellicose personality.

By 1870–71 more than half the Teton or Lakota Sioux were living on reservations along the Missouri River in Dakota and Montana territories, the buffalo so few that without government assistance they would have starved. Even Red Cloud, victor in the Bozeman Trail War of the 1860s, reluctantly accepted reservation life and American hegemony. For chiefs who visited the Great White Father in Washington, trains took them through cities with combined populations in the millions, an understandably demoralizing experience. Only one group refused to accept the overwhelming odds against independence: a relative handful

[5]For example, could anything have been more foolish than taking a canoe through the Columbia River's rapids, something that Native tribes avoided?

of Teton Sioux, Northern Cheyenne, and Arapaho, the followers of the warrior and spiritual leader Sitting Bull, a Hunkpapa Teton Sioux.

Each year buffalo herds further shrank. Other than solitary bull outcasts, few remained in western Dakota, eastern Montana, and northeastern Wyoming territories by the 1870s. Certainly it is speculative how long Sitting Bull's followers or indeed any of the other semi-independent tribes—Crows, Flatheads, Nez Perce, Métis (mixed-blood Canadians), and others—might have continued their lives based on hunting.

In addition to all this, another ominous development was inaugurated on January 1, 1870. Men in Philadelphia signed an agreement calling for the financing and construction of a second transcontinental railroad. Over three-fourths of the Yellowstone River would be followed from present-day Glendive to Livingston, Montana. The effect would be to further cut off and reduce, once and for all, the dwindling buffalo herds and those who depended on them.

This study, then, *Road to War: The 1871 Yellowstone Surveys,* the chronological first of three volumes,[6] is the story of the Northern Pacific Railroad and its efforts to construct the nation's second transcontinental railroad and what Sitting Bull's followers did and did not do to block it.

---

[6]M. John Lubetkin, *Custer and the 1873 Yellow Survey* (2013) and *Before Custer: The 1872 Yellowstone Surveys* (2015), both University of Oklahoma Press publications.

PART I

The Northern Pacific Railroad

CHAPTER I

The Northern Pacific Is Launched

The Northern Pacific Railroad, headquartered in New York and operated from St. Albans, Vermont, was created as part of the Pacific Railway Act of 1864.[1] The company was a wartime sop to New England and northwestern states that felt that they would be shut out by the Sacramento-to-Omaha route of the transcontinental railroad. Unlike the first transcontinental railroad act (1862), the 1864 act was generous in giving away "empty" land—some 50 million acres (about equal to New England and Long Island)—but provided no financial incentives or guarantees as it had for the Union Pacific and Central Pacific's transcontinental efforts.

The actual grant was open-ended, but subject to completed federally certified miles. The acres were allocated in a checkerboard pattern parallel to the road.[2] Track would stretch from Lake Superior to Puget Sound, with the assumption being that a community on St. Louis Bay (Superior, Wisconsin, or Duluth, Minnesota) would be one starting point, Tacoma or Seattle, Washington Territory, the other.[3] The route was estimated at 2,000 plus or minus 50 miles, although most of Washington, Idaho, Montana, and Dakota had never been examined for railroad construction.

---

[1]The Southern Pacific completed its transcontinental route a month earlier, in August 1883.

[2]In territories the Northern Pacific was granted 25,200 acres per mile of certified track, but track length varied by the route chosen: X under one option, X + 25 under a second—a difference of 630,000 acres (926 square miles). Also, because of overlapping land grants such as the St. Paul and Pacific, nobody actually knew how many acres had been granted, with estimates ranging from 47 to 60 million. My 50 million–acre estimate is based on the final construction. For land grants, see Middletown et al., *Encyclopedia of North American Railroads*, 581–82. For Northern Pacific grants, see Crutchfield, *The Settlement of America: Encyclopedia of Western Expansion*, 373.

[3]In September 1873, the Northern Pacific chose Tacoma.

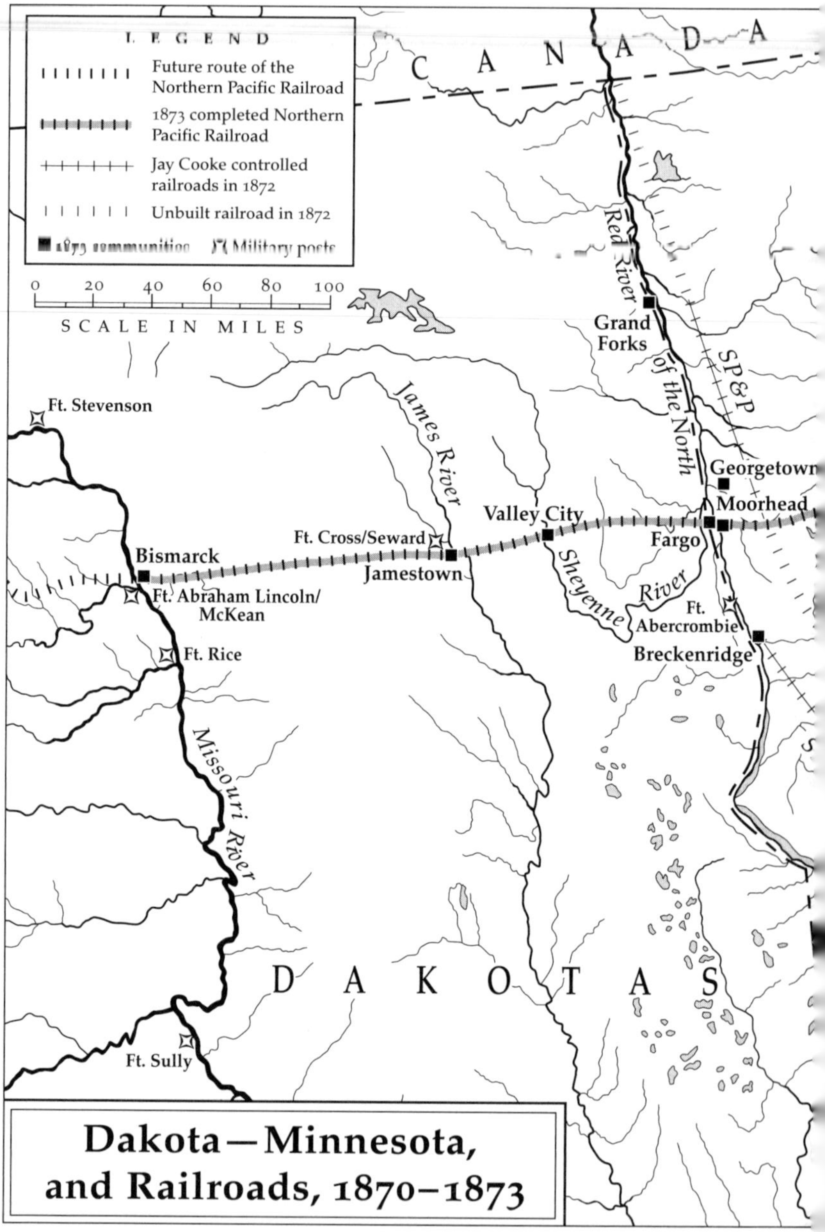

Dakota—Minnesota, and Railroads, 1870–1873

Map by Vicki Trego Hill adapted from an 1883 Northern Pacific Railroad map courtesy of author's collection. *Copyright © 2006 by the University of Oklahoma Press, Norman. All rights reserved.*

The most important thing to realize was that the Northern Pacific made absolutely no business sense in 1864 or even 1870. The blunt Cornelius Vanderbilt correctly described the Northern Pacific as a railroad that "ran from nowhere to nowhere."[4] Certainly no large American railroad was less rooted in financial logic. No large cities were connected, and the railroad's route contained not a single community above 10,000.[5]

The planned track ran through 250 miles of Minnesota with fewer than 10,000 white people within 50 miles of it.[6] From Brainerd, Minnesota, to Bozeman, Montana, the line crossed 900 "vacant" miles excepting army posts, a few trappers, and Indian traders. Montana numbers were slightly better; over half of its 21,000 people lived within 50 miles of planned track. From Missoula, the railroad took a 415-mile triangular route before reaching the Columbia–Snake River junction near Oregon. Excepting Walla Walla (1870 population 1,394), these miles were unsettled. In short, despite significant gold and silver strikes in Montana and Idaho, and the large Canadian fur trade, the land contained less than one person every 20 square miles; nowhere near the 600,000 skyrocketing population of California and Nevada.

Then why, the reader should ask, did Northern Pacific construction begin in 1870? Why not wait until the frontier had pushed farther west and hostile Indian tribes had disappeared?[7] The answer, in fact, came from a man who literally believed he was "God's chosen instrument." Just as he had helped save the Union through the sale of war bonds, Jay Cooke (1821–1905) believed he had been selected to "build" the railroad. This was no cinema-mythical Iowa cornfield where a farmer is "told" to build a baseball field and "they will come." This was to be the longest railroad in the United States and possibly the entire world (Trans-Siberian construction was still twenty years away), and Jay Cooke, the "Financier of the Civil War," felt God was pointing the way for him.[8]

---

[4]"Interview with . . . Vanderbilt," *New York Herald,* September 19, 1873.

[5]Portland, Oregon (1870 population 8,293), was not on the original route.

[6]Indian populations and military posts are excluded.

[7]Disease and overhunting doomed the buffalo, especially the Indians' practice of concentrating on younger female buffalo in their hunting.

[8]Cooke literally believed that he was "God's chosen instrument." His lifelong interest and association with the Northwest, coupled with Grant's not selecting him in 1869, meant only one thing: he would finance the Northern Pacific. See chapter 1 of my book *Jay Cooke's Gamble.* Summary information on Cooke is found in most encyclopedias focusing on business, Civil War, railroad, and western history.

Cooke could not have existed today. Slightly mad by current standards and clearly eccentric 150 years ago, he was nevertheless a hugely successful banker who as a teenager had arrived penniless in Philadelphia from Sandusky, Ohio. By skill, common sense, and hard work—and never resorting to the ethically dubious—he made a small fortune before the Civil War. After the war began, the super-patriotic Cooke began selling war bonds to the rich, realized he had a formula, and in 1862 began selling to the middle class. By war's end he had raised over one quarter of every dollar spent without a hint of dishonesty.[9]

But with Cooke's sales commissions miniscule, how did he obtain his sudden wealth? Cooke had access to military information before any other banker. He knew when to buy or sell. As his success mounted, more insiders banked with and fed him information. By 1865 Cooke was America's leading banker, one of its richest men, and venerated by the public and military alike.

Cooke, who was exceptionally youthful looking until his mid-forties, was nevertheless stubborn and doctrinaire—not surprising qualities from one who believes he is obeying God's will. After one two-hour meeting with him in 1862, Lincoln avoided him whenever possible.[10] In his unpublished autobiography, Cooke told the story of how, speaking to a congressional committee, he actually stood during his testimony and chastised the congressmen, waving his finger at them like an Old Testament prophet. It was something unusual then and impossible to contemplate today, but it nicely illustrated the power he commanded.[11]

Nevertheless, by 1869 Cooke was bored simply making money. He wanted and needed intellectual challenges. With Grant's 1868 election Cooke, who felt he was close to the president-elect, appears to have assumed—like many others—that he would be selected treasury secretary.[12] Then on March 5 came a bombshell: Grant's nominee was a dry goods merchant. I believe that Grant passed over Cooke because, since God trumped Grant, Cooke couldn't be counted on as a "team player."

---

[9]My ballpark estimate is about 27.5 percent, to say nothing of the assistance he gave to states and other war bond sellers.

[10]"Jay Cooke's Memoir," 35–36, 107; Sandburg, *Abraham Lincoln: The War Years,* 2:602.

[11]The legislation Cooke was supporting failed.

[12]Cooke "loaned" Grant an unknown amount of money before the '68 election. He was also a subscriber—one may assume a large one—to a businessmen's fund that purchased a home for Grant after the war.

Had Grant selected Cooke, the Northern Pacific would have quietly disappeared, becoming little more than a historical footnote. There would have been no Yellowstone surveys and, in turn, Sitting Bull's followers would have lived in relative peace until their ecological world imploded. While Yellowstone National Park had just been "discovered," without Cooke's pushing it through Congress, it would have been years or decades before—if ever—it became a national park. And George Custer, sitting in Grant's doghouse? He would not necessarily have disappeared from sight, but he might not have reemerged until the Spanish-American War. And, without Cooke, it's difficult to conceive of large-scale northern European immigration in the 1870s and '80s.

What *did* happen was that Yellowstone became our first national park; warfare with the Sioux broke out; millions of acres in Minnesota, Dakota, Montana, and central Washington were converted to agriculture; and Scandinavian, German, and Russian migration began. For Canada, the British secured the financing for its transcontinental road, linking Vancouver to Halifax every bit as securely as San Francisco to New York.

* * *

Within a month of Grant's decision, Cooke was cautiously approached by Northern Pacific president John Gregory Smith (1818–91). Smith combined an attractive personality, an especially strong education for his era (University of Vermont, Yale Law School), and a tendency to make quick decisions. He became Vermont's two-term war governor and its leading Republican figure for three decades. In 1851 his father took over the Vermont Central Railroad (VC) on a fluke, after selling his tiny feeder railroad to the larger VC under an agreement that stipulated that if certain annual obligations couldn't be paid, Smith would take over. Between the president's fraudulent expense accounts and the treasurer's selling stock that he printed himself, Smith Sr. took possession. Then father and son cooked the books for a decade, fighting off lawsuits until the war began. After his father's 1858 death, Smith gradually grew the VC. By purchasing a feeder line here, building a dozen miles there, VC became one of the nation's top ten railroad systems, reaching 734 miles in 1871.[13]

[13]For Smith see R. C. Jones, *The Central Vermont Railway*, 83; Frey, *Encyclopedia of American Business History and Biography*, 365–66; *Dictionary of American Biography* (*DAB*). The Smith-Cooke relationship is a major category in Larson's and Oberholtzer's biographies of Cooke.

Like so many New Englanders, Smith looked west. If railroads excited him, the construction of a *northern* transcontinental railroad was his holy grail. Smith played a key role—as a Republican governor he was in a position to do so—in the maneuvering that led to Lincoln's signing the legislation creating the Northern Pacific. A year later Smith became the Northern Pacific's president when its founder, Josiah Perham, resigned after failing to raise money, all records fortuitously destroyed in an office fire. Besides the Northern Pacific and politics, Smith managed his Vermont Central and a railroad equipment manufacturing company on a hands-on basis, looked after his St. Albans hotel, newspaper, and two banks, and fulfilled his Episcopalian leadership obligations. Smith's two banks are of singular interest, becoming the 1864 target of the Great St. Albans Bank Raid by Confederate irregulars. Smith, then governor, lost over $125,000 in cash and securities, recovering only some of the money. In hindsight, it appears that he never fully regained his financial equilibrium—with disastrous, compounding consequences when Northern Pacific's construction began.[14]

After the war Smith also failed at raising ample money for the Northern Pacific. Although directors and friends contributed $250,000, progress dragged. Smith hired the respected but aging railroad engineer Edwin F. Johnson (1803–72), a longtime northern transcontinental advocate. Johnson's 1867 contribution was a "practical" route, a distillation of previous Corps of Engineers studies, but his 1,775-mile estimate proved 15 percent too low, illustrating how little was actually known.[15]

By 1867 Northern Pacific surveying began in Minnesota west from Thompson Junction. Minnesota's surveyors were led by Ira Spaulding (1818–75), a well-known and thoroughly able wartime combat engineer.[16] Spaulding, however, had been badly wounded in 1862 and like so many others he continued to suffer, seldom appearing in the field. To what extent Spaulding had real influence in selecting the Northern Pacific's final route across Minnesota is unknown, but I believe it unlikely.[17]

With Cooke's interest and the success of initial 1869 negotiations, Northern Pacific activity dramatically increased. In Minnesota some

[14]For the St. Albans Raid and bank robbery, see *Jay Cooke's Gamble*, 309n17.

[15]Johnson's estimate; Smalley, *History of the Northern Pacific Railroad*, 149–50.

[16]For Spaulding see Hunt, *Brevet Generals in Blue*, and Malles, *Bridge Building in Wartime*.

[17]With Spaulding's 1872 "resignation," the surveyors chipped in to buy him an expensive gold watch—a Rolex by today's standards. It is unknown whether Spaulding was involved in 1870–71's graft, but some thought he was.

$25,000 was spent on a mostly public relations junket that included authors (one book resulted), newspapermen, possible investors, Minnesota's governor William Marshall, and the (likely) husband-hunting daughters of some participants.[18] When this "survey" reached the Red River, most turned back, although some, Marshall included, went as far as Fort Stevenson on the Missouri, some 275 miles to the northwest.

Additionally important work was conducted at Cooke's request: an "eyeball" survey from Puget Sound to the eastern side of Bozeman Pass.[19] This "reconnaissance" was to ascertain the feasibility of Johnson's route or any other, for that matter. This work was directed by Milnor Roberts, an acclaimed railroad engineer who had previously consulted for Cooke.[20] The group was led by local guides and, as necessary, protected by modest army contingents. If Cooke had harbored any doubts, Roberts's final report that fall erased them.[21] Significantly, it raised the estimated mileage to be built but lowered estimated construction costs to $85.6 million.

Cooke quickly agreed to proceed, and the contract was officially signed January 1, 1870. Such was the confidence in Cooke that railroad historian Robert Riegel would write, "No one doubted but that if Cooke took hold of the project, its success was assured."[22] However, what Cooke did not realize was that Minnesota's route had not been selected. Despite Cooke's enthusiasm quickly becoming known, Smith failed to make decisions that would be critical in 1870. Apparently beset by Vermont Central problems, Smith postponed selecting a final Minnesota route, choosing construction contractors, and ordering ample equipment—strategic errors of the highest magnitude.

---

[18] Coffin, *Seat of Empire*. Charles C. Coffin (1823–96), a wartime correspondent, was a staunch believer in a northern transcontinental road, and for 230 pages he praises the route's potential. More interesting is the book's dedication to Smith, "Governor of Vermont during the Rebellion, whom I first saw tenderly caring for the sick and wounded in the hospitals of Fredericksburg."

[19] It is unclear whether Cooke or the Northern Pacific paid for this group. Called Bozeman's Pass in the 1870s.

[20] The team included Edwin Johnson, Jr. (his father was too frail to travel); Thomas Canfield, a Smith business associate who later claimed the group's leadership; Sam Wilkeson, a nationally known wartime correspondent and the Northern Pacific's secretary (but more loyal to Cooke than Smith); and William Moorhead's son. Complete with Indian scares, this story would make a fascinating short book.

[21] W. Milnor Roberts's 1869 *Special Report of a Reconnaissance*; Thomas H. Canfield's 1889 autobiography, *Life of Thomas Hawley Canfield*.

[22] Riegel, *The Story of Western Railroads*, 122.

Until 1870, Smith's record was one of continual success, his problems invariably caused by events beyond his control. Yet his railroad experience had been on a small stage, and he had suffered few defeats from which to learn. Smith had never faced well-financed, knowledgeable business competition or the management problems associated with large-scale construction. Intelligent, but apparently unaware of his limitations; ambitious, but not having sufficient time for all his endeavors, Smith, like the public, vastly overrated Cooke's wealth.

* * *

Northern Pacific groundbreaking ceremonies occurred February 15, 1870, in a snow-covered Minnesota field. Nevertheless, the ceremony was a sham: no real construction began until August. I do not feel I am being overly cynical by speculating that the delay was caused by land speculation motives: the desire for "insider" profits from the development of new communities. The selection of Duluth over Superior is but one example, and then came the all but comical shenanigans that went into selecting Brainerd—literally like the old shell game—which should dispel any thoughts that engineers had a final say.[23] The eventual road, a 250-mile arc swinging south from Duluth to Fargo-Moorhead, might have been 25 miles shorter over easier-to-build terrain. Later Smith wrote to Cooke admitting that "there may have been very grave mistakes in the location of the road," but by then it was far too late.[24] Large speculative profits were made in Duluth, Brainerd (named for Smith's in-laws), smaller communities, and both Fargo (named for William Fargo of Wells Fargo fame and an NP board member) and Moorhead (named for William Moorhead, Cooke's partner and brother-in-law).[25]

Competitive construction bids were not requested until mid-April. After a suspiciously short evaluation period, winners were announced,

[23]Nelson, *The Northern Pacific Railroad in Brainerd,* 9–10.

[24]Harnsberger, *Jay Cooke and Minnesota,* 80.

[25]William G. Moorhead (1811–95) married Cooke's older sister, Sarah. After her death (ca. 1859), Moorhead became increasingly negative and a burden on Cooke, who attempted to find him meaningful work. His 1870 attempt to raise money in England failed miserably, and as chairman of the St. Paul and Pacific's executive committee (1871–72), his strategic decisions doomed the Northern Pacific, directly leading to James J. Hill's Great Northern Railroad. For Moorhead, the only source is Oberholtzer, *Jay Cooke.* One will look in vain at Wikipedia, and my efforts at the New York Public Library and in Moorhead, Minnesota, proved useless. His death notice in two Philadelphia newspapers is perfunctory.

but then the companies had no available work crews. Not until mid-August, with two-thirds of the construction season over, did crews from the just completed St. Paul–Duluth line (Lake Superior & Mississippi Railroad) become available.

Almost immediately, workers were caught flatfooted by Minnesota's swamplands. Minnesota has almost 12,000 lakes over 10 acres in size and an unknown number of smaller ones predominantly located in a 150-mile-wide belt scraped flat by glaciers. Here the gradient per mile was measured in *inches,* not feet, leaving no perceptible movement of ground water. The land was interwoven with soft woods, underbrush, moss, vines, and overhead canopies blocking sunlight. Underneath "solid" ground were invisible networks of faster moving streams; lakes and Tamarack bogs could be crystal clear from bubbling springs or black with foul-smelling, pestilence-ridden standing water. Cornelia Meigs, daughter of a surveyor, wrote:

> Sometimes stretches [of bog were] three to five miles wide, but all . . . [were] depressions in the root entangled ground, filled with black muck which was not water, for no one could swim in it, nor land, for no one could walk upon its surface. . . . [When a] wind blew over it [one] could see great heaving ripples, sinister and unbelievable, go across the surface . . . a dark expanse . . . with stunted evergreens [and] bright insects hovering in the damp air.[26]

If the work was unpleasant, for the few dozen, mostly younger, upper-class surveyors came enjoyment from the physical challenge of being tested by nature. Letters show adventurous humor in the face of life-threatening situations, despite one surveyor's life being lost in a sink-hole.[27] Equipment and supplies were lost or rotted; horses were useless; only lighter Indian ponies could assist at the "front." Campfires were often impossible, and sleep was difficult. Another unhappy discovery: the geography was an ideal breeding ground for flies and mosquitoes in the stagnant water that came with hot, humid summers. This contrasted with winter, when Minnesota is bitterly cold.

Based on the company's pre-1870 surveying, one would have assumed that the Northern Pacific's construction crews knew what they would be facing. However, on a practical basis, there is no reason to believe that contractors were prepared for the problems they would face. In

---

[26] Meigs, *Railroad West,* 12.

[27] January 8, 1906, letter from J. O. Perkins to George Brackett, Brackett Papers, catalog P-1547, Minnesota Historical Society, St. Paul.

April 1870, as if speaking to Northern Pacific officials, respected railroad engineer Benjamin Latrobe, Jr., wrote in the *Railway Gazette:*

> Construction of road bed over *boggy* ground is often an interesting problem for the engineer. . . . [R]ailways crossing our western prairies [in] deep, swampy spots have been successfully crossed by various expedients. The principle on which they all . . . depend begins [in] provid[ing] a wide surface of bearing upon the yielding quagmire which will in fact *float* the superincumbent weight of track and trains [just] as a vessel is buoyed up by the water under and around it.[28]

The basic requirement for heavy ballasting was shoring up the sides with stout wood, best driven by pile drivers. Here the Northern Pacific seems almost criminally negligent, for it purchased only *one* pile driver and *four* steam shovels, the latter of limited use in swamps.[29] In 1870 the railway paid contractors by "certified" track miles. While one assumes there were inspections, with Spaulding frequently ill, how often did he visit and how carefully did he scrutinize the work? Work crews had little incentive to wait for rock to arrive, and all too often, ballasting consisted of trees, brush, soil, and likely even pressed-down leaves. While most remained in place during 1870–71's winter, it should have surprised no one that sections of roadbed sank or entirely disappeared during the spring thaw. Among other disasters, there is the (perhaps) apocryphal story of a locomotive sinking into the muck before finally disappearing.[30]

For the thousands of construction workers, scores died from accidents, complications from amputations, rampant diseases, alcohol, drowning, and freezing weather. Regarding the cold, it is doubtful that either the railroad or contractors had ever considered the risks of constructing the line during the winter months, and the workers paid the price.

⁂ ⁂ ⁂

[28]Latrobe, "Engineering: The Introduction of Railways." Benjamin Latrobe (1806–78) was the son of the Capitol's architect and by midcentury the leading U.S. railroad engineer. Today railroad passengers between Washington and Baltimore still take his bridge across the Patapsco River. See Middletown et al., *Encyclopedia of North American Railroads,* 583–84, and *Dictionary of American Biography.*

[29]The steam shovel was patented in 1839 by William Otis (of elevator fame) and originally designed for railroad construction use.

[30]I could find no confirmation of this story, although it is something the railroad would want covered up. The cover of Cornelia Meigs's *Railroad West* (1937) illustrates the purported incident.

If Smith and his investors were overconfident about construction, the same could not be said concerning hostile Indians. On the Northern Plains perhaps 1,000 warriors still lived nomadically, with additional thousands joining them in more hospitable months.[31] These Indians conducted hit-and-run warfare against civilians and stole horses from the army with impunity. Nevertheless, with the decline and retreat of the buffalo, fewer participated each year.[32] Yet, given their culture of individual courage and bravery, parties of young warriors continually set out to prove their personal worthiness, as often as not by harassing whites. By 1871, large areas of western Dakota and eastern Montana had become a no-man's-land, nominally under "hostile" Indian control but, without buffalo, effectively empty on a day-to-day basis.

Even without the Northern Pacific, it is difficult to believe that the ongoing ecological implosion would not have wiped out the buffalo by the late 1870s. However, this is supposition. The fact of the matter was that in 1871 there was still the charismatic Sitting Bull to be reckoned with. It was Lt. Gen. Philip H. Sheridan who had the overall responsibility for protecting the surveyors. He was in full accord with the Northern Pacific's goals and bent to his "supporting" task with a will.[33]

As important as actual Indian strength was the perception of it. White Americans had grown up hearing about Indian savagery and brutality exemplified by scalp taking, the treatment of captured white women (in fact, many were raped), and their pagan religious beliefs. Yet the military skill of Indian warriors was overrated. Other than by ambush, the Indian had difficulties with civilians possessing repeating rifles (especially Civil War veterans) and more often than not was ineffective in the face of infantry-cavalry discipline. As was seen in the 1872–73 fighting connected to the Northern Pacific surveys, the Indians' lack of self-control (usually premature rifle fire) saved whites (including George Custer) time and again from serious losses.

---

[31]Kingsley Bray, *Teton Sioux Population History.* My number is based on Sitting Bull's Lakota/Teton Sioux followers with Northern Cheyenne, Arapaho, and smatterings from other tribes. During the summer this number was invariably tripled by reservation Sioux.

[32]Sheridan, *Record of Engagements with Hostile Indians.*

[33]Lt. Gen. Philip H. Sheridan (1831–88), West Point '53. Numerous biographies, articles, and encyclopedias cover his remarkable career. His purported feelings concerning the Indian, repugnant today, shroud his energy and effective combat decision making. Despite putting on weight and wearing ridiculously tight uniforms, he was still at his best during the early 1870s.

However, given the tendency of the press to amplify Indian numbers and dangers (something that sold newspapers), Indian resistance was of the highest concern to those associated with the Northern Pacific. Investors could not be expected to place money in a venture that was subject to the disruption or destruction caused by Indian attacks. If the army would protect their surveyors, it was nevertheless the railroad's responsibility to convince investors that hostile Indians were not an issue.

Narrative of Richard Relf: The First Northern Pacific Surveys

Richard Howard Relf's account describes the earliest Northern Pacific surveying. While this was written a quarter century after his experiences, the material nevertheless rings true. Little is known of Relf other than he was likely raised in Minnesota and served in the war, being born in the early 1840s. In 1906 he attended a Minneapolis reunion of the 1870–73 surveyors and twenty-five years later a reunion of late 1870s surveyors.[34]

When Gen. Ira Spaulding came to the Head of Lake Superior, in the last days of June 1867, to start the first actual surveys ever made for the Northern Pacific Railroad, he met with a cordial welcome from the little remnant of the people of Superior [Wisconsin]. Most of these had been waiting a dozen years or more for a Moses of some sort, and had seen their boom-days' population of the summer of 1857 dwindle from several thousand to as many hundred.

On his way up the lake, the General had landed one party at Bayfield, under Mr. Ruggles, to run a line from there to St. Cloud and thence west.

He brought with him to Superior Col. W. H. Owen, chief of party, and young Edwards and Boice to handle level, rod, and chain. Among his outfit was a transit and a level; but he had no one to run them, nor had any one of the party much idea of the country to be traversed. Here, then, was an opportunity for me to put to good use the dozen years which I had spent in government and railroad surveys and wagon-road building to the west of the Head of Lake Superior.

Mr. Thomas Clark . . . who during the summer of 1858 had run the first line for the Mississippi and Lake Superior Railroad from St. Paul to Duluth, was induced to take the level. Thomas Bardon, then a stalwart

[34]Relf is mentioned in a variety of Minnesota documents, but there is no definitive source.

stripling in his teens, and now one of Ashland's most substantial businessmen, was elected to straighten out the chain, and J. W. Hacken to act as commissary. Thus equipped, and with an ox team for transportation, we started out for a hard tramp.

Mrs. Spaulding and Mrs. Owen, who were with the party, took quite an interest in the outfitting of the camp equipment, and will be remembered for their contribution of a large can of cod-fish, nicely shredded and seasoned, all ready for cooking. Our chief cook, who was a good Catholic, never let a Friday go by without varying our diet of pork and beans with some of it. The General had seen too much of [military] life to care for it at his age, so preferred the steamboat and railroad via Chicago and St. Paul to St. Cloud.

Gen. Spaulding was a kindly man, genial and much respected. He died some fifteen years ago. Col. Owen was a good executive, though slightly inclined to attempt to carry into camp some of the training he acquired during the war in the quartermaster's department. His engineering abilities were immaterial as none were required on this survey, but he was about as devoid of the instincts of woodcraft as possible, and soon learned to keep to the rear or within call. His death occurred in Washington City about a year and a half ago.

The old Point Douglas military road gave us a good start to the state line, some fifteen miles out. . . . After following the road . . . to where the Crow Wing road left it, the latter was taken for a few miles. The military road was bad enough, but when this road was attempted, the oxen and wagon were soon swamped and when dug out were sent back to Superior. As soon as half-breed and Indian packers could be procured, the party cut loose from the road and started "due west."

Being on the height of land, and the watershed between the St. Croix on the southeast and the Mississippi on the northwest, plenty of open swamps or floating bogs were encountered. Those had undoubtedly at one time been lakes, some of them quite deep. For several years previous the summers had been very dry and the water low in these swamps, and the fires had burned the moss and roots down to the soil for quite a distance around the edges. This wet season had filled the swamps compelling us often to wade out sometimes almost waist-deep before getting onto the floating mass—which was anything but reliable, and several comical rescues were witnessed. Our intrepid head chainman had to take the lead and keep to the line, while the rest of us could steer around whenever any open water was in the middle of the swamp. So he was the one most often in need of brush and poles to help him out.

The line ran some half dozen miles north of Mille Lacs, and nearing the Mississippi came upon several good size lakes and fewer swamps. Here less progress was made, having to hunt country and dodge lakes, which necessitated climbing trees to see what was ahead.

Our provisions were getting low and Commissary Hacker had to be sent on to Crow Wing to see about supplies and get a boat to help us across the Mississippi river. Early one morning, when ready to start, in throwing his hand (fortunately his left) upon his pack to adjust it, it came in contact with the blade of his ax, scalping it all the way across for an inch and a half. Of course we all looked to the chief, with his army experience, to soon fix it up, but he would not look at it. So, as soon as the terrible bleeding could be checked by compression of the arm, I found a buckskin needle and some linen thread in my "housewife," and with swamp water—all there was—cleansed it as well as we could and sewed it up. The bandaging was not an artistic "job" but seemed to have answered the purpose. He stood it like a major and in an hour started off.

Several weeks afterwards when the party reached the river, Hacker was there with his boat and two men, and his hand in as good condition as though the "first aid" had been performed by an expert. Here we got our first mail and learned that Gen. Spaulding and his party were at Crow Wing.

Our crossing was at the foot of French Rapids; a couple of miles above where the road was finally located in 1870 and Brainerd was built. Again we took a "due west" course and in a few days butted into the height of land between the Mississippi and Crow Wing rivers. Sending the party into camp, I climbed to the top of this elevation and, following it south to where it was broken by the Crow Wing river, from the top of a tall tree had a magnificent view of both valleys. Returning to camp as soon as possible, I sent a half-breed to Crow Wing for leave to back out to the river and deflect enough south to clear this point. The man was back by the middle of the forenoon. Gen. Spaulding wrote, "No time to back up." So the line skirted the foot hills around the point. In office at St. Cloud, a few months after, I was asked to fill in the cut-off with an imaginary line and profile I guessed near enough for all practical purposes.

After that it was plain sailing up the valley of Crow Wing River. . . . From this point to a few miles beyond what is now Staples, the constructed road is very near our line. It was on this stretch of line that two little incidents occurred that may be worthy of notice—one of them very personal. In stepping over a down balsam, my leg, about half way to the knee, came in contact with a broken limb that went to the bone, and for a week or so I was in pretty bad shape. Finally the party had to leave me at the half-breed road house at the crossing of Crow Wing River, Col. Owen taking the party ahead. Being somewhat at a loss what to do, I consented to put the leg at the tender mercy of an old squaw medicine-man. She concocted an immense poultice of all sorts of Indian herbs with a ground work of slippery elm and juniper berries. With this she kept me in limbo till the next morning and then invited me to hobble out of the house onto the grass and lie down flat on my back. She was talking all the while very nicely, apparently, though most of it was rather muddling to me. The villainous-looking knife she had was not very reassuring; though it was evident she was prepared for an assault upon the seat of my trouble. Very soon she quietly seated herself across my knees, with her face to my feet, and the knife did its part. Then with both hands she grabbed around the incision and brought a ton or two of pressure, it seemed to me, to bear upon it. No matter how much yelling and squirming was done, there was no let up and no getting away. When both were well-nigh exhausted, she let go and with some rags dressed the wound. I found a conveyance to take me to Otter Tail City, and from there on horseback explored the country from the foot of Otter Tail Lake back to the party and, giving up the horse to Col. Owen, resumed my place.

The other was an amusing incident more than otherwise, and occurred while I was laid up and can be told only as it was told to me. One morning while on their way to work, the party was scattered along the Crow Wing and Otter Tail road when it was met by an immense bull moose, who by his occasional calls was evidently in search of his mate. None of the party were in possession of anything more formidable than a jack knife or an ax, and the moose seemed to know it, for he stalked majestically along the road while they all took to the bush or got behind trees. Figuratively, this was the first time the Northern Pacific had to give up the right of way.

From the foot of Otter Tail Lake to the Red River the country was open—except until after crossing the Otter Tail River the brush was bad—and the party made rapid progress. We struck the river at Ten Mile Point above old Fort Abercrombie, now McCauleyville, and ran up the river to Breckenridge as it was called even then, although there was only the burned remains of an old saw mill there.

Gen. Spaulding had secured offices in the courthouse at St. Cloud, and there for a couple of months the two parties were engaged in making up maps, profiles, estimates, and reports. My field days ended in March 1868 by a fall that has left me on crutches ever since. When Gen. Spaulding started construction at what is now Carlton, he gave me office work, and when he moved his office to St. Paul, I went with him and was with him all that summer.

Source: "Narrative of Richard Relf," George A. Brackett Papers, catalog P-1547, Minnesota Historical Society, St. Paul.

The Northern Pacific's Groundbreaking

INAUGURATION OF THE NORTHERN PACIFIC RAILROAD: CEREMONIES AND FESTIVITIES ON THE OCCASION OF BREAKING GROUND

Duluth, Minn., February 16, 1870

Another milestone on the road of progress was established yesterday, one of the important indices that marks the rapid and wonderful advance of the nation in material and moral greatness. It was quietly announced, sometime ago, without any flourish of trumpets, that work on the Northern Pacific Railroad would be commenced at the Dalles [rapids] of the St. Louis [River], on the 15th of February; and yesterday, equally as silent, the first sod was broken in this great enterprise. . . . The event was too grand to be uncommemorated [and] an impromptu celebration was therefore devised. The day was mild and bright and seemed singularly auspicious. . . .

An early start was made on the morning of the 15th, and the river road along the line of the LS&M [Lake Superior & Mississippi Railroad] taken as a short cut, but which, as usual, proved the longer, in consequences of mistakes of way, heavy grades, etc. But the loss of time was amply compensated by a view of the grand scenery of the St. Louis, and a survey of the conflict of the indomitable will of man with the obstacles of nature, as exhibited in the building of this road over apparently insurmountable heights and valleys. At eleven o'clock the camp at the Dalles was reached. Here it was learned that it was necessary to take a tramp of some two miles and a half before the [grounds] could be reached. Taking up the march, in Indian file, with a plentiful supply of "spikes," we passed the embryo town of Thomson . . . in all its forest grandeur, and came upon a natural roadbed that had been cleared for the LS&M . . . exactly twenty-five miles in distance from Duluth. We struck through the woods due west, and after a further tramp of a quarter of a mile we were greeted by shouts of welcome [from those] in attendance from St. Paul, Twin Lakes, and vicinity waiting our arrival.

A bonfire was roaring in the center of the group; near were the implements of work, and in the background was a large body of laborers eager for their share of the duties of the day. At 12 o'clock the assemblage was called to order. . . . [After speeches] the meeting broke up with cheers for the Northern Pacific, Jay Cooke, Gen. Spaulding, and the ladies present. Capt. Starkey immediately put his woodchoppers to work and by night nearly a quarter of timber, some 150 feet wide, was felled to the ground. He has the contract to hew down twenty miles of the road and has commenced the labor in good earnest.

Source: St. Paul Weekly Press, *February 24, 1870.*

Account by Col. Hiram Hayes

Hiram Hayes (1831–1918), a Maine native, was living in Superior, Wisconsin, by the mid-1850s. As a surveyor, he had an on-and-off association with the Northern Pacific over the years. He was invited but did not attend the 1906 surveyors' reunion in Minneapolis.[35]

October 23, 1911
Mr. O. D. Wheeler

My dear Sir:

I have your inquiry regarding "the time the construction of the Northern Pacific Railroad was first begun." The *place* was about ¾ of a mile westerly from the Northern Pacific Junction . . . in dense wood. It was site of a paper town, as then proposed by some exploiters, and a name was afterwards given to it—"Komoko."[36] An imaginary branch of the road was to start from Komoko and run to the Bay of Superior. The town and the branch were of course myths.

[35]Fox, *Regimental Losses in the Civil War*; Heitman, *Historical Register*; Powell, *List of Officers of the Army*.

[36]The name still exists, for today there is a Komoko Road in Carlton.

It was in the month of February 1870 that the work began there. . . . Speeches were made around the fire—a bon fire heaped with crackling limbs and burning with great alacrity. The deep snow melted and ran in torrents of water. The snow liquefied and so did the crowd. The earth thawed incidentally, and so did all present, for the occasion was one of hilarity and rejoicing for the start that was made. . . .

The ground being well thawed, Col. J. B. Culver,[37] a veteran of Chickamauga and other fields, shoveled the wheelbarrow full of dirt, and I myself wheeled it to the dump—thereunto qualified, as having been a quartermaster of some of the forces at Chancellorsville, Gettysburg, Atlanta, Franklin, and Nashville, and many other minor occasions. I mention this only to say that soldiers of the Civil War had returned to civil duty and were ready to shovel dirt or trundle a wheelbarrow. . . .

Gen. Rosser, a Confederate cavalry officer of much renown, was at Komoko that day, booted but not spurred, wading in snow and not in gore. He was employed by the Northern Pacific in its Engineering Department. This signified the return of amity and fellowship as between North and South, which had been fighting three million or more of men all the way from [the] Potomac River to the Rio Grande.

Time has buried the historical spot referred to, and most of those then gathered on that day in February 1870. That was not the only memorable thing connected with the N.P. at which I have attended. When Perham, the first [Northern Pacific] president, was seeking its incorporation and land grant in the very early sixties, I sympathized at least, and somewhat cooperated with him in the city of Washington.[38] . . . When the surveys started from Lake [Superior] for the west in the early seventies,[39] the engineers made my office headquarters at Superior, and such maps, acquaintance with the country, and some personal activity were at their disposal.[40]

Source: Brackett Papers, Catalog P-1547, Minnesota Historical Society, St. Paul.

[37]Joshua B. Culver (1830–83) was colonel of the Thirteenth Michigan Infantry and first mayor of Duluth.

[38]Josiah Perham (1803–68) was the first president of the Northern Pacific. Like Hayes, he was from Maine. Could there have been an earlier family connection?

[39]Hayes likely meant the late 1860s and 1870. By the winter of 1870–71, most of the surveyors were working in west-central Minnesota.

[40]Hayes's last paragraph, discussing Wisconsin and the Northern Pacific some years later, is omitted.

Jay Cooke Entertains in Brooklyn

Only a handful of contemporary descriptions of Cooke during this period survive. This low-key event undoubtedly was in keeping with the concept that "selling" was impermissible at a gathering of a social nature.

THE NORTHERN PACIFIC RAILROAD: MR. JAY COOKE'S VIEWS AS TO THE PROJECT.

Last evening Mr. Henry Bowen, of the *Independent,* gave to a few hundred prominent gentlemen, mostly residents of Brooklyn, an opportunity both for pleasant social intercourse and for becoming acquainted with the greatest railway enterprise of the age.[41] He accomplished both of these objects by inviting the leading capitalists and businessmen of Brooklyn to meet, at his residence [a luxurious Greek revival–style building] on the Heights [overlooking the East River], Mr. Jay Cooke the eminent financier. The hour specified was half-past seven, and before eight the spacious parlors of Mr. Bowen's house were filled with as fine an assemblage of the "solid men" of our neighboring city as could well be gathered together.[42] Bankers whose names are known and whose notes are taken as readily in London and in the European capitals as in New York, were there; some of the ablest representatives of our strongest business houses; merchants of world-wide fame; capitalists who have furnished many a railroad with the indispensable means, and representatives of the Press—all responded cheerfully to M. Bowen's invitation, knowing that Mr. Cooke might have a word to say well worth the hearing.

Among the gentlemen present were . . . [Scores of names given.]

After the guests of Mr. Bowen had enjoyed the opportunity of a personal introduction to Mr. Cooke and a brief period of general conversation, Dr. Fields of the *Evangelist* called their attention to what he supposed to be the special object of the gathering.[43] He alluded eloquently to the services rendered by Mr. Cooke to the nation in the most trying period of the war and said that he seemed to be the man of all others to carry through the most important and grandest railway

---

[41]Henry C. Bowen (1813–96) was a businessman, strong abolitionist, and newspaper publisher and editor.

[42]The reader must use his/her imagination to picture this scene of society's *crème de la crème.*

[43]Henry Martyn Fields (1822–1907) was a clergyman and for forty years editor and publisher of the *Evangelist,* a Presbyterian newspaper.

enterprise of the age. Mr. A. A. Low also expressed a desire to hear what Mr. Cooke might have to say on this matter.[44] Mr. Bowen, in his introduction of Mr. Cooke to the [guests], said that he had taken something of a liberty in thus bringing business affairs into a social gathering, but he had become so impressed with the value and interest of Mr. Cooke's views on the great enterprise he was now forwarding [*sic*] that he felt sure his guests would also be pleased to hear what Mr. Cooke had to say.

In response to the unanimous and heartily expressed wish of all present Mr. Cooke came forward. A large map of the United States was hung up at the end of one of the parlors and Mr. Cooke proceeded, with its occasional assistance, to show some of the peculiar advantages of the Northern Route. His remarks were more in the nature of free and offhand talk than a systematically arranged speech, and were probably more impressive from this very fact. By no means an orator or given to rhetorical flourishes, Mr. Cooke talked on his favorite theme like a man who is [so] full of interesting facts that his constant difficulty is that of selection—"an embarrassment of riches." He does not possess his subject, but it possesses him; absorbs him and makes eloquent in spite of himself, and eloquent in just the way that cautious financiers with confidence in an enterprise which has so evidently captivated so practical a man.

He alluded to the history of the Northern Pacific Railway enterprise which—years before the war—engaged the thoughts of the leading men of the South; which during the war acquired a marvelously liberal charter and land grants, through the persistency of one man [Josiah Perham], and which was to be the greatest undertaking of the age. It was called "Northern," but was really "Central," for its track lay two hundred miles south of the center of the land of this continent.

He deprecated any purpose to exalt the advantages of the Northern over the Central route [the transcontinental railroad completed twenty months earlier], and said that he regarded the securities of the Union and Central Pacific as perfectly safe and among the best possible investments. But the superior natural advantages of the Northern route were evident. Its eastern terminus, at Duluth, on Lake Superior, was four hundred miles further west than that of the other route at Chicago, while the indentation made by the waters of Puget's Sound brought the western

[44] Abiel Abbot Low (1811–93) came from a distinguished family and was a leading merchant. A son, Seth Low, became New York City's reform mayor and was closely associated with Theodore Roosevelt.

end of the route still nearer. Altogether about six hundred miles were thus saved in distance between the water ends of the route.

And this is not all. The Gulf Stream of the Pacific which sweeps through between China and Japan, strikes our coast at Puget's Sound, and makes a direct continuation of the Northern Pacific route. Along this ocean stream all the vessels bound from China for San Francisco have to sail, and they have to make a southerly voyage of eight hundred miles after reaching the neighborhood of Puget's Sound. A vessel leaving China and Japan for San Francisco is now obliged to sail within eighty miles of Puget's Sound. . . . When the Northern Pacific Railroad is completed and the proposed telegraphs are constructed, the cargo of this vessel will be [unloaded] at New York, and the announcement of its sale telegraphed to its shippers sooner than the vessel can now be signaled off the Golden Gate.

[From this point on, Cooke's remarks become more wishful speculation than facts and are significantly shortened.]

The Northern Pacific lies across a country which is susceptible, the whole distance, of profitable cultivation. The whole country is fertile, well supplied with wood, splendidly fitting for grazing purposes, and with the finest weather on the Continent. . . . There is little snow except in Minnesota and Dakota, and there it does not come in violent storms but falls early and stays all winter. No snow sheds will be needed on this route [unlike the Central Pacific]. . . . The gradients of the Northern Pacific will be remarkably easy. It crosses the Rocky Mountains at a point where the range is narrow and low. . . .

One great feature of the enterprise, and that which has engaged Mr. Cooke's special interest, was its land system. . . . The total land grants amount to 60,000,000 acres.[45] [Cooke then discussed land sales and its management as well as its plans "for the encouragement of the best class of emigration." Not stated but certainly understood by Cooke's remarks, emphasis was being placed on Anglo-Saxon/Nordic immigrants and not those from Mediterranean countries.]

[As for the bonds, Cooke] desired to be understood, however, that as the financial agents for the [Northern Pacific], the firm which he represented did not propose to make any promises which could not be filled. They regarded the bonds as the safest and soundest securities in the market. If they did not they would never lend their names to the enterprise. But he was not prepared to state the exact time of the

[45]The actual figure was about 50 million acres.

1871–1872: Northern Pacific / Jay Cooke–Controlled Railroads in Minnesota

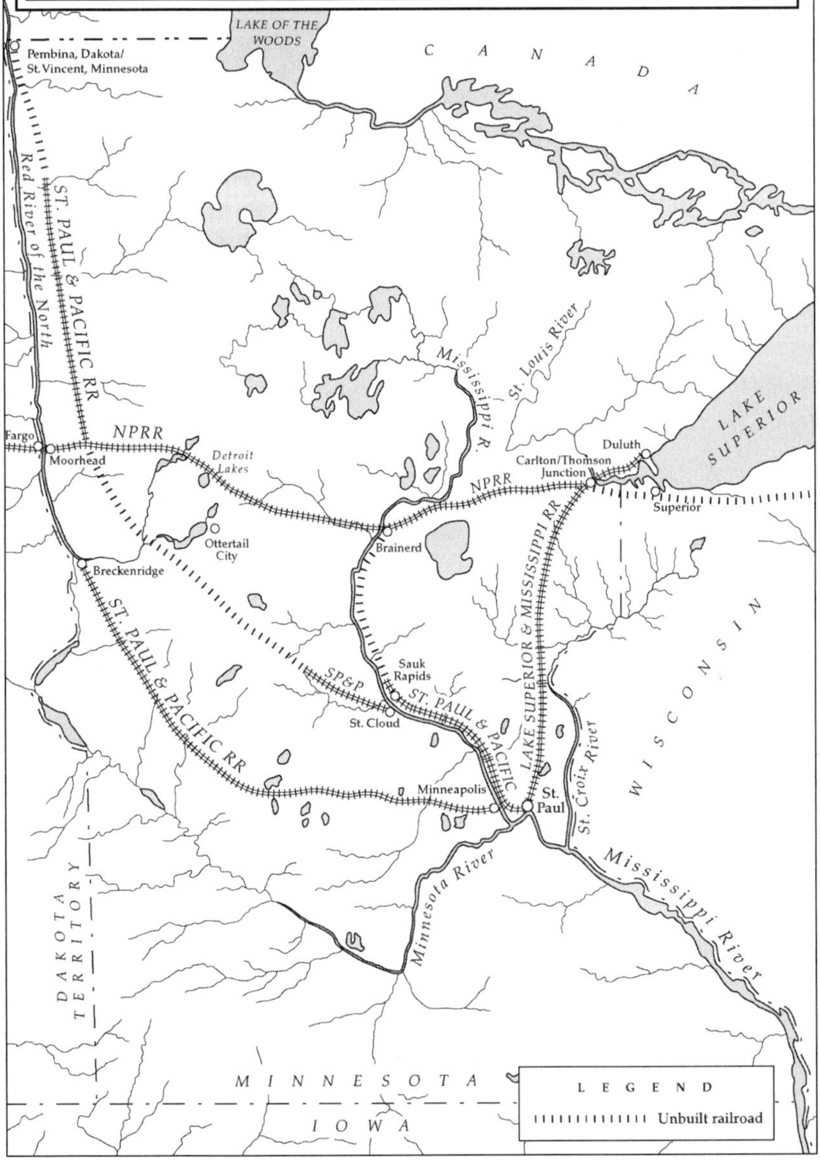

Map by Vicki Trego Hill adapted from map in 1873 Duluth pamphlet by H. T. Johns, courtesy St. Louis County (Minnesota) Historical Society.

completion of the road. If he was asked for his personal opinion, however, he would say that within four years he expected that the trade of the Indies would be carried over this route.

Mr. Cooke's remarks were listened to with the closest attention throughout and evidently impressed themselves with great force on the shrewd businessmen present. After the guests of Mr. Bowen had partaken of generous collation [light meal], Gov. Ashley of Montana enforced some of Mr. Cooke's remarks as to the climate of the country along the Northern Pacific route and as to the fertility of the land. He was satisfied that Montana was to become the great wheat region of the United States.[46] The guests of Mr. Bowen are indebted to him for one of the pleasantest and most profitable evenings they have lately spent anywhere.

Source: Brooklyn Evening Mail, *February 3, 1871, Minnesota Historical Society, M-522.*

Ira Spaulding's First Instructions to Surveyor Edward Jordan

Engineer's Office
St. Paul, Minn.
May 23, 1870

Dear Sir:

You will please proceed to Ottertail City as soon as practicable for the purpose of making a Topographical Survey of a portion of the country which will be indicated to you on the map before you start.[47]

---

[46]James Mitchell Ashley (1824–96). Ashley had been a five-term abolitionist Ohio congressman, playing a key role in the passage of the Thirteenth Amendment and the articles of impeachment against President Andrew Johnson. When Ashley was defeated for reelection in 1868, Grant appointed him territorial governor of Montana. Ashley served barely a year before resigning and was no longer governor at the time of the article. See *DAB*, *NCAB*, 11:79, and Wikipedia.

[47]Ottertail City (often spelled "Otter Tail" by contemporaries) had been a central trading area for Indians and French Canadian trappers when all traffic was by lake or river. From here there was a short, low portage from which a person could canoe to the Gulf of Mexico or Hudson's Bay. If the latter, downstream another portage led to Lake Superior. Not until mid-1871 did the NP decide not to build through Ottertail City; the road was then relocated north on a straight line between Wadena and Perham. Based on various river and community descriptions in Wikipedia and WPA guides.

If the line run by Mr. Kimberly from the Mississippi to Ottertail has not been connected near Ottertail with the line run by Mr. Smith from St. Cloud to Ottertail and thence to Georgetown, you will please connect these lines and then use Kimberly's line as your base east of Ottertail and Smith's line as your base west of Ottertail. To be of any value, your work must be done as rapidly as possible consistent with sufficient accuracy for our purposes.

The object of the Survey is to obtain the information necessary to enable us to locate the line of the Rail Road upon the best ground within the belt of the country to be examined, having in view the extensions east and west. Make your first examinations from Ottertail City to the west base of Leaf Mountains. All time and labor expended in detailed surveys, beyond what is necessary to obtain the information mentioned above, would be a waste of money and must be avoided.

The work to which you are temporarily assigned is on a portion of the 4th Residency, Minnesota Division, and when the Resident Engineer in charge of that portion of the line arrives in the vicinity of his work, you will please report to him and act under his orders. In the meantime, please report to me here, as to Col. Wm H. Owen, my principal assistant.

Mr. George A. Brackett of Minneapolis will furnish you camp equipage, cook, utensils, provisions, transportation, etc. Your party will consist of, besides yourself, 2 chainmen, 1 picketman, 2 axemen, 1 cook, 1 teamster: 8 in all. Make all your arrangements with an eye to economy and dispatch. Wages per month for chainmen and picketman will be $50. Axemen $40. Cook and teamster as agreed by Mr. Brackett.

No hotel bills will be paid by the Co. except in case of absolute necessity, and when ordered by competent authority.

Funds will be furnished you before leaving St. Paul. At the end of the month, you will make up your payrolls and vouchers, send them to me by mail, and draw on me at 5 days sight for the balance due. Take vouchers for all expenditures amounting to $5 and over, and let your vouchers explain as far as practicable the object of the expenditure.

Please advise me often of your progress.

Yours Truly [etc.]

Source: Jordan Family Papers, courtesy Mark Jordan, Gorham, Maine.

Sheridan Warns against Indian Attacks

A great many of the settlers in Montana have been murdered, and five or six hundred head of stock captured and run off within the last fifty days, and much bitter complaint has been made by the settlers on account of non-protection, the few troops stationed in Montana being insufficient to meet the wants of the case.[48]

There has also been a great deal of trouble along the Missouri River, and a number of people murdered in the vicinity of the military posts. The friendly Indians and the agents and the employees at Big Cheyenne, Grand River, and Whitestone agencies have been in jeopardy on several occasions, as the wild Indians have, at times, had their own way, driving the employees into the agency buildings, taking possession of the annuity goods [for reservation inhabitants], and taking the cattle. Steps have been taken to remedy these evils, as far as we can, by the erection of block houses. The post at Fort Buford has been in a state of siege for two or three years. . . .

Although there have been numerous depredations in the Department of Dakota and some, in fact, in all the departments, still the condition of Indian affairs is very much better than last year. The policy of reservations adopted by the Indian Department [Office of Indian Affairs, Department of the Interior] is, in my judgment, the only policy that will put an end to Indian murders and depredations. I think that it may be necessary to punish some of the Sioux and Cheyenne, as other tribes south had to be punished, before peace can be fully established and the reservation system made a success; but every effort will be made to avoid any necessity of this kind, with the strong hope that the savages may settle down on their reservation and adopt a more peaceful and civilized life.

The Indians have run riot along the lines of our western settlements and the emigrant and commercial lines of travel for many years, murdering and plundering without any punishment and the Government has, heretofore, sought to give protection to some of its best interests by making presents to these savages; or, in other words, while it found it necessary to enact the most stringent laws for the government of civilized whites, it was attempting to govern a wild, brutal, and savage people without any laws at all or the infliction of any punishment for the most

---

[48]Based on contemporary newspaper articles—not all of which agree—I find that the number of settlers killed in the period Sheridan refers to was less than a dozen.

heinous crimes. This system was not a success. If a white man commits murder or robs, we hang him or send him to a penitentiary. If an Indian does the same, we have the habit of giving him more blankets.

The Indian is a lazy, idle vagabond; he never labors and has no profession, except that of arms, to which he is raised as a child; a scalp is constantly dangled before his eyes, and the highest honor he can aspire to is to possess one taken by himself. It is not to be wondered at, therefore, if he aims for the honor when he grows up, especially if there is no punishment to follow the barbarous act.

The Government has always been very liberal to Indians, especially when they have settled on reservations; the lands allotted to them have been of the very best character, making them perhaps by far the richest communities in the country.

The system of supplying the wild band under the present management is working well; the Indian gets all that the Government intends him to have; he cannot now plead bad faith; and, if he does not now give up his cruel and destructive habits, I see no other way to save the lives and property of our people than to punish him until peace becomes a desirable object.

Source: Army and Navy Journal, *December 11, 1869.*

CHAPTER 2

Initial Minnesota Construction

Actual construction of the Northern Pacific in Minnesota did not begin until mid-August. Construction was divided into three distinct phases. First, after the route was finalized, contractors would construct a roadbed. With only a handful of steam shovels and one pile driver, almost all this labor was manual. In Minnesota laborers were white—Irish, German, or American born—and down on their luck.[1]

The second phase of construction was the actual placement of wooden cross ties and iron rails. This work was rapid but far more dangerous than roadbed work. Accidents were frequent as the wooden cross ties or sections of iron fell on feet, legs, hands, and arms. Fatalities or amputations resulting in death were common. From a variety of sources one learns of sliding piles of ties or rails and dangers of every sort. Bridge building was a separate component, with contracts going to specialized companies that did equally if not more dangerous work.

Finally there was the actual testing of the track with single or multiple locomotives and usually loaded freight cars. Each phase required certification and then payment by the railroad. The overwhelmingly critical problem was that of stable roadbeds where the wetlands began. This required filling land with a nonperishable mix that was sent by rail. One simply takes the approximate dimensions of any section of fill to realize the enormity of the task: 12 feet wide at the top for single track, 25 feet wide at the base—with the muck's depth determining the final amount needed. Given the weight of locomotives (32.5 tons),[2] an aggressive construction schedule, and very little gravel or rock available,

[1]Cheaper Chinese labor was not used in Minnesota between 1870 and 1873.

[2]The figures do not include tenders carrying water and fuel.

contractors frequently deceived the Northern Pacific by using shoddy materials that did not survive Minnesota winters.

The problem was that the nearest rock fill came from the Duluth area, the southern end of the Mesabi Range. Here was rock aplenty: iron, copper, and minerals beyond number, quartzite, metamorphic conglomerates, various "hard" rocks, and folded lava formations. However, breaking this into manageable pieces was difficult, and transporting it to "the front" presented enormous logistical difficulties given the day's technology.[3]

Being unable to secure even a modest number of workers until August, when the Lake Superior & Mississippi was completed (from St. Paul to Duluth), two-thirds of construction season was over. It seems safe to assume that even if contractors had the same day laborers involved, the transition lost even more time. The "good news" was that most of the 1,600 men hired were within 25 miles of the NP's starting location. These men who cleared ground, dug, filled, and so forth were accustomed to arduous labor.

Not surprisingly, laborers lived under deplorable conditions. Most construction companies provided tents, but little if any planning had considered winter work. Firewood and planking to line tent walls reached workers slowly. When the LS&M, now owned by Cooke, announced that it would no longer carry liquor, rioting quickly followed.

On October 22 the *Duluth Minnesotian* reported that 30 miles had been graded and 17 miles had tracks. What followed, however, was the worst single decision that Gregory Smith was to make: to continue construction throughout the winter. There is no way to avoid one of nature's most immutable laws: when temperatures fall below 32°, water will freeze and expand. It is the same reason we don't let children put soft drink cans in freezers. While building *over* frozen wetlands will *temporarily* see good results, come spring, thawing occurs; the land contracts, and everything on its surface will shift or sink once the ice melts and begins flowing.

Thus there was the illusion of construction "progress" that winter. On March 15 Northern Pacific personnel proudly telegraphed the *Railroad Gazette* that the Brainerd Bridge over the Mississippi was operational 94 miles from Carlton and that "completed" road bed extended at least (sources disagree) 25 miles westward. Despite the vicious cold, work

[3]An initially large amount of rock from the "cut" through the hill to reach Duluth was available, but even this would have represented only a small portion of the Northern Pacific's needs. For the area's geology, see *WPA Guide to Minnesota,* "Geology" section beginning p. 11.

crews had expanded to at least 3,000 laborers by April 1. If anything there was a shortage of locomotives (four of the nine being "pony" engines and most requiring frequent repairs) and only 130 flatcars and 26 boxcars.[4] Yet, despite everything, morale seems to have been high.

On April 13 the *St. Paul Daily Press* reported, "The work on the Northern Pacific Railroad is being prosecuted with extraordinary vigor." The thought could not have been more positive, the just-beginning spring thaw decidedly less so.

Construction throughout the Winter of 1870–71

The completion of the Lake Superior & Mississippi in mid-August meant that work on the Northern Pacific could finally begin. However, within months, construction bogged down. The Duluth Minnesotian, quite fearless in a Northern Pacific–dominated town, soon blew the whistle. Other articles and internal letters discuss progress and point to the massive problems the railroad would soon face.

Light Dawning:
The Beginning of a Swindle, We Hope!

It is announced that W. Milnor Roberts, of Penn. (at present Engineer of the great [railroad] bridge across the Mississippi at St. Louis), has been appointed Chief Engineer of the Northern Pacific Railroad, and [Daniel C.] Linsley, Chief Assistant Engineer Construction, of the East Mississippi Division.

Engineer Roberts is a Pennsylvania Engineer of high reputation and is the same who was sent out as the Confidential Engineer of a Cooke & Co. in 1869, to make a thorough examination of the proposed route of the Northern Pacific, preliminary to that banking house accepting the financial agency of the Company and "before (to use Jay Cooke & Co.'s own language) they would institute measures for the sale of the Securities of the Company, or become identified with the great work." Mr. Roberts' able report to and from the Pacific Ocean is well known—and . . . it was upon this favorable report that Jay Cooke & Co. assumed the Financial Agency.

[4]*Railroad Gazette,* January 28 and March 18, 1871, *Duluth Minnesotian,* February 25, 1871, and *St. Paul Daily Press,* April 13, 1871.

That the distinguished Engineer, whose relations with Jay Cooke & Co. have been of a confidential and trustful nature, has been placed in control of the Engineering of this great national work, we regard as an auspicious sign. It was about time that Jay Cooke & Co. came to the rescue of themselves and their Bondholders who are supplying the money to construct the line to the Red River—their rescues from a most corrupt, villainous, scampish combination of forty thieves, embodied in the "Northwestern Construction Company," with ramifications and affiliations, as there had been too much reason to believe, amongst the highest of the Company itself—outside, however, as we hope, the Directors!

The Line [route] adopted, and being constructed, is one entirely different from that upon which Jay Cooke & Co. assumed the Financial Agency—it is a line of a Ram's-Horn pattern; engineering to suit the plans and pockets of the Construction Company aforesaid; winding around every feeble obstruction; running south in order to run north, and north to run again south; with the general contour of a bent bow and the special shape of a Malay creese. . . .

[The route] is at least 50 miles longer than it needs to have been had the original and *direct* "Jay Cooke line" *north* of Sandy Lake been adopted. It is only necessary for any *honest* man or Engineer to examine the line being worked upon and *projected* to comprehend the *ulterior* purpose of the scoundrels who have been diverting this great national enterprise into a swindling, money-making job, into which present fortunes and ultimate town-site specifications co-mingle. The five or six millions of dollars which Jay Cooke and his friends have raised will not, under the *present Line,* and the shameful *style* of railroad building adopted by the Northwestern Construction Company suffice to put the Road two-thirds of the distance to the Red River of the North and then nothing will be left to purchase rolling stock!

We are in hopes from the new appointment of Engineers that Jay Cooke has at last gotten his eyes open to the Swindle attempted upon him and his friends; and that the immediate abandonment of the present, almost impracticable, very costly, very crooked, bent-bow line will be found the truest economy, even though the work already done should be thrown aside as useless; for the direct line north of Sandy Lake will save two million dollars in the cost of construction to the Red River, besides the saving through the centuries of the extra wear and tear in running [operating] the other crooked and longer line. Though some 30 miles are said to be graded, and the iron is laid on 17; yet only a mile and a half out from [Thomson] Junction is said to be *finished;* the rest is incomplete, not leveled up, laid upon corduroy, and is *humbugging* railroading![5]

We shall watch the developments of the next few months with great interest; and report to the public and the Northern Pacific Bondholders from time to time!

Source: Duluth Minnesotian, *editorial, October 22, 1870.*

Northern Pacific

The *Minneapolis Tribune* of the 12th [of November] says: "Track-laying on the Northern Pacific Railroad is still progressing west of the [Carlton] Junction, and will continue as fast as possible all winter. Twenty-five miles are now laid. Grading, of course, progresses uninterruptedly beyond the end of the track, and from the Mississippi River [Brainerd] west on the Western Division. There are about 3,000 men employed along the line, and the force is increasing every day. Sixty miles have been graded west from the Junction. At the close of this month, one hundred miles of grading will be finished and forty miles of track laid.

There are parties of engineers at work constantly between the Red River and the Missouri, making surveys, profiles, and locations; and from the Pacific Ocean westward [*sic*] the great work is being mapped and profiled preparatory to construction. The most remarkable feature of the work on the Northern Pacific Railroad will be that it will not cease all winter. The contract calls for the completion of the road [to Red River] by July 1 [1871], and there is little doubt, judging from the rapidity of the construction so far, that the road will be finished within the contract time.

Source: Railroad Gazette, *November 19, 1870.*

Thomas Rosser to Ira Spaulding

December 25, 1870

Genl.:

The delays in furnishing the machinery . . . makes it necessary in my opinion to materially change the programme for constructing and operating our road during the winter and spring.

---

[5]Thomson, Thompson, and Carlton Junction are used interchangeably.

Three [of the four] small engines are reported in bad condition and should be sent to the shop for repairs, and this would leave only one small ["pony"] engine and two large [Baldwin] engines, of our own and one hired, of 25 tons, to perform the large amount of work necessary to put the track in a condition of safety by spring.[6]

The ground is already frozen too hard for operating with steam shovels, and the two which have hitherto been employed have been so seriously impaired by the efforts to work them [in] this extremely cold weather that they have been laid aside for the winter; and consequently there will be no work done this winter except by hand, which owing to the post [*sic*] will progress slowly, and by using all the available force in the country and all the machinery we are likely to collect, we will be unable this winter to prepare the road bed for transmitting heavy trains of iron and ties to the tracklayers when the frost goes out [of the ground] and the swamps become soft.

[Here Rosser discusses moving up all the supplies to a point closer to Brainerd.][7]

The transportation of this [150 miles of] iron to the front will occupy two 25-ton engines seventy-five days, providing there are no accidents or delays from snow, etc., and if large numbers of ties are to be hauled from the rear . . . it will require two 25-ton engines to supply the track layers and one [engine] to each twenty miles of unfinished road in the rear, making the services of seven or eight 25-ton engines absolutely necessary to complete the unfinished work in the rear, and allowing that one mile of track is laid daily. . . .

By adopting this plan of operation and making the necessary provisions for carrying it into effect *immediately,* the work will not be materially delayed during winter and not *cut short by the floods of spring*—but unless these or some other vigorous measures are adopted, I predict that the work will be cut off in the spring and weeks and perhaps months lost in patching hurriedly.[8] . . .

Most respectfully . . .

Source: Northern Pacific Railroad, Secretary's Department, unregistered letters received and related records, undated and 1864–76, M-459, Minnesota Historical Society.

[6]The 25-ton engine was the standard weight immediately preceding the Civil War. The Northern Pacific standard Baldwin engine, built in the early 1870s, was approximately one-third again heavier, in the 33-ton range.

[7]Rosser writes of a Mud River location, but today there is no stream by this name near Brainerd.

[8]He predicted correctly, as it turned out.

Northern Pacific Line

It is of no use of the people here and at the Junction grumbling and scolding about the Northern Pacific R. R. nor carrying freight or passengers to the Mississippi at present. The frost leaving the ground has invited the track in many places of its winter-constructed road bed to sink further into it, and there would be no guarantee, neither for the lives of the one nor the safety of the other, if the managers opened the line to contracts for either kind of transportation. All had better possess their souls with patience until the line is ballasted and surfaced up, and then all things will be done safely and in order. Superintendent R. H. Morford has just been out on the line—returning to Duluth last night—and it will take two or three weeks yet to put the line in workable order.[9]

Source: Duluth Minnesotian, *April 15, 1871.*

Roberts to Linsley

Portland, Oregon, April 20, 1871[10]

Dear Sir;

. . . In regard to the stand you took with the contractors relative to their . . . hurtful system of conducting their work, you have my hearty approval. It seems as if the larger and more *imposing* these contracting corporations of men, the smaller becomes their soul and the more contracted their views, but I am really surprised that a man of Mr. Canda's mechanical repute should permit such defective bridge work to pass through his hands.[11] Perhaps had he been the sole contractor, and his name thus associated more directly and personally with the works, he would have been more careful.

All these things only go to confirm my lifelong experience that unless a R.R. Co. is weak and *must* sell themselves, it is folly to introduce a fifth wheel between them and the real men who do the work. Literally the Company that does that is *sold.* Possibly a portion of the trouble sprang from the system of the [Chief] Engineer in the beginning [i.e.,

[9] Robert J. Morford was an Ireland-born Northern Pacific official who lived in Brainerd, but no other information could be found.

[10] Roberts's letter was sent to New York, not Minnesota, and one assumes that it wasn't received for weeks.

[11] In 1875 the Brainerd Bridge collapsed, killing a number of people. It is not known to which Canda brother (Charles J., 1838–1914, or Ferdinand E., 1842–1920) Roberts was referring.

General Spaulding], leaving too much discretion and power with the Contracting party. . . .

The heels-over-head system (or want of system) in having a non-professional engineer or manipulator of miles, measuring ahead and establishing "points" for this great railroad line, if persisted in, will *ruin it*; and you and I, who will be held responsible, may lose all chance of doing justice to the Company and to ourselves.[12]

Look at that case to which you specifically call to my attention—the "Ottertail" location![13] . . . I purposely decline to mince this thing with you. I give the naked truth: and I will add that if any such portion as certain gentlemen would inaugurate in to prevail, that it will *ruin the company*. I mean nothing offensive to anyone; but I do mean to stand by my opinion. You cannot bring about some reasonable approach toward a correct system of engineering this great work—if other unrelated policy is to prevail. I shall be ready to wash my hands of the responsibility; but I hope, and I think with good reason, the engineers will be allowed to do the engineering. If so all will be right.

Source: Minnesota Historic Society, NPRR *microfilm 522.*

President Smith to D. C. Linsley Concerning Construction Problems

November 21, 1870

Dear Sir,

I arrived here Saturday night and found [your letter] of the 15th inst. I regret exceedingly to learn of the delinquencies of the contractors. After the very positive assurances given me by Mr. Balch and Mr. Robertson particularly, as well as by other gentlemen of their Co[mpany] I was led to believe that the work would be pushed with great vigor and that in its character it would be such (to use their own language) as would be not only entirely acceptable to us, but also to any committee of railroad gentlemen who might choose to invite to examine it as they had a liberal

[12] By "points," I believe that Roberts is referring to river crossing points where cities would be located (such as Brainerd and Fargo-Moorhead) and where Northern Pacific insiders engaged in land speculation.

[13] The Ottertail route was soon to be moved to the north following complaints by Roberts, Linsley, and possibly Spaulding.

contract. I was determined to give us first-class work. I could not ask for stronger assurances than these gentlemen gave me. It is of the utmost importance to the negotiation of our security here as well as abroad that this work should be driven with all possible dispatch, that it should be well and credibly performed. Their own reputation saw hope of further contracts from us. It would seem [that] it could impel them to this course.

At all events you must not let the work drag nor must they be permitted to fight it. There is one matter I wish you especially to inquire into, and that is the amount of estimates made for the work. The last estimate was two to five dollars a man equal to over fourteen completed miles of road for that month.

The total amount of payments made to them will not compare with the amount of work done, if your statements are at all correct. I wish you to give this matter a very thorough overlooking and be able to report when I come out. Also be able to give me the manner of making up these estimates.

I intend if possible to get away from here the first Monday of December. I shall reach St. Paul as soon as may be by traveling days—I cannot travel at night.

This will give me all the time necessary to meet them and get back by the 20th [of December] at which time I must be here. I expect to take Mrs. S. with me. . . .[14]

I hope you were pleased with [meeting] Mr. [Milnor] Roberts. Everything is going well here. A telegram from home says that they had sleighing there yesterday. (Sunday.)[15]

In great haste . . .

J. Gregory Smith

Source: Minnesota Historic Society, NPRR Secretary's Letters, M-459.

Tent Towns and New Cities

Construction workers were paid at least once a month. Three thousand workers, clearing ten dollars or more a month, meant that for a few brief days, significant amounts of cash were available in the temporary tent cities. Liquor

[14]An unclear reference to a possible Minnesota house for Linsley to live in has been removed.

[15]Indicates that the letter was possibly written from New York.

stores, saloons, and "bordellos"—a pleasant word for the unusually wretched conditions in which prostitutes operated—immediately sprouted with predictable results.

The Northern Pacific Railroad Riot
Twelve of the Ringleaders
Awaiting Trial at Fort Ripley

The number of men engaged in the recent riot on the Northern Pacific was about two hundred, and the amount of damage caused by their violence is about $1,000. Twelve of the ringleaders were arrested by the Sheriff of Crow Wing County, turned over to the military for safe keeping, and are now confined at Fort Ripley.[16] The date for their trial has not yet been determined, and remains to be decided by General Hancock and the Attorney-General of this state. All the rioters but those who were arrested were paid the amount due them after the proportionate amount of damage caused by each had been deducted [from their pay].

Since the arrests were made, and the payment of the men, quiet has prevailed and the work has progressed rapidly.

Source: St. Paul Weekly Press, *January 12, 1871.*

From the Northern Pacific

Major A. Brackett arrived home [St. Paul] yesterday from a two-week tour on the line of the Northern Pacific, where he has been routing the gamblers and liquor dealers.[17] He started from Minneapolis about the 15th of July accompanied by M. M. Cruikshank, assistant, and Geo. W. Sweet, attorney of the N. P. Railroad.[18] Operations were commenced

[16]Fort Ripley, an active military post between 1849 and 1877, was located on the Mississippi's eastern side, some 20 miles southwest of Brainerd.

[17]Maj. Albert Bruce Brackett (1826 to 9/22/92) was affectionately called the "Old Major." From Maine, in 1864 he led "Brackett's Battalion" in a saber-drawn cavalry charge that shattered the Sioux defenses at Killdeer Mountain. A federal marshal in the 1870s, he was constantly doing the NPRR's dirty work. Brackett could count on a wide circle of veterans and admirers throughout Minnesota. See obituaries in various Minneapolis–St. Paul newspapers.

[18]"Colonel" George Washington Sweet (1823–98) was a onetime state legislator, early developer of Sauk Rapids, and associated with Northern Pacific land development/speculation in the early 1870s. Sweet was apparently an associate of Thomas H. Canfield. Wikipedia.

by them at Oak Lake on Tuesday of last week. At that point they found about fifty "hard tickets," twenty-five of the number being desperados like "Jack O'Neil," "Buffalo Jack," "Red-headed Jack," "Limber-heel," etc., who have held the respectable portion of that community under a reign of terror, drawing their revolvers upon anyone who had the temerity to refuse to surrender money or anything else that might be demanded of them; openly and at will robbing and plundering and leading the life of highwaymen.

Notice to leave was at once served upon these characters. They held a consultation to decide whether they had better obey. . . . On the following day they did go. . . . At Oak Lake, Major Brackett arrested Jack Wellwood, alias "Lying Jack," and S. B. Pinney, formerly a lawyer in St. Cloud, for selling liquor to the Indians.

At Buffalo River he arrested Louis Berg on a similar charge. A crowd of Berg's sympathetic friends attempted a rescue, but finally abandoned the undertaking. At White Earth Reservation Henry Banlean and Clem. Fairbanks were arrested; at the second crossing of the Otter Tail, Nicholas Hendry; at Prairie Lake, J. Knowles, and at Otter Tail City, Antonio Mayo, Charles C. McCloud, and J. Bourrett were arrested—all upon the charge of selling liquor to the Indians. These prisoners were put in irons, and started for St. Paul. . . .

Messrs. Brackett and Sweet then started across the country for Crow Wing, making all possible haste to reach that point before the parties they were after should hear of their coming. They were barely successful, for a courier in the interests of the gambling and liquor selling fraternity arrived there just as they did. Messrs. Brackett and Sweet at once proceeded to business, arresting Allen Morrison, John Geo. Morrison, Albert Fairbanks, Joe Reed, and Louis La Fontaine, all for selling liquor to Indians. These prisoners the Major saw safely under lock and key in the St. Paul Jail yesterday morning and last evening. Mr. Cruikshank arrived with his prisoners, and they were also furnished quarters in the same public institution.

The penalty . . . is imprisonment for a term of two to five years, and a fine of from $1,000 to $5,000.

At Detroit Lake the officers attempted to arrest Chas. Tobin, but the fellow broke and ran. Major Brackett fired two, and Col. Sweet three shots at him, but there was a thick growth of brush in the locality and Tobin made good his escape.

. . . Major Brackett served notice upon all parties along the entire line of the road, to discontinue the sale of liquors of any kind within the five-mile limit prescribed by the law passed last winter, and he will return immediately to enforce that order.

Source: St. Paul newspaper,[19] *August 1, 1871.*

From Red River

Major A. B. Brackett returned from an absence of twenty days to the Northern Pacific and Red River country yesterday morning. . . . He reports Moorhead as a bustling, driving, thriving village of some hundreds of inhabitants already. From twenty-five to thirty buildings are in the process of erection, several are completed, and others contemplated. . . . All of the gamblers, pimps, bullies, and harlots that have been following up the N.P. road have been driven out of Moorhead, and are now located at Fargo, the new town on the Dakota side of the Red River.

Source: Minneapolis Tribune, *October 12, 1871.*

Moorhead: A Specimen of Western Growth, Business Prospects, etc.

Special Dispatch to the St. Paul Pioneer

Moorhead, Oct. 11.—The census of the city of Moorhead, Minn. [shows] the population is 220, who occupy 49 buildings, one of which is a hotel, 80 by 112 feet, three general stores, the largest 24 by 48 feet, with four warehouses attached, and all were filled, several restaurants and saloons, one wagon-shop, bakery, livery stable, shoe shop, two meat markets, one wholesale liquor store, one hardware store, carpenter shops, and fifty to one-hundred wagons loaded with merchandise passing through town daily on their way to the settlement down the [north flowing Red] river.

Source: St. Paul Pioneer, *October 12, 1871.*

---

[19]Either the *St. Paul Press* or the *Pioneer,* my notes being unclear.

Northern Pacific R.R.
Serious Riot at Oak Lake— Arrest of Some of the Leading Desperados— The Marshal Still at Work

Special Dispatch to the St. Paul Pioneer

OAK LAKE, Oct. 24.—A serious riot has been in progress at this place to-day. Major Brackett is on the ground, and has six of the leading desperados, viz: Blinkey Jack, Buffalo Jack, and four others, now in irons, and is going for the rest of them. One man who was wounded is not expected to live. General [Alonzo Jay] Edgerton is here assisting the Marshal.[20]

Source: St. Paul Pioneer, *October 25, 1871.*

From Brainerd
The Roughs on the Rampage— A Series of Shootings—Several Persons Wounded—Brackett Sent For

Brainerd, Minn., Nov. 26, 1871

To the Editors of the St. Paul Pioneer

About eleven o'clock last night an affray occurred between two roughs at a house of ill-fame in the suburbs of the town. After several shots were exchanged they clubbed each other with their revolvers. When the smoke cleared up and order was restored, it was found that one had a ball hole in his head and a few cuts on his face and head, while the other was less injured.

Not long after this affray occurred, one which threatened a more serious result took place in Frank Dunn's billiard saloon. D. S. Shemaway entered the saloon, took a drink, and turning to Dunn's woman, insulted her by calling her all sorts of names. Dunn "took it up," and after a little conversation, revolvers were drawn and nine or ten shots exchanged.

---

[20]Bvt. Brig. Gen. Alonzo Jay Edgerton (1827–96) was a respected Minnesota attorney who in 1871 became Minnesota's first railroad commissioner. What his connection was, if any, with the Northern Pacific is unclear, and the reason he was assisting Marshal Brackett, other than being a good/leading citizen, is unknown. See Hunt, *Brevet Generals in Blue*.

When the shooting commenced one lamp only was burning in the room, but was extinguished by the second shot. At the commencement of the affray there were several persons in the room, but they made their escape through the different outside doors as soon as possible, not wishing to take any part in the play.

Shemaway was wounded in the left side, but not serious, I think, as he has appeared on the streets this morning.

Major Brackett has been sent for, and is expected sometime to-night. The roughs along the line of the Northern Pacific Railroad do not like the looks of the Major, for whenever he appears on the streets one can see groups of them together, and hear them asking one another, who is Brackett after.

Source: St. Paul Pioneer, *November 29, 1871.*

Ned Jordan: Letter to a Young Lady

Detroit Lake, January 14, 1871

My dear Nell Hillhouse:[21]

. . . So far I have not explained where I am, what I am, how I am, or how I came where I am.

After stopping in Geneva [New York] and having a long and interesting talk with your Father in regard to the future prospective greatness of the Northern Pacific Railroad, and after enjoying myself in many other delightful ways, as you know I called on you in Albany. Homeward bound and home [Portland, Maine] at last reached, there I reveled in being considered and treated as company; no errands to perform, nothing to do except to tell the natural experiences of a Californian life, wondered at by believing sisters and slightly scoffed at by unbelieving brothers.

I hardly talked myself out . . . when I was ordered to report to St. Paul, Minnesota, without a moment's delay more than specified. My [railroad] passes carried me by way of Montreal where I was detained for two days; to be fleeced by cabmen and hucksters. . . . "Beware of Montreal[!]"

[21]Little is known about Nell Hillhouse other than she was the daughter of Thomas Hillhouse (1817–97), adjutant general of the New York Militia in 1861–62, New York State comptroller, assistant treasurer of the United States, and a banker. He held other public and private offices and owned considerable land in Geneva. Wikipedia.

Finally having arrived in St. Paul I was most disagreeably surprised by the non-appearance of my baggage—neither would I hear anything in regard to it during the three days I was allowed to equip myself and party for a trip into the northwestern wilderness of Minnesota.

I was given a topographical party with orders to examine a portion of the country in the vicinity of Ottertail City. Eight days travel with my outfit brought one to that place, and each day was the counterpart of the other. Across a new country with only a compass for a guide, rain, rain, rain with four or five "stuck in the sloughs" describes the trip. When I was asked by Gen. Spaulding if I was used to getting out of difficulties, [I told him] he should have seen me in a slough, with the horse and wagon hitched on a hundred feet of rope with fifteen men knee-deep in mud, pulling and shouting like fire Jakeys,[22] or else he should have seen me ferrying swollen rivers swimming the horses and rafting the outfit. Ottertail City at length reached proved itself but slightly better than its once rival town Leaf City in which I had quite an adventure.[23]

I noticed on the map that my route was laid down and passing through Leaf City, a city laid out in blocks and squares. I stopped before a grand hotel, only the hotel was not evident; and what seemed still more strange I could see the men clustered around the wagon instead of being inside getting a drink as was their custom at each real hotel. But upon a thorough examination, I came to the conclusion that the multitude of stakes I saw dotted broadcast over the prairie were only symbols for hotels, churches, court houses, etc., and upon more mature reflection I put it down as one of those paper towns of the land excitement of 1857 consisting of not one solitary house or building of any sort and never having existed. . . .

Ottertail, the metropolis of the northwest section, deserves special mention. At the time of my arrival it consisted of two stores, three dwelling houses, and a sawmill. At different periods of the year there are scattered about the streets and squares (for it is a regularly laid out

---

[22]An older definition is "sailor," so likely Jordan meant it like lower-ranking "firemen."

[23]Today there are at least three Leaf Lakes in Minnesota, as well as an East and West Leaf Lake. The community of Leaf City, to which Jordan referred, appears to have been on one of the latter two. Beginning in the late 1780s, there was competition between American and British fur traders, the land's ownership not settled until after the War of 1812. A handful of trading post buildings were built on the north side of the lake and used by different owners until shortly before the Civil War, their chimneys still standing in the 1890s. As the reader will see, this does not appear to be the same Leaf City that Jordan encountered, although the two were close. Was Jordan exaggerating in his letter, something not unusual when attempting to appeal to a young lady?

city) the portable habitations of the noble Redman, the Lo's.[24] I was quite fortunate in seeing Ottertail in its Gala season.

The big medicine man of the Chippewa tribe was present together with some 300 Indians and they were holding a high carnival. They formed a long rectangular arbor and in the middle they placed a feast of stewed dog, baked beans, and fish; around the perimeter of the arbor the assembled Indians squat. I should have remarked that this Big Medicine is sort of a secret society in which all their traditions are kept. . . .

Their proceedings were nearly as follow: The novitiates started from one end of the enclosure accompanied by the Big Medicine and play hop, skip, and a jump over the feast of stewed dog, fish, and beans until they and the accompanying whoopers and shriekers grew faint from exhaustion. The arbor figure being finished, the novitiates went off reveling in the inspirations they had received from the Big Medicine, some few accompanying him into the woods to gain knowledge of the use of "pisew herbs" (see Carlton's History of Minnesota).[25] This continued for three days, only twice varied by the pretended cure of infantile Sickness. As near as I could tell the cure consisted of Big Medicine taking the patient in his arms and carrying him through such a terrible hubbub as to completely disgust the evil spirit and ensure his departure. Or, in other words, to exorcise the evil spirit by hideous sounds rather than by religious symbols.

I was exceedingly loathe to leave Ottertail, but I had soon exhausted its central topographical features [and] also that of its suburbs, and nothing was left but to push through a dense growth of timber forty miles wide—full of lakes, swamps, marshes and mosquitoes. I packed three horses with thirty days rations; one blanket per man and cooking kit consisting of one frying pan, one bean pot, one coffee pot, knife and fork, cup and plate to [each] man, and started to cut our way through at the rate of one mile per day.

All this was very interesting, time passing quickly in our contest with Mosquitoes and Tarmac swamps. Most of the Tarmac Swamps, so called, are floating forests of trees, and beneath the network of roots and moss there is generally a mud lake from 10 to 20 feet deep. One has to only step on the interlacing roots to walk along quite safely. My Indian pony was adept at this; he carried a pack of 200 pounds and jumped from root to root, occasionally floundering but always recovering.

---

[24]"Mr. Lo" or "Mrs. Lo" was the *cool* expression for an Indian, and Jordan makes full use of the idiom and slang of his day.

[25]Jordan's note in the original. I have been unable to identify the book.

But the horses were different. A misstep would send them through the sod only to be got out by slipping poles beneath and lifting them by main strength. This together with an occasional disappearance of the head of some unlucky chap to be extricated in the same beastly manner gave a variety that was not to be harkened after, but which serves its purpose in giving spice to our life. For fifteen days this life continued, the men growing cross and surly from the prolonged hardships of wet clothes, disturbed sleep and from the incessant warfare with mosquitoes. But finally a welcome messenger arrived and delivered orders for me to report immediately in the metropolis of Ottertail.

On the way in, I learned that an engineering corps for the 5th Residency had arrived in Ottertail and that I was to report to its First Assistant.[26] My appearance as I presented myself before the swell flag tent of the 5th Residency was decidedly picturesque. Rents in my pantaloons were held up with thin strands of bark; my shoes, or the soles of what were shoes, tied in sandal fashion with bark. My stockings consisted of merely anklets of cotton and everything betokened a rough ragged rascal. After making several of the young engineers faint with the prospect of what they were likely to become when they got away from the supply station, I went to the store house and got on my outfit and became high toned as became the 5th Residency.

You can hardly form an adequate idea of what fine material you sometimes find in the engineering corps on this road. For instance, in the one I found myself assigned to, I found several elegant gentlemen. A Mr. Johnson, a "Sig," and son of the Chief Engineer. A Mr. Meigs from Washington, son of Quartermaster General Meigs.[27] A Mr. Eastman, son of General [Seth] Eastman, of the Regular Army.[28] Messrs. Swan and Patterson, bankers' sons from New York and Philadelphia, respectively.

[26]For administrative purposes, the Northern Pacific divided sections of Minnesota into "residencies" or districts.

[27]Montgomery Meigs (1847–12/9/1931) was to become one of Jordan's closest friends. He had the best formal education of his day, including Harvard and two years of mathematical studies in Germany. See *New York Times* obituary and various 1920s editions of *Who's Who.*

[28]Frank Eastman (d. 1884). Sadly, Eastman—energetic, affable, and skilled—became an alcoholic and was fired by Rosser during the latter part of the 1872 Yellowstone survey. See my book *Before Custer,* 211. Seth Eastman (1808–75) was a West Point graduate and became one of the country's best-known artists. Too old for combat duty, he was assigned administrative tasks before having to retire in 1863. Brevetted as a brigadier general after the war, Eastman was called back to "active" duty to paint over two dozen pictures in the U.S. Capitol and other Washington buildings. See *Dictionary of American Biography* and most encyclopedias dealing with western history and nineteenth-century artists.

A Mr. Bailey, graduate of Yale. Messrs. Mores and Smith, protégés of Judge Rice, vice president N.P.R.R.[29] And, in fact, a swell party.

Looking around I found each member the possessor of a Saratoga trunk and expecting transportation for the same. But the N.P.R.R. was hardly willing to furnish that, and they were hardly willing to tote the trunks themselves, so they were obliged to conform to the dimensions of a "Kennebecker," or in other words a bag of clothes about the size of a Christmas pudding bag. In this they packed their more necessary articles and were off for a seven-month camping survey.

"Blood will tell." These young knobs, laughed and sneered at by the rough common men of the party, were more willing and suffered the many little disagreeable duties with less complaint than the very men hired for *tough* [work]. I remember well their first severe initiation: it was in crossing a wide boggy river bottom. You must understand that these young men on account of having had no experience occupied very low positions in the corps. They were chainmen, flagmen, explorers, etc. As they stood on the bank of the Ottertail River with orders to cross, they were dubious but jokingly determined. Morse headed the [36-pound iron Günter] chains and waded and partly swam the river proper and reached the boggy shore. After trolling Smith across (Smith couldn't swim) spoon hook fashion, they commenced the amusing part of their trip. Watching them through the telescope, I saw Morse disappear and immediately come up shouting. Smith! Keep to the left—keep to the left—there is an air hole here! The sounder reported 26 feet and no bottom—Smith looking back to me yells—it will break through—I am not going across! Keep a firm hold of the chain Smith and I will troll you through, only be careful that a big pickerel don't grab you, thinking that you are a little pony—*Ka-win coucoush* Morse. The last in Chippewa, "not for fork."

Smith landed safely and several chains [later he goes] on with varying floundering success when suddenly Morse disappears again and on rising swears that someone pulled his shoe off when he was down. Twenty-six feet and no bottom, called the sounder—. I guess I will let the shoe remain. Smith was trolled across this and other places and finally they reached the other side. Handing over my instrument to the toter to take it across at a ford a mile up the river, I started across on the line. It was

[29]Richard D. Rice (1810–82), had been a Maine Supreme Court justice and active in railroading. He appears to have been thoroughly dishonest, and being placed in charge of West Coast construction had even more leeway.

like walking on a feather bed; at each step I took, it billowed up before me, threatening to engulf me constantly. But the secret of success was in rapid motion, the same as Phin. will explain it to be in skating over thin ice; therefore, I did not humor the boys on the other side by going through. On the west bank I found Meigs a drowned slimy rat and in his account of himself said that he experimented on a splendid place to cross as he supposed and found it decidedly soft.—back up and swing to the north, this crossing is impracticable, came from the chief. And three times that day we crossed the Rubicon. That evening was full of merry bantering in the aspirants' tent and full of growls and complaints in the tent of the "hoi polloi." Thus we went on, traveling and running preliminary lines and finally locating the line, which I am now constructing.

I had many little adventures by canoe and land, full of excitement and interest. My *particular* friend was Meigs with whom if acquainted I feel very confident that even you would feel an interest and make a quadruple out of the triangle of Ben Chew, *the impulsive Falken*,[30] and myself formed. [Meigs's] fine family, his good connection, his travelled manners (having been a student in Europe for two years), and his estimable self make him a very choice companion. On one of our returning trips from the Red River of the North, Meigs and myself took one of the party that was an old Chippewa scout, and started across the country with a canoe and hunting equipment. We followed the chain of Buffalo Path Lakes,[31] carrying the canoe on our heads across the connecting portages; and through lakes and rivers we travelled for a hundred miles or more, living upon the fish and game that the country afforded in plenteous quantities. Several times we snagged our canoe and had narrow escapes from dangerous swims. Birch bark and Indians were plenty and it took but little time to make our craft sea worthy after these accidents.

The Indians were all reported friendly, but our natural distrust of them made our trip exciting. Similar trips give a glowing color to my life here but do not let Phin. think but what the bitter in the real life far exceeds the sweet.

But the real fact is that the bitter experiences as I look back upon them afford the keener relish. The wading of brooks, marshes and rivers during the latter part of the cold fall months, the astonishing cold of the

---

[30]Unidentified.

[31]The name "Buffalo Path Lakes" does not exist today. There is a Buffalo Lake just north of Detroit Lakes, but these seem further east than Jordan's description.

winter make it as terror indeed, and a weakner of one's constitution. For the last month the temperature has ramped from 10° to 26° below zero.

I am now in new quarters. A log house, Meigs architect, forms the headquarters of the Fifth Residency, myself acting as Resident Engineer with a First Assistant commission. Thus I have traced myself to my present abode.

For my long continued silence to one who has expressed herself interested in my welfare, I owe an apology. Sad changes have taken place in my family circle,[32] and a sad retrospection constantly intrudes itself when I think of those delightful times when no broken family ties served to mar its enjoyment. My father was becoming rejuvenated in the promise of his sons. One of them, the mainstay of his youth, with every prospect of a brilliant career, has been taken away. . . .

How often I think of the most trivial details—even to the mending of my coat by your best of mothers, to many instructive talks with your father, bearing as he did my plodding ignorance. . . .

With much love to all . . .

Source: Transcribed from the original in 1954 by E. C. Jordan, Ned Jordan's namesake and great-nephew. Courtesy of Mark Jordan.

---

[32]One of Jordan's older brothers, Henry, a Bowdoin graduate and physician, had died in October, possibly of tuberculosis.

CHAPTER 3

Initiating the Yellowstone Surveys

The railroad distance between Bismarck, North Dakota, and Bozeman, Montana, when completed by the Northern Pacific, was fractionally under 600 miles, yet not a foot had been surveyed before 1871. While the Army Corps of Engineers had mapped the Yellowstone River portion of the route, no one knew how many tunnels or bridges might be needed or if there was a suitable route through North Dakota's Badlands.

As for the Bozeman Pass, a major accomplishment of Milnor Roberts's 1869 "eyeball" survey was his crossing it and, by taking primitive measurements, satisfying himself that track would be feasible. (Then he made a management decision that any angler can appreciate; he spent a day trout fishing in the Yellowstone.)

In turn, the Badlands ran perpendicular to the planned Missouri-Yellowstone route. Fear of the Sioux had seen even the bravest prospector give it a wide berth. It was here that General "Alf" Sully had waged a brutal campaign against the Sioux in 1864. He established Fort Rice on the Missouri, decapitated three Sioux prisoners, killed hundreds of Sioux at Killdeer Mountain, and routed them a second time at the Battle of the Badlands.[1] However, Sully's only engineer was killed during the

[1]Alfred Sully (1821–79) was a West Point graduate (1841), Mexican War veteran, and brevetted Civil War major general. The son of the artist Thomas Sully, in California in the early 1850s Sully fell in love with the 15-year-old daughter of a large ranch owner. Sully impregnated and married the girl, but after the child was born, the family apparently poisoned his wife and "accidentally" suffocated the baby! As for the beheadings, the only real question is whether the Sioux were alive or dead at the time of decapitation, accounts leading to logical conclusions for both. In the late 1860s on the Kansas Plains, Sully ran afoul of George Custer and Sheridan, and his career ended ignominiously. See his grandson Langdon Sully's fascinating *No Tears for the General: The Life of Alfred Sully, 1821–1879*.

campaign, and the only maps produced afterwards were misleading, as the North Pacific's surveyors would discover.

For whatever reasons, the Northern Pacific's Board of Directors seemed hesitant to survey this 600-mile gap. We can only speculate that—with all their other problems and competitive pressures—they didn't want to call public attention to likely Indian opposition. However, by early 1871, internal pressure was mounting. Roberts, for example, had written to fellow engineer D. C. Linsley in April.[2]

> Your views about the surveys of the Yellowstone [etc.] . . . are exactly those which I have formed from the facts before us, and I yet hope that the Company may feel in a position to devote time, money, and engineering talent to the thorough development of the region through which the road must pass, *without delay.* (Minnesota Historical Society, M-459)

To what degree the May 15 news of a third transcontinental railroad spurred the Northern Pacific into action cannot be known. However, the Southern Pacific's announcement was a direct shot across the Northern Pacific's bow. "When a railroad is projected," the *New York Daily Tribune* quoted them, "there must be a flourishing line of villages to tempt capital from its ordinary business routes."[3] The article continued by saying that construction was technically easy and over flat terrain, that prime farmland was already at $100 an acre, and that all costs would be lowered by Chinese labor. Ultimately the Southern Pacific had its own problems, but it went on to complete its track a month before the Northern Pacific.

Not until June did the Northern Pacific begin a series of frantic activities to put two teams of engineers in place working east from Bozeman/Fort Ellis and west from Fort Rice. The decision apparently caught Milnor Roberts by surprise; documents show him complaining that he had had to hire staff for the western survey that he did not know.

The subject had been discussed among the military for months, but the date when the Northern Pacific's first formal request was made is uncertain. On August 15 the army formally issued orders and began

[2]Daniel C. Linsley (1827–88), assistant chief engineer, came from Vermont where he or his family likely knew Smith. Joining the NPRR as a surveyor in Washington Territory, he appears to have been promised Edwin Johnson's job but lost out to Roberts. Close to if not brilliant, he was nevertheless detested by the younger surveyors and feared by Rosser, who reported directly to him. He worked exclusively in Minnesota in 1871, and apparently construction problems would have been greater without him. See *National Cyclopedia of American Biography*, 16:233.

[3]"The Third Railroad to the Pacific," *New York Daily Tribune,* June 6, 1871.

shuffling troops to Fort Rice from five Dakota posts: Forts Abercrombie, Randall, Ransom, Sully, and Wadsworth.[4] Regarding the western survey, the necessary cavalrymen and supplies were at Fort Ellis.

* * *

The leading military and railroad personnel on the surveys were not the stick figures one sees so often in history books. Excepting the Quaker, Milnor Roberts, most were hard drinking, violent, but intelligent combat survivors. Key army (with 1871 rank) and Northern Pacific personnel included the following:[5]

Maj. Gen. Winfield Scott Hancock (1824–86), West Point '44, commander of the Department of Dakota and hero of Gettysburg for stopping Pickett's Charge. Hancock was on the outs with Grant, his West Point classmate, as well as Generals Sherman and Sheridan, the latter whom he particularly despised. Headquartered in St. Paul, Hancock commanded almost 3,000 officers and men and was responsible for 369,023 square miles (Dakota, Minnesota, and Montana), leaving slightly more than 1,200 square miles (larger than Rhode Island) per soldier. Despite Hancock's huge ego, bolstered by his strong showing at the 1868 Democratic presidential convention (he was the 1880 nominee), and his unhappiness at the last-minute nature of the surveys, he was fully supportive of the Northern Pacific.

Col. David Sloane Stanley (1828–1902), West Point '52. Throughout 1870–71 Stanley commanded the 22nd Infantry as well as the District of Dakota from Fort Sully. This command contained the majority of reservation Sioux and 46 percent of Hancock's troops. While he did not take the field, he personally oversaw final preparations for the eastern survey.

Maj. Joseph Nelson Garland Whistler (1822–99), West Point '46; commander of the eastern Yellowstone survey. Whistler distinguished himself in the Mexican War, but when the Civil War began, he was stationed in Texas, captured, and not exchanged for over a year.

[4] *Army and Navy Journal,* August 26, 1871.

[5] Sources include *Dictionary of American Biography*; *National Cyclopedia of American Biography*; Thrapp, *Encyclopedia of Frontier Biography*; U.S. Military Academy, *Annual Reunion*; Warner, *Generals in Blue* and *Generals in Gray*. Biographical materials for Irvine and Clement are to be found in the South Dakota State Historical Society.

He saw desk service until 1864 when he was seriously wounded during the Richmond campaign, never seeing combat again. Whistler came from an old army family; lobbying by relatives and friends saw to his becoming a brevetted brigadier general after the war. His first cousin (not brother, as some sources state) was the artist James McNeil Whistler. While well liked by many, in 1871 he was burnt out, a functional alcoholic often too inebriated to read a compass, which cost the expedition at least an extra 55 miles marching and four days in the field. The famed diarist Col. Philippe Régis de Trobriand had written four years earlier:

> [Whistler's] whole family is in poverty [from the cost of sending daughters to schools in the east], poverty in which not even appearances can be kept up. . . . [He] will probably ask for some post in detached service which will put him close to Georgetown [District of Columbia] near Washington, where he will leave his family. But he probably will not get it, for this type of work is very much sought after, and the old soldier has spent his life on the plains far from the political world and sources of favor [and] cannot exert enough influence to make his plans succeed.[6]

Maj. Eugene Mortimer Baker (1836–84) commanded the garrison at Fort Ellis, Montana Territory, which included four companies of the Second Cavalry. Rugged, well-built, and physically impressive, Baker was a skilled combat officer and, by 1871, self-confident, perhaps to the point of alcohol-induced stupidity. Baker came to Phil Sheridan's notice during the 1864 Winchester, Virginia, campaign. The primary reason he did not receive a brigadier's star was his bad luck of being in the federal cavalry where advancement was slow. After the war Sheridan gave him difficult, distasteful assignments. For leading expeditions against "hostile Indians" in Oregon and Idaho in 1866–68 ("mop up" operations against a demoralized, poorly armed foe), Sheridan brevetted him a lieutenant colonel.

In the winter of 1870–71 Baker led a Sheridan-ordered raid against "hostile" Blackfeet Indians, attacked the wrong camp, and killed 170 men, woman, and children. He then released 140 survivors into the bitter winter, without supplies and where, one assumes, many more perished. Baker suffered zero casualties. The more one studies this "fight," the

---

[6]De Trobriand, *Military Life in Dakota*, 53. French-born Philippe Régis de Trobriand (1816–97) was as able and colorful a bon vivant as could be imagined. He was a brevetted major general and commanded a division, seeing heavy combat, including Gettysburg, during the war. De Trobriand's *Military Life* is justly considered a western classic.

uglier it gets, although it increased his popularity with hardline Montana residents. "He was," a classmate wrote in Baker's obituary, "one of the most successful commanders of such expeditions that our service has produced, a consequence of which was that he has been most violently abused by the ruthless press of our country."[7]

Over the years Baker's drinking accelerated. Not being able to peer into his subconscious, we have no idea what psychological price (if any) he paid for his handiwork. "Unfortunately," his classmate continued, "Colonel Baker, like so many officers of fine physique, believing that nothing could injure his constitution, neglected such precautions as he might have taken and broke down sooner than he had the slightest idea that he could."

In 1871 Baker, who never took command in the Yellowstone valley, was at times dysfunctional, as Roberts's letters show. Baker never married and, other than formal military documents, he left behind no personal writings. Baker's brief "comments" on the survey are in his annual report (see chapter 7).

CAPTAIN EDWARD BALL (ca. 1824–84) commanded two companies from the Second Cavalry on the western survey. Ball enlisted in the army in 1844 and participated in the Mexican War. Ball was of average height and without a formal education. But by staying in the Second Cavalry he slowly advanced, finally becoming a captain in 1865. Ball was promoted to major in 1880. Four years later he retired, dying six months later. Ball does not appear to have married. His formal report, clear and concise, is in chapters 5 and 7.

CAPT. JAVAN BRADLEY IRVINE (1831–1904). Born in New York's Finger Lakes region, Irvine moved to St. Paul, where he became a jack-of-all-trades. About 1857 he and friends hit upon the scheme of floating carefully packed ice down the Mississippi to Memphis. They raised $15,000, but Memphis was reached only after delays and unseasonably hot weather that melted the ice. Now broke, Irvine turned to carpentry and in 1861 attempted to join the First Minnesota Volunteers, which rejected him. Undaunted he nevertheless stayed with the regiment unofficially. At Bull Run, in the smoke of battle, he became lost and blundered into a Confederate regiment where, with only a bayonet, he captured the unit's colonel, the highest ranking prisoner of the day. Unsure what

[7]U.S. Military Academy, *West Point Annual Reunion,* June 12, 1885, 61–63.

to make of him, the regular army took him off the First Minnesota's hands, made him a lieutenant in the quartermasters, and ensured that he saw no further action.[8]

After the war Irvine was transferred to the Twenty-Second Infantry. He became Company A's captain and a good friend of the regiment's colonel, David Stanley. Strongly pro-abolition, idealistic, and devout, but with a quick temper, Irvine's candid, frequently angry and fearful (of Indians) diaries and letters are in chapters 4, 6, and 8.

William Milnor Roberts (1810–81) was the key Northern Pacific participant on the western survey. Beginning surveying as a teenager, his experience included canals, tunnels, railroads, and bridges. Roberts had married a daughter of the chief justice of the Pennsylvania Supreme Court and was related by marriage to both Union and Confederate generals. Later a daughter married Capt. G. W. Yates, who fell with Custer.

Cooke had used Roberts as a consultant before the war. Their mutual enthusiasm—neither suffered fools gladly—for the Northern Pacific brought them remarkably close. Roberts's appointment as chief engineer to replace the enfeebled Edwin Johnson was an absolute necessity. Roberts's honesty became obvious when, shortly after being appointed, he was sent to inspect Puget Sound construction and overrode one of Smith's cronies' orders for expensive, unnecessary equipment.[9] Roberts clearly presented a dilemma for Smith: how could he prevent the engineer from discovering Minnesota's corruption and waste? Smith's Machiavellian answer worked perfectly: Roberts was physically kept out of Minnesota throughout 1871, and one reason after another was found to send him to work in Montana or on the West Coast.

Physically, Roberts was a sixty-one-year-old marvel with a wife half his age. A baby girl was soon born, but in the spring of 1871 she died at eighteen months while her parents were in Washington Territory. Of average height, Roberts was wiry, possessed exceptional stamina, forgot nothing, could sleep or read in the saddle, and aside from being partially deaf (from caisson sickness while building the St. Louis bridge), he was

[8]Irvine couldn't have been luckier, for few regiments suffered heavier casualties. At Gettysburg, of the First Minnesota's 262 officers and men entering battle, 215 (82 percent) were killed or wounded, the highest losses any Union (and perhaps Confederate) regiment experienced in one battle.

[9]After Roberts began work, Smith invited him to St. Albans. On arriving, Smith told Roberts that his plans had changed, and then Smith left half an hour later. This studied insult perhaps best illustrates their relationship.

in perfect health. Roberts's subordinates loved him, for he was a gentle manager, leading by suggestion. Roberts hated only two things, killing and alcoholics, thus dooming his relationship with Major Baker before it started.

Thomas Lafayette Rosser (1836–1910). Rosser, the leader of the eastern surveyors, was born in Virginia and raised as a teenager in Texas. He had a weak education before entering the then five-year West Point curriculum. At twenty-four he was weeks away from graduation when he resigned to join the Confederate army. A huge man for his day, 6' 2" and weighing over 200 pounds, he was slim-hipped and graceful. A protégé of Jeb Stuart, Rosser became colonel of a Virginia cavalry regiment (1862) and was placed in command as a brigadier general of the famed Laurel Brigade the next year. A terror in combat, he is said to have sliced one poor Yankee in half. He personally killed a score of men and participated in more than 100 battles and skirmishers. At Appomattox, Rosser was a major general, leading the last Confederate unit breaking through the federal encirclement commanded by his West Point friend George Custer. Rosser let himself be captured (versus the ignominy of surrendering) a month after Lee's capitulation.

Married in 1863 after a whirlwind courtship and after the war with a growing family, Rosser found himself without permanent employment until February 13, 1870.[10] Once working for the Northern Pacific his natural leadership—the overused word *charismatic* being truly applicable—quickly shone. While Rosser suffered from chronic depression and worry about being discharged, literally being in the saddle again with men to command brought out the best in him. Rosser's diaries and a report survive. They are reproduced in chapters 4, 6, and 8. Of Rosser, the surveyor Edward Jordan wrote:

> His force and directions and his ability to enlist the best labors of others he soon showed by and over those who possessed perhaps more technical engineering capacity. He was the man [above] all others to organize the various Yellowstone Engineering Expeditions attended as they were by large military escorts, and I think perhaps the bravest man I ever saw.[11]

---

[10]Rosser to his wife the evening of February 13, 1870. Collection 11171 g-h-g, box 16, Rosser Letters 1867–73, University of Virginia, Charlottesville.

[11]Jordan's letter, to a friend, was written in the early spring of 1873, but no date is available. Jordan also wrote a letter of recommendation to Rosser for his friend, but received a letter back (May 21) from Rosser stating that there was no room for the friend, but there was still room for Jordan!

Edward Dutchman Muhlenberg (1831–83), leader of the western survey, was born in Pennsylvania, a direct descendant of Henry Muhlenberg, the eighteenth-century patriarch of the American Lutheran Church. Muhlenberg graduated from Yale in 1850, afterward surveying in Pennsylvania. With the advent of the war, he joined the Union artillery, distinguishing himself at Gettysburg and other battles. Later he worked for railroads in Texas and Pennsylvania. Exactly when he joined the Northern Pacific is not clear, but he needed the influence of Pennsylvania senator Simon Cameron—a Lincoln cabinet member and GOP leader—to secure his position. Considering his strong paper résumé, there obviously was something wrong, which in his case was alcohol.

Basil Clement (1824–1910) was lead scout on the eastern survey.[12] Born in St. Louis but part Indian, Clement spent his adult life as a trapper, boatman, army scout, and interpreter (he spoke Sioux). In 1870 he was selling wood to steamers making their way up the Missouri. It is not known if Clement had even seen a locomotive by 1871, and he certainly didn't understand the basic requirements of railroad construction. It was one thing to take a wagon train through an uphill gap, but would that same pass permit a railroad? What is certain is that Rosser didn't trust his judgment. Clement and Northern Pacific were fortunate that Sully's campaign had left a trail of nonbiodegradable debris (unexploded artillery shells among others) that stretched to the Yellowstone and couldn't be missed. Clement was physically unattractive, heavy-boned and squat with slits for eyes; like so many others he drank heavily, which didn't seem to affect his judgment, but it did make him less than pleasant to be around.

President Smith's Instructions to Roberts

With the decision to conduct the Yellowstone surveys, Smith sent the following letter to Chief Engineer Milnor Roberts. The need to be formal when issuing instructions aside, the letter appears designed to keep Roberts in Montana and other western territories as long as possible.

[12]Clement's French Canadian name was pronounced *Claymore* and *Clemmo,* the latter being what the surveyors called him. Information and photographs can be found at the South Dakota Historical Society in Pierre.

June 20, 1871

Dear Sir;

The Board of Directors have instructed me to cause the line of our Road to be surveyed from the Missouri River to the Columbia, and have appropriated for that purpose the sum of eighty thousand dollars.

In pursuance of said vote, you are instructed to proceed at once to organize a sufficient number of parties to accomplish the surveys between these points within the current season.

You will commence the work from the eastern end, at a point in the line of survey recently made under charge of Engineer Linsley in Dakota, which shall be common to a line running due east & west and a line running via the Missouri River.

From this point you will proceed on as nearly a due east & west course as the nature of the country will admit, till you strike the valley of the Yellowstone, thence following the main valley of the latter river to Bozeman Pass. Thence you will explore all the principal passes of the Rocky Mountains accessible at this point—and thence crossing the Columbia up the Valley of the Yakima River to Puget Sound.

Should time and the limitations of the appropriation permit, you will also survey a line from the Columbia into the Skagit River, & thence to Puget Sound.

In the organization of your parties, and in order to accomplish the work within the pursuant season, it may be well to start parties from the west working eastward, as well as from the east working westward. The organization & arrangement of parties however is left to your sound discretion.

In giving general instructions, owing to the want of information as to the nature & character of the country to be traversed, it is impossible to define any given route to be followed. You will therefore be left to the exercise of sound discretion in the selection of the best & most feasible route between the points indicated, namely the Missouri River and the Columbia via the Yellowstone valley—and from the Columbia to Puget Sound: the object of the Company being to obtain reliable & full information of the country between those points.

The passes through the Rocky Mountains being of special importance, you will, as far as practicable, make personal examination of these, so as to be able to render a full and complete report on the subject, & to indicate to the Board your judgment as to the best and most desirable of them for the purposes of our Road.

In the prosecution of the work you will be careful to keep as nearly as possible within the limitation of the appropriation.

It will probably be unsafe to carry on the work of these surveys between the Missouri River and Bozeman Pass without a proper military escort. Negotiations are now in progress with the Government to supply this, and it is hoped that a sufficient military force will be detailed and placed at your disposal.

Arrangements will also probably be made with the Government, by which you can purchase, at Government cost, at their Military Posts, supplies for your parties in case of necessity. Ample provision should however be made by you for such supplies before starting your parties, as this will undoubtedly be the safer course.

You will from time to time as you may have opportunity to communicate with me fully as to the progress made by the several parties in the field, and when your labors are completed, you will submit to me a full & complete report of your work, accompanied by maps & profiles. The Treasurer of the company will be instructed to answer your drafts and to arrange with you for the necessary funds.

You will keep accurate accounts of all the property purchased and expenditures made, returning the accounts & vouchers with your report, turning over all the property remaining after the work is completed as you may be hereafter instructed.

After the parties for the line above defined are properly organized and in the field, should the limitations of the appropriation in your judgment justify it, and there should be sufficient time remaining of the season to warrant it, you will put into the field a sufficient force for an exploring survey of the Northern line, so called, following the valley of the Missouri River. Submit your report thereon to the Board.

The latter however is deemed of secondary importance, & will not be undertaken to jeopardize in any manner the work of the other line.

Yours Truly,
J. Gregory Smith, President

Source: Minnesota Historical Society, M-459.

General Hancock to President Smith concerning the Yellowstone Surveys

Winfield Scott Hancock minced no words concerning his unhappiness about the timing of the eastern survey. There is no mention of the western survey's more limited requirements. In this letter he did everything possible to discourage Smith, but after receiving his formal orders, he fell into line. Note how even at this late June date nothing had been settled.

June 28, 1871

Gov. J. Gregory Smith, St. Albany, VT:

Your dispatch received, should I receive an order from the War Department to furnish you from my command with escort between the Missouri River and Yellowstone, I would collect if I had time to do so about six companies of infantry (about 300) men, which I consider to be the maximum I can furnish and not too large for the service, even if it be large enough.[13] I had hoped when this reconnaissance was to be made I should have troops enough and time enough for preparation to enable me to furnish a much larger escort, one which would intimidate the Indians from making any resistance to the required surveys, should they feel so disposed, and about which we are not at all certain. The country to be examined is one which, to my knowledge, has not been traversed by white men for several years past, and I consider it a dangerous one for parties of an inadequate strength to enter, and make a full and sufficient examination of [and] for your purposes. When General Sherman and I conversed upon this subject last winter, he considered an adequate and appropriate force for their purpose to be (8) eight companies of cavalry and (3) three or (4) four of infantry. I concurred with him in this view and see now no reason to change my opinion.

Signed,
W. S. Hancock, Major General, USA

Source: Minnesota Historical Society, M-459.

[13]Ultimately seven companies were sent. See chapter 4 for details.

Military Posts and Indian Agencies,
Department of Dakota, 1869–1873 (Officers and Men)

Districts[a]	*1869*	*1870*	*1871*	*1872*	*1873*
Montana					
Fort Shaw	NA	278	186	394	NA
Fort Ellis	NA	271	291	271	NA
Fort Benton	NA	65	48	63	NA
Camp Baker	NA	72	51	62	NA
subtotal	879	686	576	790	NA
Fort Buford	NA	285	167	428	NA
Middle (Dakota)					
Fort Sully	NA	234	253	268	NA
Fort Rice	NA	250	268	254	NA
Fort Randall	NA	205	223	245	NA
Fort Stevenson	NA	98	132	122	NA
Fort McKeenb	—	—	—	111	NA
Lower Brulé Agency	NA	111	51	56	NA
Cheyenne Agency	NA	191	114	91	NA
Grand River Agency	NA	182	115	124	NA
Old Ponca Agency	NA	118*	—	—	—
Whetstone Agency	NA	118*	57	—	—
In Camp [temporary]	—	—	—	54	—
Crow Creek Agency	NA	120*	—	—	—
subtotal	1,243	1,912	1,380	1,753	NA

Military Posts and Indian Agencies, Department of Dakota, 1869–1873 (Officers and Men) *(continued)*

Districts[a]	*1869*	*1870*	*1871*	*1872*	*1873*
Minnesota					
Fort Ridgely	NA	1	1*	—	—
Fort Snellingc	NA	104	93	78	NA
Fort Ripley	NA	79	56	53	NA
Fort Abercrombie**	NA	110	56	57	NA
Fort Wadsworth**	NA	98	123	57	NA
Fort Ranson**	NA	88	68	—	NA
Fort Totten**	NA	182	110	104	NA
Fort Pembina**	NA	144	86	92	NA
Fort Cross	—	—	—	103	NA
subtotal	246	806	593	544	NA
Temporarily Attached	NA	—	—	399	NA
Recruits en route	NA	317	429	504	NA
Grand Totals	**2,368**	**3,721**	**2,978**	**3,990**	**4,148**

Source: Annual Report of the Secretary of War on the Operations of the Department for the Fiscal Year Ended June 30, 18– *(varies by year).*

Note: The Department of Dakota was under the command of Winfield Scott Hancock from the spring of 1869 through the end of 1872. Alfred H. Terry commanded the department both before and after Hancock. Both officers reported to Philip H. Sheridan.

*Last year troops were stationed at agency or fort.

**Actually located in Dakota Territory.

[a]"District" lines did not necessarily correspond with state or territorial boundaries.

[b]Fort established in 1872 and renamed Fort Abraham Lincoln in 1873.

[c]Figure likely includes one company plus Department of Dakota staff and the staffs of some regiments, such as the 7th Cavalry in the fall of 1873.

Kingsley Bray's Estimated Teton Sioux (Lakota) Population History, 1805–1881

Tribal Division	*1805*	*1825*	*1839*[a]	*1855*	*1870*[b]	*1881*
Brulé	2,400	3,000	3,450	3,120	4,050	5,700
Oglala	1,000	1,500	2,250	2,950	3,600	4,800
Miniconjou	2,000	2,200	2,080	1,715	1,620	1,290
Two Kettles[c]				650	990	740
Sans Arc	800	900	880	1,090	1,170	870
Sihasapa	700	900	890	1,055	1,050	1,090
Hunkpapa	1,600	1,500	1,770	2,330	1,890	1,620
Totals	**8,500**	**10,000**	**11,320**	**12,910**	**14,370**	**16,110**
"Warriors"[d]	1,700	2,000	2,264	2,582	2,000[e]	NA[f]

Source: Kingsley M. Bray, "Teton Sioux Population History, 1655–1881," Nebraska History *(Summer 1994), table 3, "Reconstructed Teton Sioux Population," pp. 174–75. Original charts also include estimates for 1849 and 1869 as well as breakdowns by men, women, children, lodges, and percentages of total population for each of the tribal divisions.*

[a]Follows the smallpox epidemic of 1837–38.

[b]The 1869 Annual Report of the Commissioner of Indian Affairs lists 17,980 but also includes the Upper and Lower Yanktonais [*sic*] Sioux.

[c]Two Kettles figures for 1805, 1825, and 1839 are included in Miniconjou numbers in the original chart.

[d]Bray estimates (p. 169) that "[t]he 'warriors' would comprise the majority of adult males [who made up 27 percent of the population], excluding the aged, and account for approximately one-fifth of the total population."

[e]Significant numbers of Teton Sioux were living all or some of the year on reservations, so the available number of warriors, even in summer, had to be smaller and most likely was in the range of 1,750 to 2,250.

[f]Not applicable, as virtually all Teton Sioux were living on reservations or in military confinement (followers of Sitting Bull and Gall).

GROWTH OF RAILROAD MILEAGE IN THE UNITED STATES, 1830–1873
(ALL FIGURES ROUNDED TO NEAREST WHOLE NUMBER)

Year	*Mileage*	*(Avg.) Annual Gain*	*Investment ($millions)*[a]
1830	23	NA	NA
1835	1,098	220	NA
1840	2,818	344	NA
1845	4,633	363	NA
1850	9,021	878	318
1855	18,374	1,871	763
1860	30,626	2,450	1,149
1865	35,085	892	1,172
1869	46,844	2,940	2,041
1870	52,922	6,078	2,476
1871	60,301	7,379	2,664
1872	66,171	5,870	3,159
1873	70,628	4,457	3,784

Source: U.S. Department of Commerce, U.S. Bureau of the Census, Historical Statistics of the United States: Colonial Times to 1970, *p. 731.*

[a]U.S. Department of Commerce, U.S. Bureau of the Census, *Historical Statistics*, p. 734. The actual category is "Stock, mortgage bonds, equipment, obligations, etc." Investment figures are not available prior to 1850.

Newspaper Stories

FROM FORT BUFORD

The Redskins have been very quiet all winter, although they did come down on Farwell the trader sometime in March last, while he was carrying provisions [upriver] from this post to Fort Peck, a distance of some 150 miles. They attacked him at a point some five or six miles from Spread Eagle Bar (a small trading place lying just halfway between Buford and Peck), and after killing one of his men and wounding another, captured all his provisions and chased him and his party clean into Spread Eagle. None of the Indians were killed. It is rumored that the principal chiefs

Regional Railroad Mileage in the United States, 1841–1872

	1841[a]	*1851*	*1861*	*1871*	*1872*
New England	589	2,800	3,697	4,898	5,053
Mid-Atlantic[b]	1,237	3,795	6,963	12,380	13,499
Midwest[c]	196	1,846	11,320	27,187	30,499
West Central[d]	0	0	0	1,201	1,804
Southern	913	2,541	9,283	13,446	14,112
Western[e]	0	0	23	1,790	2,137
Totals	2,935	10,982	31,286	60,902	67,104

Source: Railroad Gazette, *July 19, 1873. The* Gazette, *unlike U.S. Department of Commerce, U.S. Bureau of the Census,* Historical Statistics, *shows construction by region. While the numbers themselves are slightly different, they clearly have the same order of magnitude. Also note that some numbers were not entirely legible.*

[a]1841 is the first year shown by the *Railroad Gazette.*
[b]Includes Delaware, Maryland, the District of Columbia, and West Virginia.
[c]Includes Missouri, Nebraska, and Kansas.
[d]Includes Wyoming, Utah, North Dakota, South Dakota, Colorado, and Oklahoma.
[e]Includes California, Nebraska, Oregon, and Washington. No track in Arizona, Idaho, Montana, or New Mexico.

of the hostiles on the Yellowstone have held a great council or war and their object was to stand by each other and attempt with all their might to defeat the plans of the Northern Pacific Railroad Company in running a railroad through their country.

Source: Army and Navy Journal, *June 24, 1871. The article was written by an Army officer who used the pen name "Tepee."*

Problems at Fort Rice

Captain L. H. Sanger, Seventeenth Infantry, commanding at Fort Rice, reports that on the 23rd of July a squad of sixty or seventy Brulés and Indians, from the Grand River Agency [Reservation], divided into three parties, made a dash from the hills near the [stockade] post, and endeavored to stampede the cattle, which were saved by the exertions of a young Sioux scout. The troops turned out very promptly, and there was some firing. A mounted [force] pursued [them] for some time, but not fully prepared for an extended scout returned.

Source: Army and Navy Journal, *August 5, 1871. This is from a larger article. The headline "Problems at Fort Rice" is mine.*

Probability of an Indian War

A letter received in this city [Sioux City, Iowa] last evening from Fort Randall [Dakota Territory] says:

"Two companies left Fort Randall for Fort Rice on Tuesday [August 22], *en route* to join the expedition sent out by the government to protect the surveyors of the Northern Pacific Railroad, operating in the Yellowstone valley. A general Indian war will follow this move. Red Cloud's [disposition], and the chieftainship of his tribe being given to Sitting Bull, bodes evil, and is a clear indication of the bad intention of the savages, Sitting Bull being extremely hostile. Agent Washburn, in charge of Spotted Tail's tribe who recently moved from Whetstone [Agency] to the Black Hills, declares his inability to control the Indians under his charge. They are marauding about Fort Kearney.

Source: Sioux City Journal, *August 26, 1871.*

Northern Pacific

A telegram from St. Paul, dated the 26th ult. says:

"A military expedition is now fitting out at St. Paul, which will have the double object of escorting the engineers of the Northern Pacific Railroad, while making the final location of the line through Western Dakota and Eastern Montana, and of repressing any hostile demonstrations of the Sioux in the Yellowstone valley. The expedition consists of seven companies of infantry—420 men—four Gatling guns, twenty mounted [Indian] scouts, twenty-five members of the Northern Pacific Engineer corps, and seventy teamsters and government employees, making a total of about 600 men. The troops will be commanded by General Whistler, and the engineering party will be in the charge of General

T. L. Rosser, formerly of Confederate cavalry fame, now Chief Engineer of the Dakota Division. . . . The latest survey of the railroad line through Dakota, crossing the Missouri and the mouth of the Heart River, wholly avoids the bad lands east of the Missouri, and traverses a fertile prairie country the entire distance.

Source: Railroad Gazette, *September 2, 1871.*

Hancock's Official Orders of August 15, 1871

By Special Orders No. 185 and 187, August 15, headquarters Department of Dakota, an escort, constituted as hereinafter directed, is detailed for the protection of a surveying party of the Northern Pacific Railroad while engaged on a reconnaissance, from the vicinity of Fort Rice on the Missouri River to the Yellowstone River, and returning thence. Two full companies of infantry will be detailed by their respective commanding officers from each of the following named posts, viz: Forts Randall, Sully, and Rice, and will be put on en route, fully supplied and equipped for the duty, in time to rendezvous at Fort Rice not later than September 6th. These companies will be filled to the maximum by details from the remaining companies at their respective stations. One company (with its commander), to consist of say forty effective men, will proceed from Fort Wadsworth to Fort Rice, Dakota Territory, where it will be added to and form part of the escort.[14] An artillery detachment of twenty men, inclusive of the proper proportion of noncommissioned officers, will be organized under the command of First Lieutenant L. E. Campbell, Twenty-second Infantry, from the companies remaining at Randall and Sully (ten from each post). This detachment will be armed with three or four Gatling guns supplied from Randall and Sully. Half of the whole number of Indian scouts at each of the posts, Forts Abercrombie, Ransom, and Wadsworth, will be detailed by their respective post commanders and assembled at Fort Wadsworth under the command of a

[14]Fort Wadsworth was in present-day South Dakota, some 25 miles due east of Sisseton and 25 miles south of the North Dakota–South Dakota state line. (Its name was changed to Fort Sisseton with the establishment of Fort Wadsworth, New York.) It is on the west side of the Kettle Lakes, chosen because of its defensible position and access to good stone, wood, and water. Robinson, *A History of the Dakota or Sioux Indians*, 366, and the *WPA Guide to 1930s South Dakota*.

subaltern officer [second lieutenant] and detailed from the post by the commanding officer. This detachment will be put in complete order for the field, under the personal supervision of the commanding officer of Fort Wadsworth. It will accompany and escort the quartermaster's train from Fort Wadsworth to Fort Rice, and on arrival there will be reported by its commanding officer of the escort for duty therewith. Commanding officers of the posts above named and of Forts Abercrombie and Wordsworth will if practicable issue to each civilian teamster sent from their respective posts one breech-loading musket, sling and cartridge box, and one hundred rounds of ammunition, taking memorandum receipts for the same, for the proper care and preservation of which they will be held responsible.

Major J. N. G. Whistler, Twenty-second Infantry, is assigned to duty as commanding officer of the escort. He will be relieved from duty at Fort Sully, and will proceed to Fort Rice in time to personally supervise the final details of equipment, supply, and organization of his command, for the completeness of which in every particular he will be held responsible. The quartermaster's supply of mule trains, now at Fort Abercrombie, complexly equipped and furnished, will at once be put en route via Fort Wadsworth to Fort Rice, where it will be reported to the commanding officer of the escort, for the transportation purposes thereof. In case this train does not furnish sufficient means of transportation for the purpose, the chief quartermaster of the department [of Dakota] is directed to hire private teams to complete the allowance necessary. Captain Henry Inman, acting quartermaster, is assigned to duty as quartermaster of the escort. The company sent on this service will be transported from Fort Wadsworth in the train ordered from that post to Fort Rice. When returning from this escort duty, the company will conduct the train back to Fort Wadsworth. During the absence of a portion of his command on escort duty, the commanding officer at Fort Randall, Dakota Territory, is authorized to order to his post such officers and men in Company D, Twenty-second Infantry, stationed at Whetstone Agency, Dakota Territory, as he may deem proper and necessary. Upon the arrival at Fort Rice of the commanding officer of the escort, Surgeon C. E. Goddard, U.S. Army, will report to that officer for duty as senior medical officer of the command. He will be relieved from duty at Fort Rice until the escort shall have completed its duties, when he will be returned to that post.

Source: Army and Navy Journal, *August 26, 1871.*

Sam Wilkeson to Milnor Roberts on the Death of His Daughter

Samuel Wilkeson (1817–89) was a graduate of Union College, 1837. He had an explosive temper, and Henry Villard, later Northern Pacific president, once knocked him out in a wartime brawl at the Willard Hotel in Washington. Although trained as a lawyer, Wilkeson spent his early career as one of the best-known journalists during the war. He played a key role in helping Lincoln receive the 1860 nomination. Following his son's death, he went to work for Cooke, publicizing war bond sales. Smith hired him to be the NP's secretary and publicist partially because of his closeness to Cooke, his letters from the banker beginning "Dear Uncle Samuel." Wilkeson was one of the five on Roberts's 1869 western survey, remaining with the NP until his death. For Wilkeson, see obituaries in the New York Times *and the* Tribune, *Union College archives, and frequent references in Oberholtzer's* Jay Cooke *and in this author's* Jay Cooke's Gamble.

New York, May 10, 1871

My Dear Mr. Roberts,

There is no medicine for such a wound as you have received. After I buried my oldest son, or man-boy or boy-veteran of 19 years, who was killed by a cannon ball at Gettysburg, I could not hear the words that sympathy or fashion whirled in a long protracted eddy about my head. They were confused sounds. I did not know what men said to me—save when the soldiers of his battery whom he commanded and whom they worshiped came and told me how brave he was, how humane he was, what a disciplinarian he was, how his battery was the best in the army, how he went into the fatal battle as if into a dance—all the residue were dead [words].

I have no words of philosophy nor religion nor custom to give you. Strengths you may get out of the great truths that the dead are not dead—that they live—that there is no death, only separation—that our children who die do but go ahead of us—and that time that separates us from them is Thank God! *such* a thin film.

How our men [who have] returned from the Columbia River all praise the loveliness and [*illegible*] of your girl! Judge [Richard D.] Rice most feelingly spoke of her—and his son-in-law Governor Goodwin, and Mr. Canfield—all of them. Within sight of you, within hearing of you, my friend, she waits for you.

Samuel Wilkeson

Source: Roberts's letters at Montana State University–Bozeman.

PART II

The Yellowstone Surveying Expeditions

CHAPTER 4

The Eastern Survey Begins

Late August to September 19

The arrival of the various contingents at Fort Rice—military, civilian (teamsters with their personal wagons), and surveyors—soon occupied the grounds in front of Rice with the largest number of men since Sully's 1864 campaign. This time, however, the army was fielding one-sixth the number, their Gatling guns were untested in battle (which proved useless against mounted Sioux the following year), and their military leader was of questionable ability. Army units had been cobbled together at the last minute, and while some company officers knew each other, most were working together for the first time.

In addition, there was no cavalry. Thus many worried, only a slow response in case of emergency was possible. If, the thinking ran, Indians ambushed the surveyors and their only fifty (or so) man infantry guard, who could help possibly reach them in time? No one needed to be told that the Fetterman "massacre" involved half again as many mounted men in December when hiding was considered impossible. But in September? Following a river where trees and brush were in abundance . . . well, officers could only shudder at the thought.

A reasonable number of contemporary diaries, letters, reports, and newspaper articles in which eastern survey participants described their daily activities, problems, and worries survive. Chapter 4's entries take the reader from the final Fort Rice preparations through September 19 just before the prairie fire that caught the column in the open. Entries begin with Major Whistler's formal report, Irvine's exceptionally candid diaries and letters to his wife, Rosser's diary and report, the diary of the lovelorn Lt. Lafayette Campbell, and newspaper stories.

Montana — Dakota, 1864–1873

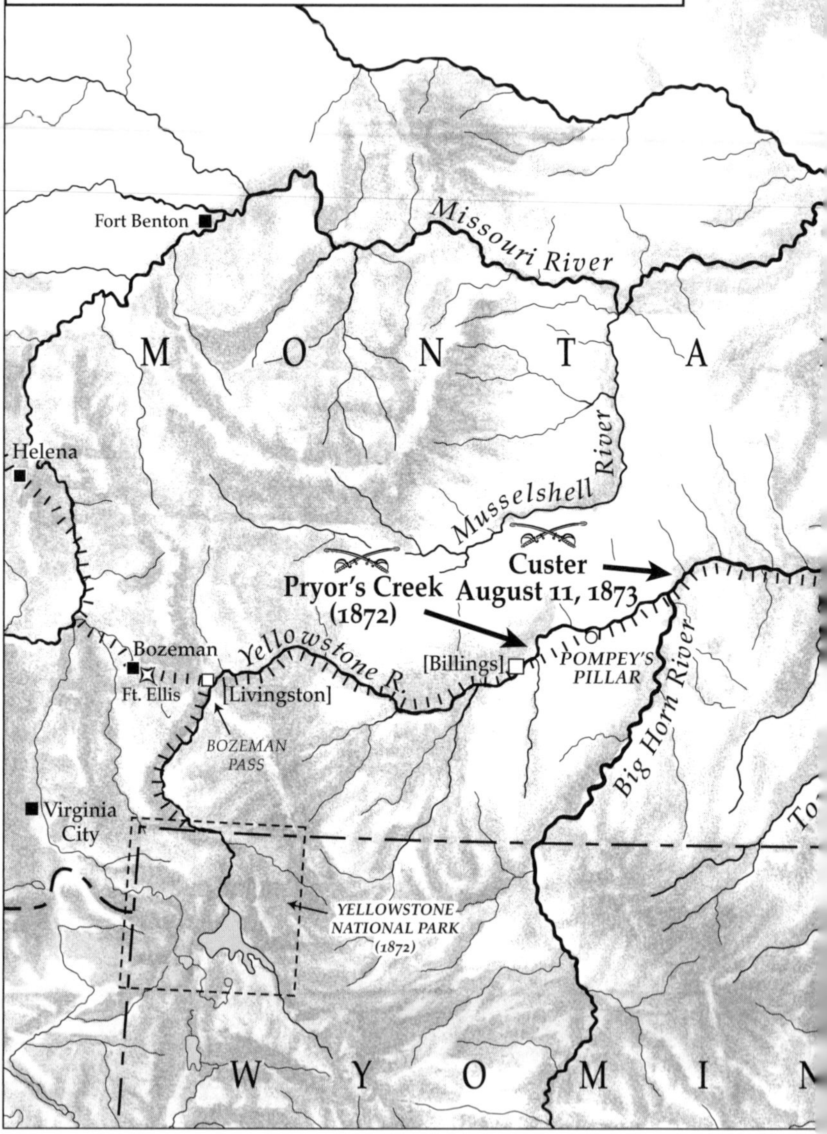

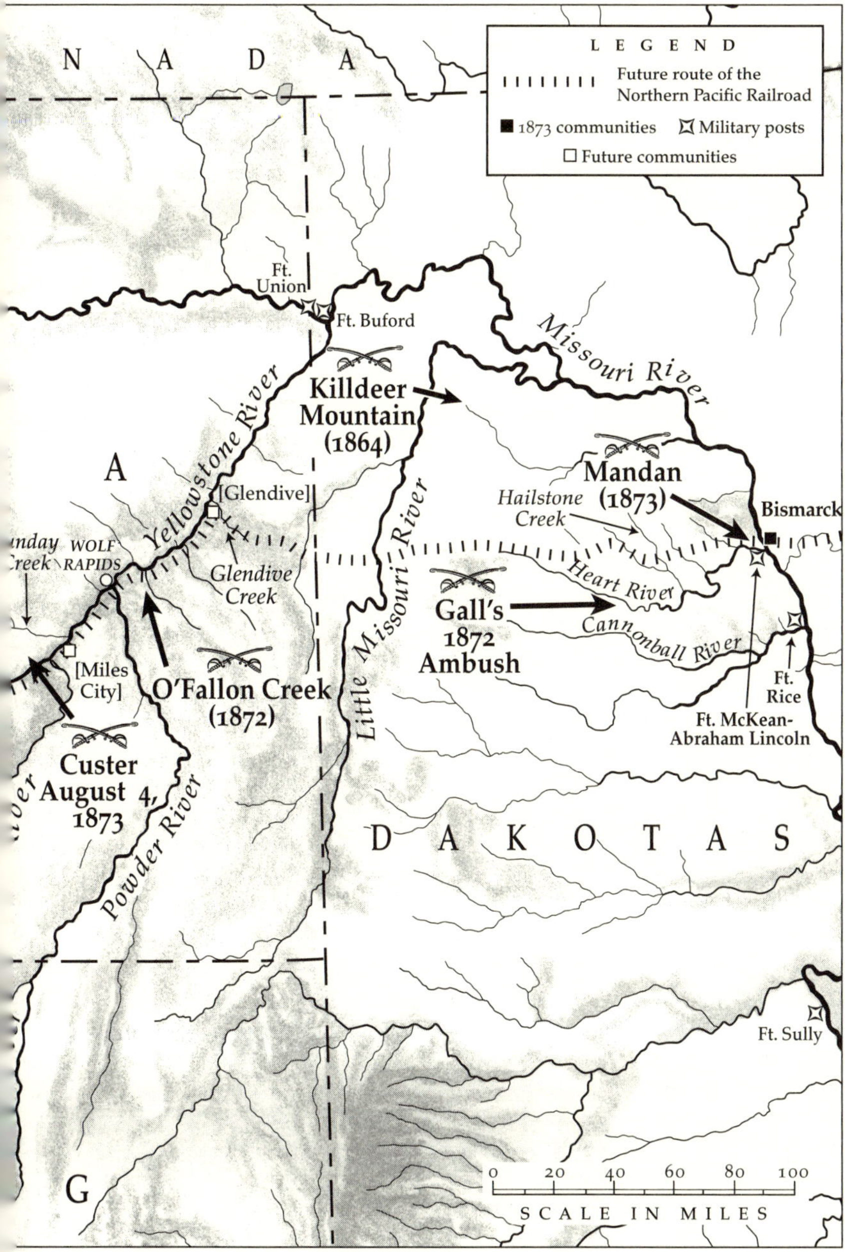

Map by Vicki Trego Hill adapted from an 1883 Northern Pacific Railroad map courtesy of author's collection.

Whistler's Report on the Yellowstone Expedition

The first of three sections of Major Whistler's report, actually written by Lt. William W. Daugherty, begins here.[1] *As can be gathered, the report falls into the everything-went-fine-no-problems-sir approach to military writing. Nevertheless, it is the most comprehensive description of the eastern survey and for this reason is unedited.*

Report of the Expedition accompanying the Engineers of the Northern Pacific Railroad from Fort Rice D.T. to the Yellowstone River and return, during the months of September and October 1871

In compliance with Special Orders No. 185 from Head-quarters Department of Dakota I left Fort Sully D.T. on the 28th August 1871 accompanied by Lieuts. L. E. Campbell and W. W. Daugherty 22nd Infantry, and the Government trains from Forts Sully and Randall, destined to form part of the transportation of the Yellowstone Expedition.

Arrived at Fort Rice D.T. on the evening of August 31st 1871. On my arrival there I found Capt. Henry Inman Asst. Quartermaster U.S. Army had arrived and crossed the River with forty-seven Government teams from Forts Wadsworth and Abercrombie, escorted by 26 Indian Scouts under the command of 2nd Lieutenant E. Turnock 20th Infantry.

Capt. Inman had been very energetic since his arrival, and his train was in excellent condition and ready for the march.[2]

---

[1]William W. Daugherty (1840–1922), from Indiana, enlisted as a private in 1861 and retired as a major in 1893. He was apparently popular and active in Indiana veterans' affairs. Heitman, *Historical Register,* Powell, *List of Officers,* and Wikipedia.

[2]No one was in more trouble than Capt. Henry Inman (1837–11/13/99). He was the son of the famous frontier artist and on his mother's side descended from New York's first Dutch settlers. Enlisting in 1857, Inman served with conspicuous gallantry and frequent wounds during various Indian wars, the Civil War, and postwar Indian fighting on the Southern Plains. As a reward, the immensely popular Inman was transferred to the quartermasters where his informal, laissez-faire lifestyle and attitude toward paperwork and cash (he was everybody's friend in a saloon) soon resulted in him selling two army horses and pocketing the money. Court-martialed but not convicted(!) by a friendly jury of his fellow officers, Hancock overturned the acquittal in mid-1871. That summer Inman was going through the appeal process, which he later lost. Dumas et al., *Dictionary of American Biography,* Thrapp, *Encyclopedia of Frontier Biography,* Heitman, *Historical Register, National Cyclopedia of American Biography,* 9:247, *New York Times* obituary, and Powell, *List of Officers.*

Fearing I could not obtain all that was necessary for the expedition at Fort Rice, I took from Fort Sully picks, spades, scythes, and water kegs.

Not knowing what was to be the amount of transportation I was to have, and fearing I would have to depend on grass for my animals, I ordered the A.Q.M. to make hobbles for all the animals, which was done out of rawhides obtained at Fort Rice.

On the morning of the 5th September 1871 the four companies of the 22nd Infantry arrived on the Steamer *Far West* and on the following day Capt. J. C. Bates 20th Infantry with his Company and citizen train of fifty-five wagons arrived and were crossed [over the Missouri] by the Steamer *Peninah.*

General Rosser and the Engineers of the Northern Pacific Railroad arrived on the 7th but could not cross the River until the morning of the 8th in consequences of the wind being too high.

On the 8th the train was loaded and I found I could carry sufficient grain for 60 days at the rate of from 5 to 8 lbs. per animal per day.

On the morning of the 9th September 1871 at 9 o'clock the expedition to escort the Engineers of the Northern Pacific R.R. under the charge of Genl. Rosser to the Yellowstone River left Fort Rice.

The morning proved clear, bright, and beautiful though the prospects were, from the lateness of the season, of an onerous, difficult, and cold trip. The cheering sun together with the pleasant strains of music at the head of the column from the band of the 17th Infantry and the presence of the Officers and ladies of the post, brightened and cheered our hearts with their good wishes. All seemed in good spirits.

The expedition consisted of the following troops viz:

Surgeon C. E. Goddard, U.S. Army Surgeon

Capt. H. Inman, A.Q.M., U.S. Army Assistant Quartermaster and A.C.S.

1st Lieut. W. W. Daugherty, 22nd Infantry, Acting Adjutant

Acting Asst. Surgeon E. C. Shirley, U.S. Army Assistant Surgeon

Company B 20th Infantry, Capt. J.C. Bates

Company I 22nd Infantry, Capt. F. Clark & 2nd Lieut. O. M. Smith

Company A 22nd Infantry, Capt. I. B. Irvine and 2nd Lieut. J. E. Macklin

Company H 22nd Infantry, Capt. D. C. Poole & 2nd Lieut. G. L. L. Ward

Company C 22nd Infantry, 1st Lieut. T. H. Fesher & 2nd Lieut. F. L. Davies

Company D 17th Infantry, Capt. C. E. Clarke & 2nd Lieut. J. Chance
Company H 17th Infantry, 1st Lt. H. Marcott and 2nd Lieut. J. M. Bivins
Two Gatling Guns under command of 1st Lt. L. E. Campbell 22nd Infantry
Twenty-six Indian Scouts under command of 2nd Lt. E. Turnock 20th Infantry

One hundred and fourteen (114) wagons constituted the train which was complete in every respect. The Engineers' train consisted of eight (8) wagons.

We soon passed out of sight of Fort Rice bearing about north west. The country passed over is very hilly and broken but well covered with buffalo grass. No timber. After travelling a distance of about 11 miles, went into camp at the head of a small stream called by the guides "Mule Creek." Plenty of water, wood, and excellent grass, sufficient grass cut for the animals during the night.

SEPTEMBER 10. Left camp about 5 o'clock A.M. weather beautiful, the Country passed through the first three or four miles was very broken. We finally reached high land, the march with the train was in four lines, and from a high point by looking back you could see a most beautiful sight, the advance guard, then the main command, with flankers on each side of the train, the Scouts on the prominent points of the flank of the train, then the rear guard, all was calculated to impress the beholder with the beauty of the scene. The direction travelled during the day was about North West, the country was rolling and well covered with grass, and antelope were seen in every direction. We passed a high Butte on our left; it is a good landmark raising about 200 feet above the plain and is almost a perfect cone in shape.

Encamped on a river emptying into the Missouri. Excellent grass both for grazing and mowing, plenty of wood and water. Distance travelled a little over 11 miles.

SEPTEMBER 11. Met with much difficulty in crossing the river. General Rosser with Lieut. Turnock and Scouts had left us the day previous to search for the "Heart River" and did not return to our camp that night.[3] Met us at this juncture as we were crossing the train. After leaving the

[3]Edwin Turnock served as an officer for two years in an Indiana regiment during the war. He entered the year with a cloud over his head for leaving a Northern Pacific survey team

river, the direction travelled is about North West and the road for 4 or 5 miles becomes a gradual ascent. The country over which our march extended this day we found to be covered with good buffalo grass which at times must have afforded a fine pasturage for buffalo and antelope, as two of the former had been seen during the morning and many of the latter.

After completing our march of nearly 12 miles, we encamped on the south bank of the Heart River. The valley of the river at this point is about ¾ of a mile wide. The bed of the river is from 50 to 100 feet wide and crosses the valley repeatedly and at short distances. We found groves of cotton wood and in the surrounding coolies and ravines, running to the river scrub oak, ash, and elm. Water slightly alkali but not sufficiently as to inconvenience us for drinking purposes.

At this point Genl. Rosser decided to run a line up the valley of the Heart River, and owing to the inconvenience we were constantly subjected to from the repeated crossings of the river, I found it impossible to accompany him with the large train; therefore, I detached one company and six Scouts to accompany him daily.

The Company acting as flankers to the working party employed, and the scouts stationed on the adjoining bluffs of the river as lookouts.

September 12. Reveille at daybreak. At 7 A.M. the Engineers started their line. General Rosser thinks he will have no trouble in getting from the Missouri to this point and will delay running a line until his return. Crossed the river above our camp, had some trouble in making a road as a great deal of quicksand was found. The teams were over three hours in getting across as most of them had to double. Finally all were across and we started in a westerly direction up a gradual slope, the teams having no trouble drawing their loads. After getting well up from the river we could see a large, well-timbered stream to our right. This stream is supposed to be the north fork of the Heart River.[4] The bluffs about a mile back are very rugged and cut into all kinds of fantastic shapes by the action of the weather. We left the high ground and started down a long ravine towards the river which we reached a little before sunset.

---

unprotected on the eastern side of the Missouri in Dakota. After a court-martial review in 1871, he was acquitted, but Hancock's comments (*Army and Navy Journal,* September 30, 1871) were so scathing that he resigned. See Rosser's 1871 diary for his view. Also see Heitman, *Historical Register,* and Powell, *List of Officers.*

[4]Actually it *was* the Heart River.

The country passed through was broken prairie. Our camp was pitched on a nice piece of bottom land near the river along the banks of which there is plenty of timber and wild fruit such as cherries and plums. The command was kept as near the river as possible during the march, and constant communication was kept up with Engineers by means of the scouts. Distance travelled 8 miles.

September 13. The command started at 8:30 A.M. but had a very hard time crossing Heart River. We were across and on our way by 11:30. The country was very bad to travel in, so cut up with ravines that it was a wonder we could get along at all. After travelling nearly 7 miles we found our guides had misled us and we had to make a turn almost back on our track. Our course was almost south east and we could see the High [Heart] Butte spoken of before. We came down a very rugged place into the valley without any accident, tried to cross the river again but found we could not without bridging, so we encamped.

The Scouts report having seen a great deal of game. Distance travelled nearly 10 miles.

September 14. Left camp at 8:30 A.M. The guides having reported the country on both sides of the river was so rough and broken that it was impossible to travel over it. I concluded to travel up the river valley. Crossed the river in about an hour, travelled up the valley for about a mile, and came to the river again; here the crossing was very bad, the banks of the river being very high, and the bed all quicksand which had to be covered with brush over which dirt was thrown, the banks had to be cut down a great deal, but with all the labor we were almost three hours crossing. After travelling less than a mile we came to a place where the point of a hill had to be dug off to allow us to get around between the bluffs and the river. We now started thinking our trouble was over but were brought to a halt by the river again in less than a mile. This crossing was very rocky. Two companies soon moved the rocks but it was almost 4 P.M. before all were across. I now found it impossible to travel along the river, so I concluded to get out of the bottom which was done after a pretty hard pull up the bluffs. Went into camp as soon as we reached the plains. The Scouts reported they had seen two Indians, who made tracks as soon as they were discovered, travelled in a south by west direction and made a little over 5 miles. Two Scouts left this morning with the mail for Fort Rice.

SEPTEMBER 15. Started at 7 A.M., made a march of 5½ miles over a fine prairie road when we reached a small stream that the guides [said] emptied into the "Muddy River." Crossed this stream and then crossed the "Muddy" about half a mile from where it empties into the Heart River. Experienced a great deal of trouble in doubling and crossing the train. After crossing this stream which we found dry, we entered again into the beautiful valley of the Heart River. The valley at this point is at least 2 miles wide and very level. The river banks are lined on both sides with cotton wood groves. After travelling up the valley for 4 or 5 miles we came to another small stream coming in from the North West and emptying into the Heart River. The Guides called it the "Little Muddy." It is well supplied with fine water. The valley of the "Little Muddy" is about a mile wide, the banks of the river being lined also with small groves principally of Elm. Finding I would be obliged to recross the "Heart River" to the south side and being ahead of the Engineers, I went into camp on the Heart River at the point where the Little Muddy empties. Found good grass for grazing and mowing. Soon after going into camp we were agreeably surprised by the arrival of the escort accompanying Dr. Shirley Asst. Surgeon to the expedition who came from Fort Rice. They also brought us a mail, and had left Fort Rice this morning.

We are almost due west from Fort Rice and cannot be more than 30 miles from that post. Distance travelled a little over 8 miles.

SEPTEMBER 16. Left camp early this morning and crossed the river in a short time. Two roads had been made which hastened the crossing very materially. After travelling over a level plateau we stared up a gorge and soon reached the high ground where travelling was good. The train was soon formed into four lines and in this order we made the march during the day.

The country over which we passed was about the same we met with on all uplands. The course about North West for the first four miles and then changed almost due west which course we kept for several miles.

After travelling about seven miles we came across a fine spring of good water. We passed some bold speers [domes] which were left to our right, our course then stood nearly south west to camp, which was reached at last, and a very poor one, as the grass had been burned off by the Indians during the summer. Engineers arrived at camp the same time we did. Game plentiful. Distance travelled over 21 miles.

September 17. Left camp about the usual hour and succeeded in getting the train across to the north side of the river. Moved in a north west direction up some pretty steep hills, soon struck the table land, where the road was good, moved in four lines. As soon as we reached high ground we could see "Heart Butte" and from our course we would pass to the left of it. We soon commenced to get in sight of broken country which it was found we had to cross. Our guides found a road down a gentle slope and after we reached the bottom, we found one of the finest streams of water we had seen since starting. It was the home of the Beaver, judging from the number of dams to be seen. *Timber was very scarce and they had used stone instead* [emphasis added]. Great roads had been made by them in the tall rank grass in going from one place to another. The water kegs were all filled with the delicious water. The distance from our night camp was a little over 9 miles. The train was sometime in getting across. After we got under weigh [*sic*] we passed some very high hills undoubtedly of volcanic origin, judging from the rocks. The route left "Heart Butte" about three miles to our right, and after winding down some rather steep places, brought us safely into camp, a distance of over 15 miles from that we left in the morning. The camp was pleasantly situated for wood, water, and grass. This region is undoubtedly a great game Country, judging from the Antelope we saw and the tracks of Elk and deer in the bottom. The weather was cold and the fire much sought after especially in the morning.

September 18. Left camp as soon as a crossing could be made over a deep ravine which ran into the Heart River. Our route led us along the bottom of the river for some distance and then up a deep canyon on each side of which there were a great many volcanic rocks.

It took some time to get the train up, which was finally accomplished, but not without breaking several [wagon] tongues. The morning was very cold and overcoats we found to be comfortable while the train was coming up. The country was about the same as that passed over before. Our course was very nearly west. When about 8 miles out we had to cross a small stream with little timber where we found plenty of good water. Here the command was detained sometime in crossing the train which made it nearly sunset when we made camp on the bluff about a mile from the river. The men were all tired and some foot sore, so I concluded to lay in camp tomorrow. Game in abundance. Distance travelled nearly 18 miles.

SEPTEMBER 19. Remained in camp this day. Genl. Rosser, the Adjutant and Lieut. Campbell escorted by the Scouts under Lieut. Turnock went out to examine the country. They crossed a large creek about two miles from camp, and succeeded in finding General Sully's trail, and soon found where he had camped, old boxes, broken material still to be found there.

The men improved their time by washing and mending their clothing.

Source: Records of the War Department, Records of U.S. Army Commands, 751 MDM 1871, National Archives.

Capt. Javan B. Irvine's Diary

Irvine's diary is 3½ by 5¾ inches and after September 14 frequently contains forty to forty-five lines per page. Because of this, cuts have been made in unclear sections, other parts represent a précis, and overlaps with letters to his wife are eliminated.

FRIDAY, September 1. Beautiful, charming day. Col. Stanley went down to the boat and finding then the *Silver Lakes* far behind he concluded to charter the *Far West* to carry our companies to [Fort] Rice.[5] At noon, [it was] announced that we were to proceed to Fort Rice on the *Far West* and started for the boat about 3 P.M. Led by the band playing "The Girl I Left behind Me."

SEPTEMBER 2. Reveille at dawn of day. Breakfast at 6 o'clock A.M. Our boat started out at daylight and ran eight miles and wooded at [Basil Clement's] wood yard by breakfast time.

SUNDAY, SEPTEMBER 3. Being the Officer of the Day yesterday was up at reveille. . . . The boat moved along nicely until ½ past 11 A.M. where we were halted. Passed the *Katie P. Kountz* coming down about 6:30 A.M. The *Kountz* was making very poor time downstream. The day has been very warm, we have ran along with but a slight detention of an hour and a half at Swan Lakes searching for a channel, finally,

[5]Fort Rice was approximately 25 miles due south of Bismarck on the western bank of the Missouri. It was established by General Sully in 1864, preparatory to his campaign against the Sioux. The post was named for Gen. James C. Rice, who had taken command at Little Round Top and then been mortally wounded in May 1864 at Spotsylvania Court House. His last words were "Turn my face towards that of the enemy." See Warner, *Generals in Blue*.

by backing down about three miles we moved over to the east and got out at a wood yard where we . . . learned that an Indian had killed a white man yesterday. A large village of Indians are opposite the mouth of Cheyenne River, then we ran up to Grand River after dark and stuck in the mud opposite about 11 P.M.

SEPTEMBER 4. Did not get the freight off until 9 o'clock A.M., but the *Peninah* pushed off before that time after unloading the troops and stores which the *Far West* will take on board to Rice. We completed the transfer of the troops and stores and pushed off at 8 o'clock A.M. Saw the two teams which started from Rice Saturday morning. Landed for beef two miles above the agency. Col. Stanley and the Capt. of the *Peninah* had some words last night about the transfer of the troops and supplies from the *Peninah* to the *Far West*.[6] Clement came on board and joined us. Overhauled the *Peninah* and passed her in a short, difficult bend at 2:45 P.M. Tied up at the wood yard of Isaiah Dorman.[7]

SEPTEMBER 5. Bad morning, dark with the mist indicating rain. Arrived at Cannon Ball River at 11 A.M. I arrived at Fort Rice at 12 o'clock fortuitously after dining on the boat and marched our companies to their campground and went into camp. The day has been cool and pleasant. Quite cool in [the] evening. Visited suttlers' store [and] started our mess.

SEPTEMBER 6. First frost of the season last night. Mr. Dickinson and Capt. Inman [spotted] the train from Minnesota coming over the hill on the east side of the river about 10 o'clock A.M. today.[8] The *Peninah*, after discharging her freight for this post, crossed the river and brought over the train which had just arrived from Minnesota [with] tents for

---

[6]The *Far West* was owned and captained by Grant Marsh (1836–1916) and was the steamer that brought news of the Little Big Horn as well as the wounded to Bismarck. A 1996 U.S. postage stamp featured a likeness of the *Far West*.

[7]Isaiah Dorman (ca. 1835–76) was an escaped slave believed to have come from Texas. While few sources agree, Dorman apparently lived with and married a Hunkpapa woman, ran a wood yard on the Missouri, and acted as a scout and translator for the army. He was with Reno's detachment at the Little Big Horn, and after their attack failed and the cavalrymen fled, Dorman's horse was hit and rolled over on him, crushing a leg. Still alive, he was recognized and apparently slowly tortured to death, one version being he was forced to drink his own blood from his coffee cup. Profiles of Dorman appear in most Custer/Little Big Horn books, encyclopedias, and magazines (especially summer 2014 and winter 2015 of the *Battlefield Dispatch,* Custer Battlefield Historical and Museum Association).

[8]Dickinson apparently was a quartermaster or sutler. Dickinson, North Dakota, is not named for him.

officers. Sergeant Bridgman arrived with his wagons from Sully this morning. Met Captain Bates of the 20th Infantry who came out with his company of forty men as escort for the citizen [wagon] train from [Fort] Wadsworth.[9]

SEPTEMBER 7. A high wind blew all night last and continues this morning, preventing the *Peninah* from crossing the wagons from the east side of the river. Captains Bates and Inman report the country lying between the Missouri and Fort Wadsworth as the most barren and desolate region imaginable; hardly sufficient to subsist a grasshopper. About noon the engineers of the N.P.R.R. with their train made their appearance on the opposite side of the river, but the wind blew so strong and the waves ran so high on the river in consequence that none of them would venture to cross the stream in a small boat. The steamer *Peninah* has been laid up all day, unable to continue the transfer of the wagons across the river. Mr. Rosser, the Chief Engineer, finally succeeded in crossing the river.

SEPTEMBER 8. Wind lulled after sunset but sprang up again and brought us slight rain after two o'clock past midnight. This morning the wind still blows heavily and the river very rough but nevertheless the *Peninah* succeeded in ferrying the balance of the train across the river by 9 A.M. The engineers encamped just west of our camp and are completing their outfit preparatory to marching to Heart River tomorrow. Col. Stanley came out and inspected the citizens' train this A.M. Weather cool and cloudy. The whole command was inspected this evening by Col. Stanley and Maj. Whistler preparatory to taking up our line of march at 9 o'clock A.M. tomorrow. Quite a chilly day.

SEPTEMBER 9. Marched eight miles today. Frost last night. Up at reveille. Packed and tents struck and wagons loaded by 8 o'clock. We move today in four columns. At 9 o'clock the band of 17th infantry came into camp. . . . [O]ne citizen wagon broke . . . and had to be unloaded . . . wagon overturned just as we came into camp, an ammunition wagon stuck and took an hour to unload. Quite chilly. The commanding officer

---

[9]John C. Bates (1842–2/4/1919) was the son of Lincoln's attorney general. He enlisted at eighteen, participated in virtually every major Army of the Potomac battle, played a major role in the Spanish-American War, and retired after forty-five years, a lieutenant general, then the highest rank ever achieved by a non–West Pointer. See Malone et al., *Dictionary of American Biography*; Heitman, *Historical Register*; *National Cyclopedia of American Biography*, 14:34; *New York Times* editorial at death, February 9, 1919; Powell, *List of Officers*; and 1918–19 *Who's Who*.

misled the column three miles regardless of the representations of the guides and scouts.

SUNDAY, SEPTEMBER 10. Sunday morning reveille at 3 o'clock A.M. Warm, clear morning: moved out of camp as the sun rose, halted about two miles out until the train moved up. Saw two antelope running across the head of the column and a small herd to the left. Marched ten miles to Lone Butte and halted. The country still very rough and broken, but the trail we followed was quite passable. Went into camp on Heart River about 8 miles from its mouth about 1 o'clock having marched 13½ miles. Mr. Rosser with twenty Indian scouts started for the mouth of Heart River this morning to reconnoiter the country and has not returned. *Some anxiety is manifest by the Major at this* [emphasis added]. Someone in advance of the columns killed an antelope. The creek we encamped on last night is designated "Mule Creek." Commanding officers not with column while [we're] marching but [he is] off hunting and cavorting over the country. Third day [and the] C.O. acts as if he were on a general hunting excursion. [He] gives no attention to the order of march but lets everyone look out for himself. . . . The teams are [*illegible*] and some overloaded. Second day C.O. mistook a branch of Heart River for the stream itself. He gives no thought to the men but marches without proper periods of rest.

SEPTEMBER 11. Pleasant clear morning: reveille at dawn of day. Mr. Dickenson breakfasted with us, and reported the theft of some soap from the quartermaster's train by some soldiers. Scouts were sent out this morning to ascertain the whereabouts of the Chief Engineer and party. . . . Gave permission for some soldiers to go out hunting but they found no game. About 11 o'clock orders were given to strike tents and prepare to march to Heart River. The stream on which we were encamped having been ascertained to be Fawn Creek and not Heart River as at first supposed. We marched across the creek and halted to allow the wagon train to cross. While waiting there the Engineer in Chief with the scouts was observed coming into camp from the west. He expressed surprise that we should have taken the little dry run as Heart River especially as he was assured by the C.O. that he had been all over the country and knew all about it. We reached Heart River after a march of 11½ miles and went into camp at sunset. Antelope were seen along the route.

SEPTEMBER 12. Marched 7¾ miles. Last night the sentinels of "B" Company 20th Infantry who were on guard fired on each other and the relief approaching them and created some excitement in camp. Almost if not a slight frost this morning, clear and calm. The engineers commenced their survey this morning and the little red flags are fluttering among the trees and foliage along the river bottom. We are supposed to be about eight miles from the Missouri River which was in sight shortly before we came into camp yesterday. Heart River is a sandy stream with but little water running in the channel. Quite large timber is growing on its borders. . . . We proceed with the train over the most feasible route for wagons. We broke camp at 11:25 A.M. and crossed to the south-east side of Heart River over a stony ridge which afforded an excellent roadbed for our wagons: it took us over two hours to cross as the wagons had to go in single file and the teams [had to] double to pull up on the east side. We suffered from the heat as we lay waiting for the trains to cross. Saw no game on the route as the escorts and hunters had frightened it all away.

WEDNESDAY, SEPTEMBER 13. Marched 10 miles. We arrived in camp last evening at sunset. . . . The engineers report an abundance of game along the river bottom on the line surveyed by them. We are camped on the Heart River. The country is very rough and broken so much as the Bad Lands but not so barren. The soil sandy, grasshoppers are plentiful, and little gnats annoyed us on the march. I was advance guard yesterday and rear guard today. We left camp at 11 o'clock A.M. having crossed the train in an hour and a half; some mishap occurred during the transit . . . a breaking of chains. . . . About ten miles out a forage wagon [overturned], but we soon righted it and reloaded and moved on three miles when a hind wheel of one of the wagons broke and [was] exchanged for another. One of the horses of a contract wagon gave out and had to be replaced by a mule. We camped on Heart River about an hour before sunset. An orderly announced this evening that a courier would be sent to Rice with the mail in the morning. Some of the wagons attempted to cross the creek this evening but were unable to do so and returned.

SEPTEMBER 14. Tis cool and cloudy this A.M. Slight wind blowing from the north. "A" Company is detached each morning to accompany the engineers in their survey, but I fear they proceed *too far in advance* to support them in case of attack. I think it impolitic and dangerous to the command to permit it as [we are] more liable to be attack[ed] in detail. The engineers should be instructed to keep within supporting distance of the main column and to proceed no further with the survey than will admit of this disposition of our forces. Today a detail of 28 men are made as Pioneer Corps to build roads and construct crossings for the train. Broke camp at 8 A.M., crossed Heart River, marched two miles and recrossed. Killed a Bull Snake 5 feet long, cut him in two with my shovel at the second crossing. . . . A pair of horses got frightened at the double teams dragging at their heels and ran away from the driver and dashed into the mule teams which stopped their mad [rush]. Crossed Heart River three times traveling seven miles and camping on the table land adjoining the river and in sight of the camp we left this morning, an antelope was around our camp this evening [and] was fired at by Major Whistler but was not hit. Company "A" went out on picket tonight occupying ten posts with four men on each. [The] Officer of the Guard made the rounds at 12 and 3 o'clock. [Two sergeants] walking the rounds every two hours. Conversing with the teamsters I learn that they get three dollars a day and . . . are every much dissatisfied with the roads. Should they break a wagon or lose a horse they will be paid a fair valuation for their loss. The roads were very bad today and little progress was made.

SEPTEMBER 15. Cloudy, damp morning with slight wind from the north. Reveille at dawn. Broke camp at 7 A.M. . . . We marched almost seven miles and came to a fine, clear series of pools of water free from the impurities of alkali. [Here] we halted, lunched, and filled our kegs and canteens, and after watering our stock [and] cutting some grass we moved on through bottom lands adjoining the Heart Creek but made slow progress for some time. Our guide, Isaiah Dorman, left us yesterday. The officers in charge gave but little attention to his counsel, made no provisions for his comfort, and cast a great deal of opprobrium on him for calling Fawn Creek Heart River. They first disregarded him as a guide and misled the column two or three miles themselves and rendered him no assistance in his endeavor to find a practicable route for the train keeping him near the train when he should have been permitted to ride ahead with two or three [Indian] scouts with instructions to leave them stationed at proper intervals to designate the route. No provision was made for his mission, but he was made to shift for himself. All this disgusted him and he left. The country over which we pass today presents the same barren, desolate appearance characteristic of Dakota; the soil sandy . . . ledges of fragile sandstone cropping out on the bluffs east for the first time yesterday. The fruit of the cactus which is shaped somewhat like the pecan nut is quite palatable. . . . The men nearly two hours crossing the dry stream from which we discovered such good water and after proceeding a mile further went into camp at 2:30 P.M. having marched eight miles. The mail from Fort Rice [arrived]. . . . Received letters from wife and Chaplain Crocker, also a bundle of underclothing from wife with newspapers. Dr. Shirley becomes a member of our mess, and [an Indian], the interpreter from Stephenson, goes with me as guide.

SEPTEMBER 16. Marched 21 miles today. Cloudy, hazy cool with slight breeze. Broke camp at 7 A.M. and crossed to the south side of Heart Creek. The banks and crossing sandy causing difficult and hard pulling for the team. Learn that the brother of Capt. Sanger, 17th Infantry, who was a passenger to Rice on the *Penniah* died there on the 12th from chronic diarrhea from which he was suffering on the boat. We came to a dog town shortly after crossing the creek, the first I have seen since we started. The town was about half a mile long. Shortly after, we came to an old Indian camp probably several years old. We ascended to the table land and stopped for the train to ascend up the steep grade we encountered. Having reached the table land we proceeded some distance without difficulty and approached the river where there was a good crossing. Suddenly the train was halted and the major commanding commenced prancing around frantically declaring that the guide did not know the country and he was going to be his own guide. He then turned the train and taking a wide circuit to the left to avoid some coulees led us at least six or seven miles out of our way. The train escort, guide, scout, guards, and all got frightfully scattered, and had there been hostile Indians, we would have been cut up without the possibility of [an] effective defense. We then found some [pony] droppings apparently made by a war party of about thirty Indians who had previously camped here. When we were turned back by the C.O., we had proceeded but a short distance when the prairie was accidentally set on fire by someone in passing. The skirmishers soon quenched the flames. As we arrived at the river, we observed the engineers and escort passing up the bottom of the other side surveying the route, the escort deployed as skirmishers. After supper Dr. Shirley came into our tent and we had a very pleasant social chat. It showered slightly this morning and was a cloudy afternoon.

SUNDAY, SEPTEMBER 17. A cool wind blew in just as we encamped last evening and continued blowing all night. This A.M. it is cloudy and indications of rain are perceptible. Started out at 6 A.M. to accompany the engineers up the river bottoms. . . . Crossed to the north side of Heart

Creek. Found some remnants of Indian tepees after reaching the table lands. We had a fine prairie to march on for five miles when we came to broken ground over which we passed [but] with the sudden breaking of a wagon wheel. Saw several antelopes, came to a series of ponds of fine water formed by beaver dams. It took us a couple of hours to cross this stream, but the good water amply compensated for the delay. [It] was the best water we had got on the whole trip. The water we used at the last camping ground was impregnated with saline matter instead of alkaline as usual. The cacti indigenous to this region produces a sweet [taste] and grow in clusters and is not larger in circumference that a five cent piece. None of the larger variety has been found this far. Camped on Heart Creek about 5 o'clock P.M. having marched sixteen miles. One of the most agreeable marches we have made. The engineers entered camp just as we did having surveyed fourteen miles.

Lt. Smith reports seeing plenty of game while crossing through the creek bottom. This region is very sandy and formerly volcanic. Have seen large quantities of cinders and the rock having evident signs of passing through great heat. Capt. Inman showed me some very fine geological specimens which he has gathered today. We have not rested much on this Sabbath Day and unless we pass more to God's commands cannot expect His blessing on our enterprise. This makes two Sabbaths in succession that we have violated by marching.

SEPTEMBER 18. Marched 18 miles. Quite cool this morning. Strong wind blowing from the north. My Company "A" is designated as escort for the Engineers today. The men late in getting [started. Had] to wait for wagons to load up our rations and property and the engineers got a half mile ahead of us before we overtook them. Introduced myself to Chief Engineer Rosser and then rode on ahead on horseback.[10] I secured two horses to pack in any game we might kill. Saw two large wolves as I ascended a bluff to take observations. Veins of lignite [coal] crop out of the bluffs along the bank of the creek. The valley is not more than a quarter of a mile in width, and the soil is very poor. The Company hunters brought in the hind quarters of two antelopes which I strapped to my saddle. We have crossed the creek sixteen times [and] it is only 9 o'clock A.M. [Yesterday] we crossed the creek thirty-two times and [the engineers] chained ten miles. Encamped at 6:30 P.M. Aside from crossing

[10]The fact that they'd been together over a week and hadn't met seems amazing but indicates his abolitionist feelings and continuing hostility toward the South and Southerners.

so often, the march with the engineers is preferable in my opinion to marching with the command. . . . It was dark when we entered camp; [the] officers and men [complaining about] the Major Commanding in prolonging the march until dark [and then] encamping on the bluff without wood or water and unable in consequence of the lateness of the hour and darkness to [find] any. Company "A" had to go to bed without coffee or their regular supper because they couldn't get water. This is now the tenth day we have marched and surveyed; most of the men and animals are quite exhausted and some sick from overwork. The officers with the train report that the commander is somewhat demoralized in consequence of the continued [lack of game], his favorite sport hunting antelope. Officers are indignant at his want of judgment and lack of administration. Rosser said it is evident that we deserve being [in trouble from] his weak and churlish direction.

SEPTEMBER 19. Marched no distance today. We rest today simply because the animals and men are too exhausted to proceed. One or two mules have died from accident and overwork. This is the coldest morning we have yet experienced on the trip, the vapor from our breath being distinguishable on the cold morning air. Mr. Rosser, Lt. Daugherty, and some guides went out this morning to reconnoiter and hunt. Sent out a party of hunters from Company "A" about 8 A.M. to secure game for the Company. Lts. Daugherty and Campbell killed two antelopes. They found Sully's trail and where he had encamped. [When the] Day began yesterday we saw Heart Butte in the distance. This prominent landmark is located on maps on the south side of Heart River whereas it is [really] on the north side. . . . The prominent formations are of soft sandstone overlaid with soft, chalky rock thickly interspersed with sand which later is washed away by the rain and storms leaving pillars of clay capped with the harder sandstone. But little timber is found on the banks of the stream and this of a dwarfish, scrubby nature. Five antelope ran by our camp about 1 o'clock P.M. nearly within range but did not stop long enough for a shot to be fired at them. About 2 P.M. a sentinel reported a fire raging in the bottom [lands] adjoining camp: the bugler sounded the alarm [and] the men were turned out without arms and after marching some distance it was found to be an old stove which the men had been using to heat water to wash their clothes: how much [better] for the Major Commanding to have investigated the affair [rather than] alarming the camp instead of looking himself. The stores have been rearranged in the wagons and three wagons have been set apart for each company; one box of ammunition must be carried in the company wagons to be ready for any emergency. The camp we occupy is very poor, being a mile from water and wood. [Someone else] selected a better camp in the bottom where there is plenty of grass, wood, and water, but when we looked for the train to descend, they observed that it had already turned back on its trail and was nearly a mile distant. It would not have taken as long to descend into the bottom and go into camp; then we would have had an excellent camp and been miles further.

Source: Javan B. Irvine Papers, State Archives Collection, South Dakota State Historical Society, Pierre.

Irvine's Letters to His Wife

On board transport *Far West,*
Cannon Ball River, 8 miles below Fort Rice, D.T.
11 A.M., Sept. 5th 1871

My Dear Wife:

So far, our Expedition is a success, and if we meet with no delay at Rice, I see no reason to complain. . . . All the men and officers are in good health and spirits.

Tell Jamie [their son] the Cannonball River derives its name from round boulders which line the shore of the river and are found in the bluff. The boulders, many of them, have the appearance of cannon balls as you look at them from the boat. We are now in sight of Fort Rice and can see the wagons of our train on the opposite side of the river. We passed some of the soldiers belonging to Rice who have charge of the [beef] herd at the mouth of the Cannonball.

We arrived at Fort Rice at 12 o'clock noon precisely, and had just landed, when the *Nellie Peck* was observed coming down. We marched our companies out southwest of the Fort and went into camp. . . . I returned to the boat and met Capt. Peck of the Steamer *Nellie Peck.* The Engineers with a train of 60 citizen wagons have not yet arrived from Minnesota, and the *Far West* will remain here two days to ferry them across the Missouri.

Capt. Inman, A.Q.M. of the expedition, has arrived with his train and I learn is a very efficient officer. He is also commissary of the expedition; he has wall tents and stores in them for all the officers and will take them along unless he is positively forbidden to do so.[11] Fort Rice is a well built post and presents a fine appearance from the outside. Tell Jamie the hounds they have here are splendid fellows, large, lusty ones.

[Salutations etc.]

* * *

Fort Rice, D.T., Sept. 6th 1871

My Dear Wife:

Our wagon train of 57 wagons from Minnesota arrive about 11 A.M. today and the *Peninah* came into port at the same time. A Company of 20th Infantry accompanied the train from Wadsworth and forms part of our expedition. We will have about 500 men and between 80 and 90 wagons all told. Our greatest difficulty will be to protect our train and animals. I am of the opinion that we will meet with disaster in this regard. We certainly have not troops enough to guard our train and supplies, but we will do our best to take care of them. We have 25 mounted Indian scouts, who are regularly enlisted for five years and drilled and disciplined like our soldiers. They will scour the country in front and on our flanks, and give notice of the presence of Indians. Capt. Inman, our train Quartermaster, is a very energetic and efficient officer. He is also our commissary and will take ample supplies and stores for officers and men. We have turned in our shelter tents and drawn common tents for the men and wall tents for the officers, which (later) are fitted with stoves. Last night we experienced our first frost and many officers complained of being chilled. I took the precaution not to disrobe when I retired, hence came out unscathed.

After discharging her freight for this Post, the Steamer commenced crossing the train, and troops from Minnesota and Capt. Bates' company arrived in camp about 5 o'clock P.M.

Thursday, P.M., Sept. 7th 1871. A high wind sprang up last night, and has continued blowing hard all day preventing the *Peninah* from transferring the wagons from the opposite side of the river and she has been wind-bound all day, unable to move. The Engineers of the N.P.R.R. arrived on the opposite side of the river about noon today, but the wind was so high and the river so rough, that no one could cross and we are as yet in the dark as to the route of the expedition. It is supposed however

[11] Wall tents were of a larger size; each side rose perpendicular to the ground before angling at 45°.

that we go up the river to the mouth of Heart River, and proceed up the valley of that stream. I suppose we will move out tomorrow.

[Salutations, etc.]

⁂ ⁂ ⁂

Fort Rice, D.T.
Friday evening, Sept. 8th, 1871

My Dear Wife:

Our entire command has just been inspected by Col. Stanley and Major Whistler preparatory to marching tomorrow at 9 o'clock A.M. for which movement orders were issued today. The engineers will level and chain [measure] the entire route; we go up Heart River about 100 miles and then cross over to the Yellowstone, striking it at the mouth of the Powder River.[12] Should this prove a practicable route, we will return, if not, we will proceed to survey down the valley of the Yellowstone to Fort Buford, and thence march home. If we find a good practicable route, the R.R. Co. will commence work with 2,000 men in the spring at the crossing of the Missouri and work both ways east and west. We have good guides and interpreters, one, Isaiah Dorman, the best in the country, honest and reliable [and] was with Genl. Sully through this country during his campaign in 1864 against the Sioux. The *Peninah* finished crossing the wagon train from Minnesota this morning and started up the river. Charlie Hamilton and Ned Anderson, the cousin of the expedition's C.O., arrived here yesterday. They proposed to accompany the expedition as sutlers, provided they could take five or ten barrels of whiskey along; but company commanders object so strenuously to harboring an enemy in camp, that they have given up the enterprise, and will not go at all. For two days after our arrival the Major commanding devoted himself exclusively to testing that five-gallon demijohn of brandy sent him on the *Peninah* and got very much fatigued. Aside from him, we have not a soaker in the command, and if success depends upon the sobriety of officers, this expedition, with the exception of the military head thereof, ought to be entirely successful; for all reprobates the idea of taking any fine water along, and I know of none doing so, save the one specified above.

Saturday morning, 7 A.M., Sept. 9th 1871. On the tented field, Fort Rice, D.T. Our tents are struck and arms stacked waiting for the wagon.

---

[12]As Colonel Stanley also thought the Powder River was the goal, one must wonder why, unless it was based on a misreading of maps or inaccurate maps.

I write this sitting on my valise on this chilly, frosty morning. We march at 9 o'clock. All leave here in the best spirits.

[Salutations, etc.]

* * *

Sunday, P.M., Sept. 10th 1871
25 miles from Fort Rice, D.T.

My Dear Wife:

We left Ft. Rice about 9 o'clock A.M. yesterday morning escorted by the 17th Infty. Band; Richard Wagner playing the cornet and the tune "Sister to the Waking Bird" and the "Girl I Left Behind Me." Yesterday we marched over quite a rough country and the wagons being heavily loaded, we had to double teams at some steep hills that we encountered three miles from Rice. We were led out of our way by the Comdg. Officer who thought he was a better guide than the one we employed at $100 per month and did not get into camp until sunset. We had reveille this morning at 3 o'clock and left camp just as the sun rose. Yesterday we traveled 11½ miles and today 13½. We march no faster than the teams walk and they being heavily loaded go at a funeral pace. Scouts mounted are sent in advance and left in rear to notify us of the presence of Indians. We have seen no Indians nor any other game except two jack rabbits and a small herd of antelope. One of our [teamster] wagons broke down yesterday and we took off the wheels and most important parts and abandoned the rest. One of the Army wagons overturned just as we went into camp yesterday. Result of careless driving, but the damage was slight. We remain here in camp tomorrow and possibly next day to enable the engineers to survey the route from the Missouri to this camp. Everybody is happy and we are all very comfortable thanks to *Quartermaster Inman* [original emphasis] who has used every exertion to provide us with everything that could make our trip a pleasant one.

I think our expedition will get through safe and without material mistake, but it will not be successful from anything the commander may do, for no one has any confidence in him and he has failed to exhibit any good sense or judgment so far in his conduct of affairs. His cousin goes with us in the capacity of bulldriver or herder. We have 104 wagons and between 350 and 400 animals and about 500 men. We have a good cook who gave us oyster fritters for breakfast and Canned Peaches and biscuit for supper. We catch plenty of clams and crabs from the river. This stream does not deserve the name of river; it can be stepped across and the water only stands in holes, there is but little timber on the creek, and not much game in the country.

[Salutations, etc.]

Source: Javan B. Irvine Papers, State Archives Collection, South Dakota State Historical Society, Pierre.

Rosser's Diary

SUNDAY, AUGUST 27. Got my appointment as Division Engineer of Dakota. Went with Gov. Smith and Mr. Linsley to General Hancock and arranged escort matters.

AUGUST 28. Left St. Paul with party for the Yellowstone. All things working well until we reached Morris station. There had some difficulty in getting supplies up the track. Finally arranged it with Assistant Superintendent.

AUGUST 29. So in hopes I would hear from my precious Lizzy [wife]. Got only a telegram.

AUGUST 30. Teams and party overtook me. Visited by Commanding Officer and ladies from Fort Abercrombie invited to attend evening. Surprised by entertainment, music and dancing. Seeing others happy make me long for Lizzy and the children.

AUGUST 31. Left Fort Abercrombie. Crossed the Upper Wild Rice [River] and move across the country a due west course. Saw but little good country until the P.M. Then saw good grass in the distance to right and left. Went into camp without water but dug a bit in the sand and found plenty. Sand gave trouble in keeping it clean. All passing off well and weather good.

SEPTEMBER 1. Broke up camp 7:30 A.M. and after marching 10 miles due west came upon the Sheyenne River about 3 miles from the bend. Took dinner thence moved around the river of the Ransom Road and encamped on Dead Colt Creek. Good water and good wood and grass. Suffered fearfully of piles [hemorrhoids].

SEPTEMBER 2. Still suffering of piles and a cold. Left camp at 7 A.M. and marched due west 12 miles and took lunch. Dug for water [at] 2½ feet found good water. Reached the Great Bear Creek 2 P.M. Broke down one wagon but had it all right in a few minutes. Left Eckelson to kill ducks and moved [to] James [River].

SUNDAY, SEPTEMBER 3. I intended last night to cross the James and rest for the day but I had great difficulty in getting over and then learned that my forager was short and the grass on the James being bad I was forced to march all day. I dined on the James then marched west. Found ground good water along the north in several places, encamped in a good valley.

SEPTEMBER 4. Left camp 7 A.M. and marched steadily all day. Stopped about 10 A.M. for water but it was not good and the horses didn't drink with a relish. Good grass for noon and at night found good water for stock. Dug a well but did not use it though got good water. Very dry.

SEPTEMBER 5. Left camp in a little shower. Quite cold. Stopped at well dug the evening before and watered from a spring near an alkali lake. Good grass for noon and night. Encamped on Beaver River. Water and grass good. Ducks and grouse *abundant.*

SEPTEMBER 6. Left camp around 7 A.M. The country much better than yesterday, found a great many antelope but killed none. Came upon the road travelled by the party from Wadsworth about 3 P.M. The road dusty and disagreeable. Rode ahead but finding no good camp camped on a high prairie. Very windy and disagreeable.

SEPTEMBER 7. Country very rough. Reached Fort Rice. 12 miles. The wind blowing a fearful gale and could not cross with wagons. Went over myself and arranged to ferry over tomorrow morning. Found officers very kind and much pleased with my reception. Spent night with General Crittenden.[13] Sent telegrams to sweet Lizzy and Mr. Linsley.

---

[13]Thomas Leonadis Crittenden (1819–10/23/93) was the son of John Crittenden, Kentucky governor, U.S. attorney general, and an 1860 presidential candidate. His brother George was a Confederate general. Thomas made numerous army enemies as a Union general; he was sacked by Grant after helping to lead the retreat at Chickamauga. Because he was not welcome in Kentucky after the war, President Johnson made him a colonel in the regular army and he was posted to Fort Rice. His son John's death with Custer (the boy was apparently captured and tortured, and his body was never officially found) finally led to a New York assignment, but by then he was a broken man. He and Rosser were to become good friends after 1871. See Malone et al., *Dictionary of American Biography*; Warner, *Generals in Blue*; Heitman, *Historical Register*; *National Cyclopedia of American Biography*, 2:169; *New York Times* obituary; and Little Big Horn documents for son.

September 8. Rose very early and paid ferryman over 139.00 dollars for doing it. Had wagons repaired and horses shod. Got supplies and clothing. Dinner with Generals Crittenden and Stanley. All passed off pleasantly. Sent letters to my precious Lizzy and Mr. Linsley.

September 9. Left Fort Rice 9 A.M. Added a note to sweet Lizzy's letter. The country rough and the march very disagreeable. Got into camp 6 P.M. after marching 11 miles. Weather warm and clear. Thermometer at noon 78°. No breeze perceptible.

Sunday, September 10. I took an escort of Indians and rode to Heart River, 20 miles. The commanding officer promising to [meet] me there. The command did not arrive and we lay out on the prairie [all night] without food, forage or blankets. Saw Buffalo. No one wants us but Indians.

September 11. Sent out scouts to discover the camp. [They] returned 10 A.M. finding it about 6 miles north. Having mistaken a small creek for Heart River I was dreadfully annoyed about the matter. Left the camp 1 P.M. reached Heart River 5 P.M. and will begin work tomorrow.

September 12. Begin running line on Heart River about 15 miles from its mouth. A beautiful valley, abundant of game, soil good, made 5 miles of survey. Soldiers complaining of sore feet and wish to halt and rest a day. I will oppose it all I can. Will write to my precious wife tomorrow. God bless her and children.

September 13. Begun line this A.M. before 6 O'clock. Party working beautifully. Ran 10 miles and 100 feet by 4 P.M. Came back 6 miles to meet wagons. Will be greatly delayed if the wagons don't get on faster. Will write to my precious wife tonight.

September 14. A beautiful day and the party working well. Ran 9½ miles by 3:30 P.M. then had to turn back on account of the slowness of the wagon trains. Had to walk 8 miles back to camp, most disgusting. The commanding officer is worthless for an expedition like this.

September 15. Dreamed of my precious Lizzy last night. Dreadfully homesick and depressed today. Everything begins to drag and it requires almost super human efforts on my part to keep things going. I have carried picket stakes all day afoot and am very tired tonight. It does appear to me that if I can ever get back to Lizzy I will never leave her again—God bless her.

SEPTEMBER 16. Started a little ahead of the wagons and judging from the post, was dreadfully afraid we would get a long way ahead and have a long walk. Therefore made slow progress—only 11 miles. I killed a black tail deer.

SUNDAY, SEPTEMBER 17. The river very crooked and the valley narrow except where we camp tonight, here it is quite broad. Ran 14 miles. The prairie is on fire. I hope we will find no hostile Indians and that I may soon return to my family.

SEPTEMBER 18. Spent a restless night last night. Dreamed about Indians and dear Lizzy and awoke a great number of times. Ran nearly 14 miles today. Country rough, wagons very late getting into camp, and men broken down. Will rest tomorrow except myself. I will go ahead with the [scouts].

SEPTEMBER 19. Several of the men sick and the horses being very tired I required the line only run up to camp. And rode out and looked up a road for tomorrow. Came in at 1 P.M. and went to the river and took a bath.

Source: Collection #1171-g-h-k, box 16, Small Special Collections Library, University of Virginia, Charlottesville.

Rosser's Report

NORTHERN PACIFIC RAILROAD.
ACROSS DAKOTA AND UP THE YELLOWSTONE.
GENERAL ROSSER'S
REPORT.[14]

BRAINERD, MINNESOTA, NOV. 1, 1871.
D. C. LINSLEY, Esq.,

SIR:—In compliance with instructions contained in your communication, dated St. Paul, Minn., Aug. 27, 1871, I proceeded, the day following, with the engineering party which I had previously assembled in St. Paul. . . .

At Fort Abercrombie . . . early on the morning of the 31st I started for Fort Rice without guard or guide. . . . I felt quite safe at this time,

[14]Privately printed in limited number, likely for Northern Pacific officials and perhaps for key investors.

with an armed party of twenty-five men. And as for the guide; I would earnestly recommend to all explorers to avoid that class of creatures called guides in this western country. You can rarely get one who has been over the exact ground you wish to explore, although they will tell you, in most every instance, that they are perfectly familiar with it, but after a few days' march they begin to grow confused and soon become a perfect nuisance. My advice to all is to leave guides behind, and if any intelligent man has ever been through the country, and furnished data for a map, take his map as your guide, and you will rarely go astray.

. . . [A]bout noon on the 7th I reached the ferry at [Fort] Rice. When I reached the Missouri, the wind was blowing a perfect gale, and the river was so rough that I could not cross, and I was compelled to encamp on the east bank of the river and await the lulling of the winds. A portion of the transportation of the escort was also caught in this gale, and was lying on the east bank of the river waiting an opportunity to cross. The steamer *Peninah* . . . was lying moored under the high banks waiting for calm weather that she might finish her work at this point and proceed on her voyage up the river.

The following morning, the wind having lulled, and the steamer having transferred the escort's wagons to the west bank of the river, I was informed that my wagons and party would be taken over at the same liberal rates that had been awarded to the Government. As there were no other means of getting over, and fearing that the winds would rise again with the sun, I felt compelled to accept this proposition, and had my party, at an early hour, on the west bank of the Missouri. For the information of all who may desire to patronize this generous steamboat company, I will state that this proposition amounted to six dollars for a light two-horse wagon, two and a half dollars for each horse, and one and a half dollars for each man. Should the R. R. Company desire to operate in the vicinity of the Missouri in advance of the track, I think it would be economy, in the event of not being able to put the necessary boats upon the river, to transport the required supplies overland.

At Fort Rice I found the District Commander, Gen. Stanley, who had accompanied the escort thus far, to assure himself that all necessary preparations had been made for the comfort and safety of the command. From him I obtained important information of the character of the country through which I had to pass, and of the difficulties which I would most likely encounter. I had left Minnesota under the impression that I could rely upon grass for my stock's subsistence, and had made but scant provision for the transportation of forage; but on conference with Gen. Stanley, it was deemed unsafe to depend upon the uncertainty of finding grass, inasmuch as it was believed that the Indians had already burnt all that they could, and would continue to give us all the trouble of this character within their power. Therefore I purchased one two-horse [wagon], and borrowed with Gen. Stanley's permission and aid one six-horse wagon. I cut down my rations as low as I could with safety, and loaded as heavily as possible with oats. By this arrangement I was enabled to take seven pounds per horse per day for sixty days, which with the grass I knew would be sufficient . . . to take me safely through. The escort which had been provided by the distinguished and courteous Department Commander, Major Gen. Hancock, had already reached Fort Rice, and, under the command of Gen. Whistler, an experienced and gallant soldier, it had been thoroughly organized, and prepared for the field.[15]

On the morning of the 9th, camp was struck, and the column, which presented quite an imposing appearance, was put in motion for the Yellowstone. From all the rumors and reports which had been circulated through the camp, an early attack from the Indians was apprehended by us all; but the precautions taken by the prudent commander of the escort to guard against a surprise gave every assurance of perfect safety and rendered our situation quite comfortable.

. . . From Fort Rice to the mouth of Heart River is only about twenty-five miles; but owing to the roughness of the country along the Missouri, we were three days in making the journey; and then we were compelled to strike so high on Heart River that I could not examine its mouth or begin operations nearer than ten or twelve miles of the Missouri River, and had to defer this portion of my labor until my return, when my wagons would be light. I rode over to the mouth of the river, however, and made a careful examination of the valley from the Missouri River to the point which I selected for the beginning of my survey. The train reached the valley of Heart River on the afternoon of the 11th, and early on the morning of the 12th the survey was begun.

As may be seen from the accompanying map, Heart River is a very tortuous stream, about the size of the Sheyenne [east of the Missouri], and possesses a valley of from a half to three quarters of a mile wide. A portion of this valley is covered with a healthy growth of cotton-wood and maple timber, and a large percent of the bottom land is not subject to

---

[15]Compare this published document with comments about Whistler in Rosser's diary.

overflow. The water in the river is but very slightly alkaline, and when I passed through it was entirely clear; but I judge that, in the spring, when full, it must be highly colored by washings from the "Mauvaises Terres," in which it has its source. The general direction of Heart River is from west to east, and is about 175 miles long. The country through which it flows is more or less broken, not only in the vicinity of the river, but for miles each side. This country is abundantly watered by the tributaries of Heart, Big Knife, and Cannon Ball Rivers. The soil in the valleys is of excellent quality, and, indeed, with the exception of the steep hill-sides and buttes, the land everywhere is susceptible of cultivation. Until burnt by the Indians, it was covered with the most luxuriant growth of grass I ever saw, and which afforded abundant pasturage for the great number of antelopes, black-tail deer, and elk which we found there. As we ascended the stream, the adjacent country became more level, and when we reached the celebrated Heart Butte, a very remarkable change was observed in the topography of the country. A few years ago, the country around Heart Butte was the seat of the Blackfeet's empire; and here the guide who accompanied the escort recognized the ruins of many a council lodge where, but a few years ago, he saw the wild chief of the tribe (Fire Heart) assemble his braves, and plan bloody raids upon their neighbors. It was here that the traders met them and exchanged merchandise for furs. Now, with the exception of these ruins, and the bleached bones of the dead strapped on decaying scaffolds and in the neighboring trees, there is nothing in the calm, wild solitude to recall a thought of the wandering tribes which once thronged these hills and valleys but have now gone hence to more western homes, in pursuit of the buffalo. A few miles west of Heart Butte we came into the coal district, and from this on to the Yellowstone, we traveled in one continuous field of coal. . . .

Specimens of this coal, with explanatory labels, are herewith sent you.

We found several mines on fire, having caught from the burning prairie and, from appearances, I should judge them to have been burning for several years.

The line of my survey was necessarily laid along the valleys, and the map and profile show frequent crossings of the streams; but on a careful location, more than half of these could be avoided. The lateness of the season demanded the greatest economy of time, and the lines which avoided timber and insured the greatest progress were adopted. The topography of the ground contiguous to the line was faithfully taken by Messrs. Meigs and Eastman, who are skillful topographical engineers;

and an examination of the accompanying map is respectfully recommended, as it clearly shows the susceptibility of the route of survey to the improvements above referred to.

Source: Milnor Roberts Papers, Collection 783, series 6, box 10, Burlingame Special Collections Library, Montana State University, Bozeman.

Lafayette Campbell's Diary

SEPTEMBER 1. This morning I am at Fort Rice [after traveling over country] and a more tired and dirty fellow never came to the Post, but I am as comfortable as possible as all the officers are very kind to me and I have all that I can ask . . .

SEPTEMBER 2 to 5. No entries.

SEPTEMBER 6. We are all excitement today as we hear the boat with the troops is to be here. She came in about 11 o'clock with Genl. Stanley & Crittenden with four companies of the 22nd Infantry.

I AM glad to see my old friend Crittenden. The consoling creature as my darling Mary calls him. Wish I could see her.[16]

SEPTEMBER 7. The weather is delightful this morning and the balmy air of a September morning. . . . Close to the Post, I am out with my mules & horses and in the afternoon try my [Gatling] guns. Find that they work very fine and I am confident that I can work them very effectively against any living thing.

SEPTEMBER 8. We are at Fort Rice today and everything is all in a jiffy as we start tomorrow morning at 9 o'clock. The order of march has just been issued. One of my guns to [go] in the advance and the other in the rear. I accompany the advance guns as I cannot think of being in the rear. I am all ready and have my things. Splendid conditions. I only wish that I could see my dear Mary.

[16]Frequent sections of the diary of Lafayette Campbell (1844–5/03/1919) contain references to Mary (last name unknown), whom he had met in St. Paul. Whether he ever saw her again is unknown, but about 1876 he married into the Dent family (as in Julia Dent Grant) and later became fabulously wealthy through a large stake in Colorado silver mines. In 1862 he enlisted in an Iowa cavalry unit and retired as a major in 1892. Based on obituaries in Denver papers, Powell, *List of Officers,* Wikipedia, and my e-mail correspondence with his great-granddaughter.

SEPTEMBER 9. This morning we are all getting ready to leave as we move at 9 o'clock. Mailed letter to my Darling. At the appointed hour we left Fort Rice. The band playing "The Girl I Left behind Me." We all start in good spirits. The Ladies (God bless them) were all out bidding us good luck and god speed. Weather delightful. . . . Traveled slow as we had a bad road and train detained us. We got into camp at 5 o'clock. I go in camp in front of the line.

SUNDAY, SEPTEMBER 10. A beautiful morning. We broke camp about 11 o'clock and crossed the River. Found it quite a job as the sand was so deep we were two hours crossing. Then passed up through a fine valley and to the highlands. . . . Our scout got two deer, three antelope, and an elk. We had part of the elk for dinner—find it to be very fine. The engineers go through the valley while we are compelled to take the highlands with the teams passed down a narrow road into . . . a fine camp. I am thinking of you, my dear.

SEPTEMBER 13. We are up today early and go up on the bluff and keep on it until the guide informed us that we cannot get down to the river. So we change course and march back down in the very way we came. I saw a fine elk today but did not get a shot at him as he was too far and ran down into the valley.

SEPTEMBER 14. We leave camp early. . . . We go on and find some almost impassable roads. We cut down the banks and get along the best that it is possible to do and then make only 5 or 6 miles.

SEPTEMBER 15. [Too illegible and fragmented.]

SEPTEMBER 16. Today I go with the engineers and try to kill some of the elk and deer there. Was unsuccessful and could find none. Saw one deer, but he was so far away that I had no chance to kill him.

SUNDAY, SEPTEMBER 17. A fine morning we broke camp early and went along finely. We are in sight of Heart Butte. We crossed a beautiful creek with magnificent spring waters. We had all our stock fill up here in order to guard against [bad luck] as it is possible that we may have to camp without water, but I think it hardly probable as we follow the river. I went on the river and Heart Butte found the top to be stone and full of wolves.

SEPTEMBER 18. We broke camp quite early and crossed a bad ravine after which we had quite a good road, although a poor country and nothing scarcely but the everlasting cactus with which the country abounds. Passed some beautiful specimens of petrifications, one very large stump, and a fine tree almost entirely petrified. I killed a fine antelope today. We left the Heart Butte to our right.

SEPTEMBER 19. Today we will lie over. Genl. Rosser is going ahead so Lt. Dougherty and I will go with him with the Indian scouts as an escort. We left our camp and traveled through some rough country and passed the famous corral made by Genl. Sully in August 1864. We find quite a number of the implements. . . . Lt. Dougherty and myself each killed an antelope. Returned to camp about 2 o'clock and found all well.

Source: Collection no. 10435, American Heritage Center, University of Wyoming, Laramie.

Eastern Survey to the Yellowstone: Press Reports and Letters

In a letter to the Secretary of the Interior, giving an account of his expedition in charge of supplies for the Milk River Agency [on the Missouri], Lieutenant William Quinton,[17] of the Seventh Infantry, reports that at [adjacent] Fort Browning, May 4, Standing Buffalo, accompanied by other leading chiefs of the Sioux, and Red Stone and Little Bull of the Assiniboine, together with some 250 lodges of Santee and Yankton Sioux, came in for a grand smoke and council, at which they expressed an earnest desire for peace, but made strong appeals for powder and lead with which to shoot the buffalo. These Indians, he reports, are but the advance guard of the Sioux nation, who are expected to settle in Montana. The Teton Sioux under Sitting Bull, and numbering 800 lodges, are moving in this direction. Sitting Bull's Band was formerly Red Cloud's. It appears that Red Cloud returned to his people with wonderful stories of what he had seen and heard while visiting the Great Father at Washington. Red Cloud saw too much. The Indians say these things cannot be, and that the white people must have put bad medicine over Red Cloud's eyes to make him see everything and anything [the whites wanted], and so Red Cloud lost his influence. The present

[17]Quinton was born in Ireland in the late 1830s. He enlisted as a sergeant in 1861, served throughout the Civil War, many Indians wars, and the Spanish-American War, retired as a brigadier general in 1902, and died in 1916. Wikipedia.

chief, Sitting Bull, who has for his chief soldier a Sandwich [Hawaiian] Islander, declares he will never make peace with the whites.[18]

Source: Army Navy Journal, *July 8, 1871.*

Indian Opposition to the Survey in the Yellowstone Country

From up-river advices we learn that a large body of Indians are now concentrating in the Yellowstone country, evidently for the purpose of opposing the survey of the Northern Pacific Railroad through their territory. Every indication now points to this end. It is estimated that there are already about 2,700 lodges of hostile Indians on the line of that survey, and that their numbers are being augmented daily.[19] It is therefore quite probable that the expedition from Fort Rice will meet with serious opposition in this enterprise, providing the Indians prove as hostile to it as indications of their movements go to show. There is far more trouble to be apprehended from these red outlaws than is generally believed.

Source: Sioux City Daily Tribune, *September 2, 1871.*

The Yellowstone Expedition

We learn from passengers by the steamer *Ida Stockdale,* which reached here yesterday from Fort Rice, that all the Indians at several posts and reservations along the Upper Missouri have disappeared and left their camps and villages in charge of women, children, and superannuated braves. No one knows for certain where they have gone to, but everybody is satisfied that their object in leaving their villages is to congregate at some point in the valley of the Yellowstone and drive back the surveying party, which left Fort Rice on the 9th inst. . . . Many of the people in the up-river country, who are familiar with the facts of the Yellowstone expedition, our informant says, are fearful for the safety

[18]Frank Grouard (1850–1905). A person of Polynesian/Society Islands (mother) and American (father a Mormon missionary) extraction was with Sitting Bull at the time, but likely had no real policy influence. See Malone et al., *Dictionary of American Biography*; Thrapp, *Encyclopedia of Frontier Biography*; and Wikipedia.

[19]The average lodge held two or three warriors. See Kingsley Bray, "Teton Sioux Population History," sec. I-C-1.

of the expedition. The Indians, we are informed, will outnumber the expedition ten to one, and they are said to be very hostile.

Source: Sioux City Daily Tribune, *September 21, 1871.*

The Yellowstone Expedition

News has been received in this city from Gen. Rosser's Surveying party on the line of the Northern Pacific Railroad. At the date of these advices of the 14th of September, the expedition was fifty-five miles west of Fort Rice, at which point the officers were felicitating themselves on the success of the march, and the fact that no Indians had been seen, and hopes were high that a good route could be found *from Heart River to the mouth of Powder River* [emphasis added]. To those who have been over that route, this confidence will be regarded as slightly premature. If Indians are to be encountered, they will first be met on the Mauvaises Terres [Badlands] and not the rolling prairies through which the Heart and Cannonball Rivers run.[20] If any engineering obstacles are to be met with, they will be found not in the Heart or Powder River valleys, but among the ridges between the source of the two rivers, through which the Little Missouri River has cut its way. The following dispatch gives interesting information in regard to the movement of Indians:

SIOUX CITY, IOWA, Oct. 3.—A few days since, a band of hostile Indians stampeded the corral of the government stock at the Cheyenne agency, Dakota, and ran off a number of ponies.[21] The Indians who left the reservations six weeks ago for their fall hunt have not yet returned. It is believed that they have all gone to the Yellowstone valley. Old Spotted Tail is now on the headwaters of Milk River with his entire band of warriors.[22] It is said he is on his way to join Sitting Bull, who is organizing a large force for the purpose of driving back the Yellowstone expedition.

[20]The Cannonball River runs roughly parallel and just south of the Heart.

[21]This Cheyenne River flowed west to east and into the Missouri slightly above present-day Pierre, South Dakota.

[22]Spotted Tail (ca. 1823–81), leading Brulé (Teton/Lakota) Sioux chief. With the Brulé decimated by warfare, disease, and the transcontinental railroad, he was not a militant leader. In fact, that winter he joined Sheridan, Custer, Buffalo Bill, Wild Bill Hickok, and Russian Crown Prince Alexis on a buffalo hunt. He is mentioned in virtually all encyclopedias focusing on the American West and Indians, especially the *Encyclopedia of Frontier Biography* entry with good sources.

Nothing has been heard from the expedition since they left Fort Rice on the 9th of last month. . . . It is generally believed here that they will be obliged to abandon their proposed survey or obtain reinforcements.

Source: St. Paul Weekly Press, *October 12, 1871.*

The Indian Country
War on the Northern Pacific
News from Western Dakota

Messrs. R. A. and W. A. Plummer, brothers, are in the city having recently arrived from military posts in Dakota Territory. . . .

The prairies of the whole region from Fort Stevenson[23] [to] Fort Totten were fired early in the present month, over a district at least 135 miles in breadth, the fires raging to an unknown distance northward. . . . The fires are supposed to have been set by the Sioux, the purpose and effect being to destroy subsistence and drive game out of the country in which whites and friendly Indians roam.

Indians of various tribes of Sioux are believed to be gathering with hostile intent, the advancing Northern Pacific railroad being their *casus belli,* and the valley of the Yellowstone the coming battleground. At least 2,000 lodges are believed to be banded together with this hostile purpose and to be marching towards the river Yellowstone to oppose the surveying party now going forward from Fort Rice. It is reported that "Setting Bull [*sic*]," chief of the Hunkpapas (Sioux), who is a terror in all that land, is marching with 500 warriors from their haunts far up the Missouri to join in the anti-railroad movement. The railroad party are reported not to exceed 1,000 men as a military escort, including teamsters and others not thoroughly effective for action; the force is one of regulars under command of General Whistler.

The preparations for departure of this party and its escort from Fort Rice caused some trouble in the camp at Fort Berthold; for as soon as it became known that the expedition was underway and that the Sioux were about to enter the field against it, the Indian scouts in the government service, who were sent for to act as guides for the party, precipitately deserted.

Source: Minneapolis Tribune, *September 30, 1871.*

[23]North Dakota, located under present-day Lake Sacajawea, roughly southwest of Minot.

Letter from Col. David S. Stanley to Gen. Winfield Scott Hancock

September 21, 1871 [Not received until October 14]

[Sir]

By mail of yesterday from Fort Rice enclosed [are] official and private letters dated [September] 14th instant from the Yellowstone Expedition. [They have not had a] hard time excepting the breaking down of one wagon. [They] had seen no sign of Indians and had feasted on elk, deer, and antelope. They found a fair valley to the Heart River, but the stream crosses from bluff to bluff, so cutting the Valley [that] the train moves on the ridge. The average day's march has been ten miles.

Mr. Rosser expresses the belief that he will be back to Fort Rice on the first day of Nov. I think that the half-breed, Clement, understands the country at the head of Heart River. [I]f he does he will show a [*illegible*] easy rail road route from the head water of the Heart River to a creek called Beaver which empties into Powder River. I have this from "Little Black Foot," Sully's only trusty guide, who would have gone with the expedition had he been at home when it started. There will be no trouble as far as route is conceived, provided they [avoid] the Bad Lands by keeping to the left of them. I do not expect to hear again from the expedition until they have finished their work. I am so thoroughly convinced by the Indians' description that a good route for a railroad exists from the mouth of the Heart River to the mouth of Powder River and that this expedition will find it, that I predict a speedy return of the expedition to Fort Rice without the long and laborious march by way of Fort Buford.

I have nothing further to report, excepting that five days ago four Indians of the Hunkpapas band of the Sioux stole eight horses belonging to citizens in the close neighborhood of this post. The horses were not missed for a day, and a few days afterward a friendly Indian overtook and recovered by bagging five of the horses. These Indian thieves belong to the camp near the Powder River and say they intend to pay frequent visits to the posts on the river to steal.

Source: NPRR *Secretary's Department, letters, M-459.*

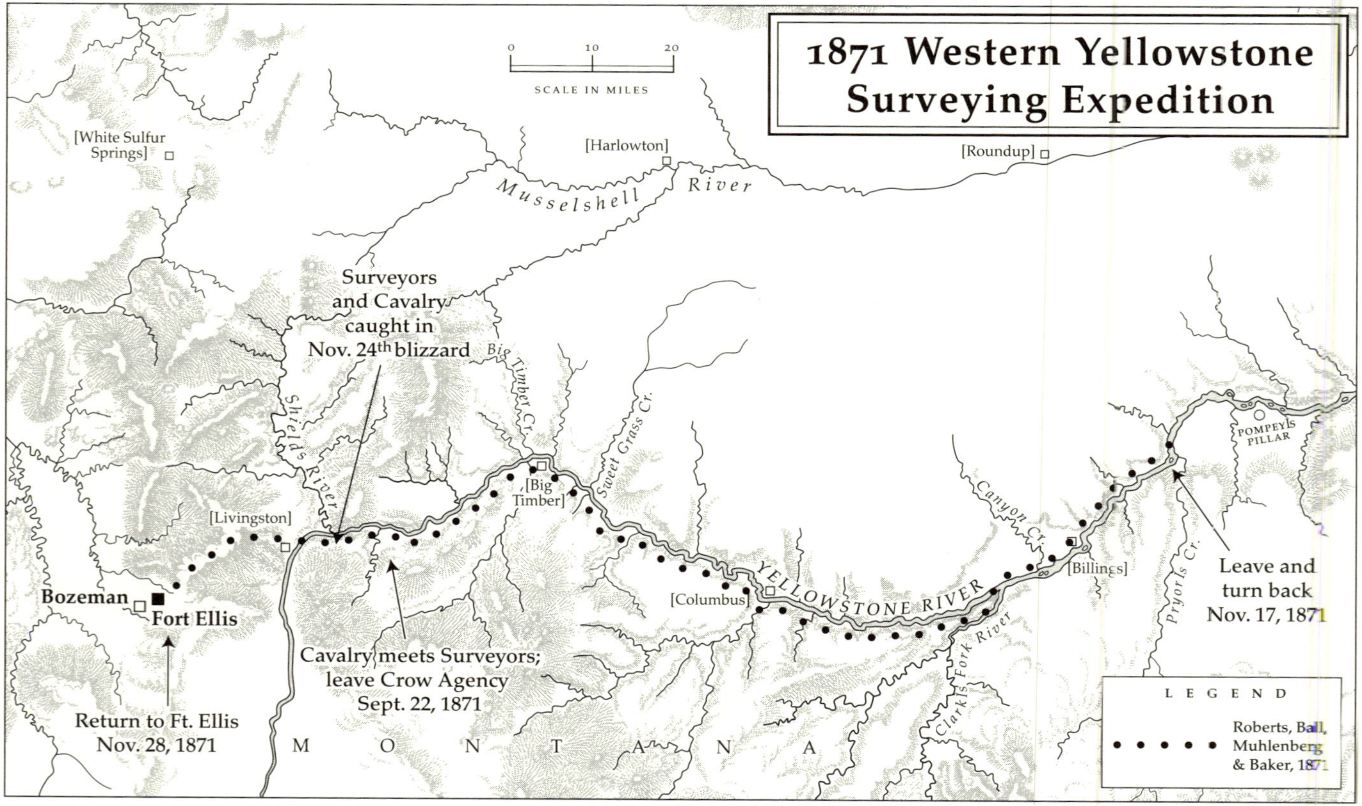

Map by Vicki Trego Hill adapted from U.S. War Department maps, 1867 and 1876, courtesy Denver, Colorado, Public Library.

CHAPTER 5

The Western Survey
Mid-September to Mid-November

Unlike the eastern survey, no air of geographical mystery existed with the western survey. By 1871 the Bozeman Pass had been crossed a thousand times by whites since William Clark in 1806. The floor of the Yellowstone valley east of the Pass had been mapped by the Army Corps of Engineers, and the Northern Pacific knew it contained no natural obstacles. This did not mean, however, that there weren't substantive technical issues and financial questions relating to which side of the Yellowstone was best for construction and how often crossings were needed.

Additionally, the Mountain Crow (Apsaalooke) had, by treaty, been given the land on the south side of the Yellowstone from Livingston to approximately where the Big Horn River entered the Yellowstone, about 60 miles east of Billings.[1] With the Crows traditionally at war with the Sioux, they were regarded as the army's and Montana settlers' strongest ally. Since no one had previously considered building a railroad, the Northern Pacific—especially Cooke and Roberts—felt obliged to prioritize a road on the northwestern side of the Yellowstone.

---

[1]The 1851 and 1868 Fort Laramie Treaties first gave the "Mountain" Crow 38 million acres, then reduced it to 8 million. Later (1882) the Crows ceded additional lands along the south bank of the Yellowstone to the Northern Pacific Railroad. For this, modest compensation (mostly federal dollars) was received over an extended period. See western encyclopedias including but in no way limited to Howard Lamar, *New Encyclopedia of the American West,* p. 385 for 1851, James Crutchfield, *The Settlement of America for 1868,* 1:202–203, David Wishart, *Encyclopedia of the Great Plains* (numerous citations), and various biographies of Indian and white leaders, western history, etc. The Big Horn River is called the Wind River in Wyoming.

As will be seen, this decision considerably slowed down work, as the surveyors had to daily cross and recross the (very cold) Yellowstone. In early November, Roberts, returning from the West Coast, was met at Fort Ellis by Baker, and with a small escort they entered the Yellowstone valley.

Chapter 5 discusses the period when the surveyors and their escort under Capt. Edward Ball first entered the Yellowstone valley in mid-September, Milnor Roberts's arrival and meeting with them, their travel almost to Pompey's Pillar, and then meeting a small Crow war party that had just stolen horses from the Sioux. Documents include Captain Ball's report and Milnor Roberts's letters and report to President Smith, his frank letters to his wife, and Montana newspaper articles concerning the Sioux which—like Minnesota and Iowa papers—assumed that Sitting Bull would take the warpath.

Capt. Edward Ball's Report

Fort Ellis, M.T.
December 10, 1871

Sir:

I have the honor to submit the following report for the information of the Commanding Officer of the post.

In compliance with Special Orders No. 144 dated Headquarters, Fort Ellis, Montana Territory, September 15, 1871, directing me to proceed to the New Crow Agency with companies F and H 2nd U.S. Cavalry for the purpose of escorting Mr. Muhlenberg and party of the N.P.R.R. down the Yellowstone River. I left this post on 11 A.M. of the 16th September 1871 and proceeded to the mouth of Shields' River, four miles west of the Crow Agency where I overtook Mr. Muhlenberg and party.

At this point I assumed the duties of escorting and guarding Mr. Muhlenberg and party on their survey down the Yellowstone River.

On the morning of the 22nd September Mr. Muhlenberg reported himself and party ready to move when camp was broke at 9 A.M., and our march commenced down the Yellowstone River.

Nothing of importance took place until the 10th October when after making a short march and pitching camp 47 miles east of the Crow Agency, a fire broke out in one of the tents in the officers' line (the officers being out at the time and attending their several duties) and although a number of men were at the time within a few feet of the tent in which the fire originated, their efforts to extinguish it availed nothing, the wind blowing such a terrific gale that not more than one minute could have elapsed from the time the fire was first discovered until it swept down to the river, a distance of 250 yards, taking the entire line of Company H's tents, burning up clothing, bedding, arms (carbines, the pistols being worn by the men at all times), camp equipage, rations, and ammunition.[2] Although the alarm was given the moment the fire made its appearance ... men who were asleep in their tents 150 yards from this point had their clothing, hands, and hair burned before they could get out.

About eight hundred rounds of carbine and pistol cartridges were exploded in the burning debris after the fall of their tents, sending their missiles in all directions, and although the greater portion of the command were busily engaged in extracting what they could from the burning ruins, yet not a man nor animal was injured.

Immediately after the fire, I took an inventory of public property, clothing, bedding, etc., belonging to enlisted men, made up an estimate of what was actually required for the remainder of the expedition, and detached Lt. J. G. MacAdams with one wagon and a small escort on the following morning to Fort Ellis, where he obtained all that was necessary for the equipment and comfort of the men, returning to the command on the 17th making a march of 166 miles with wagons over a rough road and through an almost continuous snow storm in seven days.[3]

The burning of this camp did not, however, impede the progress of the survey, as everything went on as though nothing had happened, Captain Tyler very kindly sharing his tents with my company and his men their clothing, bedding, etc., with the sufferers of my company.[4]

The survey of Mr. Muhlenberg was made to a point on the Yellowstone River 110 miles east of the Crow Agency to which point I escorted him,

---

[2]Edward J. McClernand (1849–1926), West Point '70. His account, *With the Indian and Buffalo in Montana*, 26, written fifty years later, states there was a fire "on the return march" and the "camp was destroyed." As will be seen, Ball's report makes no mention of a second significant fire at any time. I have previously questioned McClernand's recasting of events; see appendix, *Jay Cooke's Gamble*.

[3]James G. MacAdams (d. 1890). Born in Canada and enlisted with a Kentucky cavalry regiment in 1863. Believed to be married, he was a captain on active duty with the Second Cavalry at his death. Heitman, *Historical Register*; Powell, *List of Officers*.

[4]George L. Tyler (d. 1881). From Maryland and enlisted in 1862. There is a good chance that he was taken prisoner at the Wilderness (May 1864) and went to Libby Prison, which broke his health. Married with three or four living children (at least two died in infancy). Heitman, *Historical Register*; Powell, *List of Officers*.

arriving there on the 14th November, giving him all the protection he required and all that was necessary.

Source: MF *339, reel 1, courtesy of Montana Historical Society, Helena.*

Milnor Roberts's Published Letters

Northern Pacific Railroad.

DOWN THE VALLEY OF THE YELLOWSTONE.
EXTRACTS FROM THE LETTERS OF
CHIEF ENGINEER W. MILNOR ROBERTS TO
J. GREGORY SMITH, PRESIDENT[5]

THURSDAY, NOV. 2.—We started from Fort Ellis at 7 A.M., with two government wagons, an ambulance, and the cavalry, &c., mentioned, in command of Col. E. M. Baker, with Lieut. Schofield.[6] The road was very muddy and heavy all the way up to the Bozeman Divide, about 14 miles, being much cut up with the teams hauling the winter's provisions to the Post. The snow had been about six inches deep, but the weather was quite mild, and it was rapidly disappearing. As soon as we passed the divide, lo! the scene changed—there was no snow left and the road was dry, looking precisely almost as it did in August, two years ago, with less dust.

A few miles below we crossed the Yellowstone by fording over three channels, the deepest being about three feet at this time. It is now said to be at its very lowest stage. At a point below, where it all runs in one channel, I made an approximate estimate or measurement of the flow [of] 211,000 cubic feet per minute—more than double the low water flow of the Ohio at Pittsburgh.

The sunset tints on the few clouds, contrasting with the blue, more than Italian sky; the grand old mountains with their sides and tops glistening with fresh snow towering in the near distance on both sides of the valley, and the valley itself reposing quietly beneath all, formed a scene of beauty which, one of the party expressively said, "was hard to beat."

---

[5]These and Roberts's other published letters were for the exclusive use of NPRR personnel and possibly selected investors.

[6]Charles B. Schofield (1849–2/01/1901), West Point '70. Despite his father's high rank (the father succeeded Sheridan in 1888), the handsome Schofield never advanced beyond captain. Cullum, *Biographical Register of the Officers and Graduates of the United States Military Academy*; Powell, *List of Officers*; USMA, *Annual Reunion.*

At the Crow Wing Agency, farming has commenced; but it was too late last season when the Agent, Mr. Pease, began.[7] The Indians raised a good crop of potatoes, very good turnips, and cabbages, and had about two acres of sweet corn, which succeeded well.

I do not propose to enter in the slightest degree into the Indian question in this letter; I merely refer to the above to show what can be done in this extreme upper portion of the main valley of the Yellowstone in the way of farming. When I say the extreme upper portion, I mean so far as the line of the N.P.R.R. may possibly pass through it, for as you are aware, we leave the Yellowstone valley proper some ten miles above the Agency and pass up a small tributary to the Bozeman Divide.

The real extreme "Upper Yellowstone" is that portion lying south of our general route and rising in the midst of those wonderful scenes of nature which have been immortalized by the pens of civil and military gentlemen.

The Valley of the Yellowstone for the ten miles above the Agency, and for several miles below, is about three miles wide. That portion lying along within a mile or two of the river is good rich soil; the residue is good soil, mixed with too much gravel, though it has pasture upon it. The uplands or slopes of the foothills on either side of the valley have better pasture—good bunch-grass. The valleys of the tributary streams also show some farming land.

SATURDAY, NOV. 4.—A fine morning with the thermometer at 36°; we started about 7 o'clock. About a mile below the Agency we forded the Yellowstone to its left bank. Here the water was in one channel, about 350 feet wide, from two to three feet deep, flowing over three miles an hour; an approximate measurement gave the flow about 220,000 cubic feet per minute. The river width, when the water is three or four feet deeper, is here nearly 600 feet, and this is as narrow as any place I have yet seen.

Maynadier, in his report of the Yellowstone, does not mention any place less than 600 feet, although I have no doubt that it is much less in some

---

[7]"Major" Fellows D. Pease (1834–10/20/1920). Pennsylvania born, the eighth of fifteen children, he left home and came west. Married a Crow about 1859 and learned their language and Indian sign language. A frequent army scout and representative, he is credited for a friendly U.S.-Crow relationship. The Crow Indian agent, he actively assisted the 1871 and '72 western Yellowstone surveys. Not to be confused with Montana Indian agent Lt. William B. Pease. See obituaries in many newspapers including *Butte Miner* and *Columbus News*. Mentioned in Yellowstone Valley histories including Mark Brown, *The Plainsmen of the Yellowstone* (1961).

of the canyons or in its narrowest places.[8] With the depth 2 feet greater than it is now at the fords, I think it could only be crossed by horse and some swimming; as in one place the water came above half an inch over the high bottom of the ambulance. Maynadier lost a four-mule team, ambulance, and nearly all of his instruments in one of his crossings. There should be a good ferry or a bridge between the Agency and the Fort. A bridge would be much the best. The Yellowstone, although it has a strong current, does not rise high. Eight feet would be a safe estimate for its extreme rise anywhere, so far as I have seen it. It will not be a costly river to bridge, as cheap piers and short spans will answer. Hold on! Whither am I going? At this rate, I'll never get a letter up down to Boulder Creek.

After crossing the Yellowstone with one party as above, we passed down a favorable flat for several miles, and there our road took up a side swale over high ground a few miles north of the river. This trail was so run to avoid what is called a canyon for a few miles below, where it would have required some work to get a wagon road through, at a time when immigrants could not afford to stop to make roads; but the canyon is of little account against the *Railroad.* There is one, however, farther down which must be formidable, according to Pierre Chène.[9] He says, "It is 20 miles long; that it will cost $40,000 to build a railroad through there." I recommend that you give him the contract over that costly part, if he will deliver us the road for that sum.

We came to the main valley again about 11 miles below the Agency, but with one view from above before we left it and one view back after we regained it. I saw it all practically, and besides we have our survey through it. About 2 miles further our trail again crossed the Yellowstone, where we forded it back to the right bank and continued on a wide flat of mixed good and gravel land all the way to this stream, the Boulder, about 28 miles by our marching road to our encampment.

The Boulder is a very considerable tributary of the Yellowstone. It is now at its lowest, or very near it; yet there is a large volume of water passing—not less than 25,000 cubic feet per minute. It is clear, and of rapid descent, and full of large and small boulders from bank to bank, showing by the shapes of the bank that it is a terrific stream when in

[8]Henry E. Maynadier (1830–68), West Point '51. Early army explorer in Montana-Dakota. Later a brevetted brigadier general for his wartime services. His father (1807–71) was on active (administrative) duty during the war and also a brevetted brigadier general. Hunt, *Brevet Generals in Blue.*

[9]Also spelled "Shane." An old, illiterate French Canadian interpreter living with the Crows.

flood. Its ford is not over two feet deep at present but very rough on account of the size of the boulders.

Whatever the survey may say, I am quite confident that thus far, in the Yellowstone valley, it is easy to build a railroad at a very moderate cost.

Major Pease, who spent two winters in this valley at the Agency above here, says it is rare to have even such a snow storm as this one, and that he has seen no considerable depth of snow in the valley at any time. He has been along the Missouri, Milk River, &c., for years, and says that there it is quite different, and that the snow and the weather are very much more severe.

Camp "Gate of Valley"

Nov. 9, 1871.—We are now about 120 miles from Fort Ellis and 83 miles below the Agency, about nine miles above the mouth of Clark's Fork. Our camp is on the left bank of the river, in a lovely valley just before entering a much broader portion of the main valley of the Yellowstone. Yesterday, about noon, we overlook the survey line and Capt. Ball's camp. Yesterday and today they have had a splendid valley to run in, and the survey advanced six miles each day. Previously they have been much delayed by having so much of the line along rough side hills and bluffs along the left bank of the river; but it was deemed prudent to keep the line on that side of the Crow Reservation. The Reservation side, or right bank, the greater portion of the route, is obviously the better side for the rail. We have notes which will enable us to judge the merits of the best line with a choice of sides and bridge crossings of the Yellowstone. The camps have generally been on the left bank, but there has been no serious trouble in crossing the river at many points. I have forded it frequently, following Capt. Ball's trail to get the best travelling.

We were at Camp Beauty, November 6th; Camp Rosebud, evening of November 7th; and Camp Ball, last evening, where we overtook the survey.

Col. Baker has today, after moving down six miles from Camp Ball to Camp Gate of the Valley, arranged with Capt. Ball to take sixty of his men and our own thirty, which, with Col. Baker, Capt. Tyler, Lieut. Jerome, Lieut. Schofield, Dr. Whitestone, Mr. Broadwater, Major Pease (Indian Agent), Blackfoot, Boyer (Guide), and myself, all armed, and several besides with pack-mules, make a force of over 100 men and horses. We leave all the wagons and ambulance with Capt. Ball and the surveying party. It is our purpose to start tomorrow morning at seven o'clock and push on to the Big Horn River, which, as nearly as we can make out from maps and guides, is about 115 miles below here. We have full rations for five days which is enough for six or seven days if we should be delayed somewhat. We expect to meet the survey on our return in five and a half or at most six days.

I call this place the "Gate of the Valley," because it is here confined between bluffs to a width including the river of about one mile, but immediately below opens out to a width of five miles.

Yesterday and to-day we have all been charmed with the beauty of the valley and its surroundings, while our animals have been reveling in splendid grass. The soil is excellent, the side valleys are good, and the uplands are certainly very superior grazing regions, and they are claimed to be good for farming.

For sheep, cattle, and horses, this region that we are now in surpasses any that I have ever seen in North and South America.[10] For several days we have seen a great abundance of game, and the camp of Capt. Ball was overflowing with fresh meat, of deer and antelope. We were moving along more rapidly and did not kill many wild animals. Today I saw an immense herd of antelope; I was on an elevated peak surveying the grand valley below and saw them about a mile and one-third off, on another grassy ridge about 200 feet above the plain.

Let me note here, if I have not done it before, that all the waters of the Yellowstone and of all its tributaries thus far down are as clear as crystal, flowing rapidly over clean gravel and boulders. There is neither mud nor sand, nor even fine gravel; the streams are so impetuous, when full from the melting of the mountain snows, that they carry along easily boulders from six to ten inches in diameter. The crossings of the river are always over that kind of water-turnpike without toll-gate, and the water ranges from two and a half to three feet deep at the best fording places we have found. There is no danger of miring at any of the streams or crossings.

Capt. Ball, the officers generally, and Mr. Muhlenberg are so charmed with this part of the Yellowstone valley that they want to continue on as long as possible. Col. Baker expressed some apprehension of trouble in crossing the Yellowstone a few weeks hence, on account of ice. We have had ice one-half inch thick in the shallow, still water, but for the last two days and nights the weather has been very mild, only cold towards morning.

---

[10] Roberts had lived four years in Brazil and perhaps had visited Argentina.

This 9th of November, the thermometer recorded thus: Noon, in the sun, 68 to 70°; morning 38°. Day before yesterday it was down to 19°, but that was only a snap of a few morning hours; by nine o'clock A.M. it was 38°. The snow, which may have fallen four inches deep, has all disappeared and the grass is dry. Capt. Ball has large quantities of hay cut every day, and feeds it to the horses in the evening in addition to their daily grazing.

The Doctor has a sinecure. Nobody gets sick; rather they are fattening. Lieut. Jerome thinks he has gained thirty pounds. He looks as if he weighed two hundred. Such days! Such nights! Such game! Such appetites! But I must not expatiate, for if our friend Mr. Wilkeson should see this he will break his heart, thinking that he should be here. Our guides say that there are fifty-five miles right straight along of fine open valley.

Source: Roberts Papers, series 6, box 10, Burlingame Special Collections Library, Montana State University, Bozeman.

"Preliminary" Report of Milnor Roberts to Gregory Smith

NORTHERN PACIFIC RAILROAD.

THE YELLOWSTONE VALLEY.

ENGINEER-IN-CHIEF W. MILNOR ROBERTS'S PRELIMINARY REPORT.

HELENA, November 29, 1871[11]
Hon. J. GREGORY SMITH,
President Northern Pacific Railroad,

DEAR SIR:

I beg leave respectfully to present the following Report in regard to the Yellowstone valley as a route for the main line of the Northern Pacific Railroad.

After striking the Yellowstone valley, it was deemed advisable to confine the actual survey line to the northern side of the river on account of the fact that south of the river the country is a reservation of the Crow Indians, but to make such observations as would enable us to determine the full engineering value of the entire valley.

[11]Sections not relating to the Yellowstone have been omitted, and the report is arbitrarily split into two sections.

It so happens that the largest portion of the most favorable ground is on the reservation side of the valley, and our transportation and many of the encampments had to be on that side. The general route from the head of the Missouri to the vicinity of Fort Ellis, about 31 miles, is remarkably favorable, mostly gentle rolling prairie work, but with some extra cutting and filling along a few miles near the outlet of the Gallatin Valley.

The total rise, from the initial point to near Fort Ellis, is 833 feet in a distance of 31 miles, or an average of nearly 27 feet per mile. From Fort Ellis to Bozeman Summit, 11 miles, the ascent is 867 feet, or at the rate of 78 8/10 feet per mile, without cutting or tunneling on the summit. From the summit to the mouth of Twenty-five Yard Creek (Shields' River) 20 miles, the descent is 1,354 feet, or at the rate of 67 7/10 feet per mile.

These 31 miles comprise the difficult portion of the Yellowstone route, both for construction and running. In order to maintain regular ascending and descending grades, to pass this divide, the line must be thrown upon the irregular and, in some places, rocky side hills, making rather costly work on some of the miles; but with a careful location, a good line can be secured. Before finally establishing the route, further careful preliminary lines will of course be traced. This remark applies to all of the lines surveyed in Montana.

At the mouth of Shields' River, at the 62nd mile [from the Missouri]: The survey had extended, when I left the party, to the 164th mile. The fall from Shields' River in 97 miles is 1,066 feet, or an average of 11 feet per mile measured by our line. The line is considerably shorter than the stream, which meanders greatly between the sides of the valley. The valley itself varies materially in width, being, for the most part, from three to four miles wide, sometimes widening out to ten miles, and at a few points, for short distances, narrowing down to about one mile.

The final line, if located along the Yellowstone valley so as to take the greater advantage of its graphical features to secure the shortest, straightest, and cheapest line, will be considerably shorter than the line we have surveyed. It is obvious that, *after fairly entering the valley from the west,* the grades will be very moderate; and with some care in locating, and with little extra cost, they may be maintained, moderately descending, or level most of the way.

My personal reconnaissance and distinct view of the valley extended to about the 220th mile, or about 61 miles below the leveling, as I left it. The leveling was carried to the 186th mile, when stopped by the inclemency of the weather. These 61 miles are rather more favorable than the average of the line surveyed above, at least 50 miles of the distance being across wide, nearly level plains—from four to ten miles wide.

This is the general description of the route for 220 miles, from the initial point, say to Pompey's Pillar Creek, a stream which enters on the right bank of the river.

From the mouth of Pompey's Pillar Creek to the Big Horn River, the air line distance is 27 miles, most of the way through a narrow valley or canyon. This distance (of about 27 miles) embraces the least known portion, in an engineering view, of the entire valley. Between the Big Horn and Powder Rivers, 106 miles, the testimony I have is concurrent that it is, in general, an open, wide valley.

The line traced by General Rosser from the crossing of the Missouri River westward ended, as I learn, at Glendive Creek. I could not locate, by that name, any stream on the Yellowstone; but . . . General Rosser's distance from the mouth of Heart River, as reported to me by Mr. Linsley, is 226 miles. This makes the total distance from the mouth of Heart River via the Yellowstone valley and Bozeman Summit to the initial point at the head of the Missouri River, 596 miles. . . .[12] Calling it 460 miles from Duluth to the mouth of Heart River, the total distance from Duluth to the head of the Missouri River would be 1,053 miles. The total (approximate) distance by our most circuitous route from Duluth to Puget Sound, 2,040 miles.

The Character of the Stream

From the point where our surveys first strike the Yellowstone, as far down as I have seen this stream, it has the same general characteristics. Its waters, and the waters of all its tributaries above Powder River, are clear and swift, running over clear, pebbly, or boulder-stone bottoms. In its lowest stage it has a large flow, exceeding 200,000 cubic feet per minute when we first touch it and increasing as we descend

In floods, there is an immense volume of water; but the river does not rise more than about 7 feet, and rarely overflows its immediate banks, which are usually not very high. Trout of the finest kind are abundant in the main stream and all of its tributaries, and the streams are yet uncontaminated by any washings from the mining operations.

Not much drift passes down. Ice rarely forms of great thickness. Some winters there is very little ice. Snow in the immediate river valley does

[12] A remarkably accurate estimate.

not usually fall to any great depth and rarely lies long on the ground. It will be easy to build bridge piers that will be safe; and as they need not be very high or costly, short spans may be adopted, thus reducing the cost of bridge superstructures. Hereafter I will present a special report on the subject of bridging the Yellowstone and its tributaries and the streams generally in Montana.

The drainage of the Yellowstone comes mainly from its southern side where the long, large tributaries enter. The streams on its northern side are comparatively small and short, draining limited territory.

The reason is that the Musselshell Valley, running nearly parallel, is but a little distance north, leaving only a narrow margin of country to drain into the Yellowstone on that side. It is only 32 miles across from the Yellowstone to the Musselshell River at a point not far below Pryor's Creek, so that a portion of the Musselshell Valley would be within the Land Grant; on the southern side of the Yellowstone its drainage is very much more extensive; the streams are longer, larger, better supplied with water, and are altogether more important than those on the north side. The Big Horn River is in fact considerably longer than the Yellowstone above their confluence and drains a larger area. From the vicinity of Shields' River, and from the Crow Agency, the air line distance, up to the lower falls of the Yellowstone, is 68 miles. . . .

The principal streams which enter the Yellowstone on its southern side, taking them in descending order, are the Big Boulder River, Rosebud Creek, Clark's Fork, Pryor's Fork, Big Horn River, Rosebud River, Tongue River, and Powder River. The area of country draining into the southerly side of the Yellowstone from Powder River upwards, including that of the Powder River, is over 45,000 square miles, or equal to the area of the entire State of Pennsylvania, so that but for the rapid descent of the main stream, *eleven feet per mile,* its floods would be of great height, as nearly all the drainage is from mountain regions. Here is the perennial source of a large portion of the flow of the Missouri River below its junction with the Yellowstone.

The principal streams entering the Yellowstone from the north are Shields' River (or Twenty-five Yard Creek), Big Timber Creek, Sweet Grass Creek, Great Porcupine Creek, and Little Porcupine Creek; but the entire drainage from the north into the Yellowstone above the mouth of Powder River is only about 5,000 square miles area, or only one-ninth of that on the south side.

The soil along the bottom of the Yellowstone and its important tributaries is generally very good. In some places it is too gravelly, but the low bottoms, although sufficiently above the floods, have a rich, black alluvial soil and yield fine grass. The burning experiments at the Crow Agency betoken that the Yellowstone valley will be good for general farming, while the uplands are admirable for grazing lands.

In many places timber, excepting cotton wood along the river, is scarce; but the mountain ranges or pine-covered hills are frequently not distant from the river on both sides, having a good growth of excellent pine timber, sufficient for building purposes, bridges, cross ties and fuel; so that with a railroad through the valley, lumber should be furnished at all points at reasonable cost.

Logs, cross ties, &c, can be floated down stream, and in the spring and early summer there is a descending navigation for boats. Two to three feet depth of water exists in the channels, even at low water; but the current is swift, owing to the rapid descent of the stream.

The saving in the *actual railroad length* between the points designated, namely, the mouth of Heart River, on the Missouri, and the mouth of Powder River, on the Yellowstone, by the Heart River route, would probably not be less than 100 miles, owing to the great curvature along the Missouri River. Taking the mouth of Heart River as the common starting point, we can compare the *approximate distances, via* the Yellowstone and *via* the Missouri, respectively to a common point west of the Rocky Mountains, at the junction of the Big Blackfoot and Hell Gate Rivers.

The Yellowstone is not at all adapted to general navigation, owing to its great declivity. The Ohio River has an average fall, from Pittsburgh to Cairo, of about six inches per mile, while the Yellowstone has an average fall of eleven feet, or twenty-two times more per mile; on this account it is not advantageous for navigation, but it is splendid for water power and for irrigation.

Source: Roberts Papers, Collection 783, series 6, box 10, Burlingame Special Collections Library, Montana State University, Bozeman.

Roberts's Letters to His Wife

Camp Crow Indians
Saturday evening, November 11, 1871

Dearest O and Darling O,[13]

I wrote you last . . . on the 9th I think. We left [Captain Ball taking] about 90 soldiers . . . with Captain Tyler in immediate command, Major Pease, guides Mitch Boyer[14] and Pierre Shane, and Chiefs "Blackfoot" and "Wolfbow" and myself, and *"Col,"* the big black dog—and a few pack horses and their drivers made a party of full 100 strong, all armed—especially his dog—to the teeth.

We travelled down all day yesterday throu' the broad part of the valley about 30 miles by our route, but probably not over 26 or 27 by the line a railroad would take, and in the evening encamped at Camp *"Lignite."*

I called it *Lignite* because within a mile or two above, on the opposite or right side of the river, in the high bluffs against which the river impedes, occur[s] [a] thick vein of Lignite—an inferior kind of soft coal, which however is said to burn very well.

I rode up opposite to them, within about 700 or 800 feet—the width of the river at that point, and looked at them. During the day we saw immense quantities of game; antelope and deer, wild geese, rabbits, and some Buffalo; this being near the upper boundary of their range this season in the Yellowstone valley. We killed one Buffalo, several antelopes, a deer, and a wild goose, so that we had a magnificent dinner or supper last evening, and breakfast this morning. We were furnished at starting with five days' rations for us *men,* but with nothing for the horses, depending on the grass of the valley for their food.

As soon as we entered the Buffalo range we found the grass thin, eaten up or nearly so, so that our animals had rather short feed last night and nothing to-day. It was a cold night, but we contrived to have big fires in front of our feet, and with a good supply of robes and blankets, slept well without tents—just as I did this time last year in Minnesota.

---

[13]These letters have been edited so as to limit overlapping with communications to President Smith.

[14]Mitch Boyer or Bouyer (ca. 1840–76). Half Indian, longtime scout also on 1872 Yellowstone survey with Custer. In the 1990s a skull was found at the battlefield and through a photographic overlay technique proved to be his. Found in virtually all Little Big Horn accounts, *Encyclopedia of Frontier Biography,* and also John S. Gray's *Custer's Last Campaign.*

Capt. Ball loaned his fine horse "Dick." I found him the best horse I have ridden for years; so that five minutes after dismounting, after riding thirty miles, with scarcely a pause, I felt no fatigue, and my appetite was, as you may believe, good. The part of the Yellowstone valley that we came through for the past few days is five, ten, and even fifteen or more miles wide in places, with good soil, easily irrigated. The river has an abundance of water for water power and for irrigating purposes; and plenty for an artificial navigation when it is at its lowest stage, as it is now; but the fall is so great (on an average of 12 feet per mile) that it would be very costly to construct a lock and dam navigation; and on any other plan it would need be only deep enough in low water for boats of very light draught. It would be difficult for boats to work up, although it might be a fair *descending* navigation for a few months—part of June, July, and August. Those explorers who have pronounced it easily feasible for steamboat navigation, created by the removal of a few *obstructions*, at moderate cost, did not understand the regimen of this stream, or did not sufficiently study it, or had not (perhaps) the requisite experience to enable them to form a reliable practical judgment.

No more tonight dearest, good night darling Milnora.

* * *

Camp "Crow Indian" Nov. 12th

I did not write much of our *trip* yesterday, having branched off into navigation. We left Camp *Lignite* early yesterday morning. It was *cold.* The thermometer at 20.

We continued along the left bank of the river occasionally crossing some gullies, over generally very good soil, but the grass is gone, used up for the season. It is said that there were 6,000 horses feeding along here last summer and large number of Buffalo. We saw quite a number of Buffalo, and shot one cow, which made good food for us—also plenty of antelope, deer, and wild geese through the day.

In the morning, between 11 and 12 o'clock, as we were crossing a deep ford of the river, one of our soldiers, named Shavers, came near losing his life. His horse fell over in the deep, swift water and fell upon him and held him under some time—long enough to make me feel very uneasy about him. Without help he would have been lost. Captain Tyler and several soldiers got to him after a while with a rope, and got him back to the gravel bar where the Command had started to cross over. He was chilled, frightened nearly to death; but they soon stripped him and gave him different articles of dry clothing, and then brought him over. It was not a good ford, and we will search for another on our return today.

Yesterday afternoon, after we had seen a number of herds of Buffalo, we thought we observed another small herd a long way off in front. I was the first to suggest that they did not move like buffalo, and after a while Major Pease took out his glass and observed (as I had said one of them was a man or a horse) Indians, on horseback. I had observed that they had after approaching retreated. They came forward again, and shortly afterwards we saw distinctly about a dozen Indians, and could hear their cry to the effect that [they] were "Crows." Soon we saw several signal poles with red flags. Major Pease rode forward, and they came up and shook hands apparently greatly rejoiced to meet us; and if their story is true, they were glad to find that we were not Sioux.

Their story is that they had stolen a lot of horses from a large Sioux camp, about fifty miles off on the *"Big Horn"* river or rather a few miles beyond it, but not near its mouth, and had sent the horses across to the Musselshell where there is a large Crow camp. They had ridden all night, they said. They were young, good looking, and had on their war paint! Without any invitation they retraced their steps and followed us into camp last night. We had no tents; neither had they; but they very soon improvised one of poles leaning together at the top, with a cloth laid around them to keep out the wind and snow which was threatening, and which came about the time. . . . We had a poor shore of pasture—after considerable search and no grain with us and no better pasture in the valley below for nearly a day's march or more. Col. Baker had last night a chill fever, so this morning we [began] to start back.[15]

* * *

Camp *MILNORA*—on left bank of Yellowstone five miles below Clark's Fork [River].

Nov. 12th evening.

Here am I, on my return. I will explain. Yesterday afternoon we had a perfect bird's-eye [view] of the wide valley, nearly level below us for more than twenty miles; so that to see anything of much account beyond the scope of our vision, we should have to travel two more days down and two more days back to reach Camp *Crow Indian*. I called it that name to

[15]A "chill fever" might better be translated as "the shakes."

commemorate our meeting with the little band of Crows whom we met yesterday afternoon and who returned with us to *"Camp Milnora."* Here we met Capt. Ball—who had moved down the valley from where we left him, about 20 miles—a few miles in advance of the Survey. They had no name for the Camp, so I call it by the name of our darling. I am in Capt. Ball's tent, having had an excellent supper with a nicely cooked young wild goose, buffalo meat, antelope, and deer meat, and good coffee. I am to sleep here tonight. Mr. Chenoworth who shared my tent on our way out—now has quarters with Mr. Muhlenberg. Mr. Frank Kneass is to return with us. We are to start in the morning.

We have killed more antelope and deer today.

Capt. Ball tells me he has with him those cattle, on the hoof, which he brought with him, but they have had such an abundance of game that he expects to take them back with him alive. It is very cold, but the Capt. has a neat little stove which keeps the tent only too warm. Our horses are happy now—having both pasture and grain—grain in small doses. This party has been out from Fort Ellis about two months, and Capt. Ball and Mr. Muhlenberg are both anxious to push on as far down as weather and forage will permit.

I have left the matter entirely with Capt. Ball. Capt. Ball and the other officers here say that *Mr. M* has worked faithfully and well since they left Ellis, and that he has been entirely abstinent. He is all right now, and they all like him. The man who was nearly drowned yesterday is one of the Battery [Muhlenberg] commanded during the war.

Mr. Chenoworth came to me this evening saying he wished to return with me tomorrow. I asked him why? He said it was filthy rough work, etc. I told him that if he wished to continue pursuing engineering as a profession, that under the circumstances, he had better not quit—that I should be done with him, too, and that it would not be many days before the whole command of Capt. Ball would return. He said he would remain. I informed upon Muhlenberg the importance of aiding Mr. Chenoworth all he could, as he had shown that he was a good worker—much better than Frank Kneass. Mr. M said he would himself help him.

Good night dearest O and darling O.

Source: Roberts Papers, Collection 783, Correspondence 1871–1874, series 2, box 2, folders 4–5, Burlingame Special Collections Library, Montana State University, Bozeman.

Newspaper Coverage

The Teton [Lakota] Sioux

This fierce and warlike tribe have come within the borders of our [Montana] Territory.[16] They number over one thousand lodges (in all, probably four thousand warriors), and occupy a tract of country in the Yellowstone valley which covers the Northern Pacific Railroad for more than 200 miles. It had been ascertained beyond a doubt that the late raiding party in the Gallatin valley was composed of these Teton Sioux, and unless the most prompt and vigorous measures are taken by the Indian Department, much trouble may be apprehended from the predatory bands which roam the country for scalps and plunder.[17]

The Indians referred to a few months since recognized the authority of Red Cloud, until his return from [Washington] concluding the treaty of peace with the Government, when, either from dissatisfaction from terms of said treaty, or through their implacable hatred of the white man, they denounced Red Cloud as having been "blinded" by the lies of the pale faces, threw off their allegiance to him, and have united under the Beelzebub of the tribe, "Sitting Bull."

They have announced their determination to oppose the survey and projection of the railroad through the country they now occupy. In this exigency, something must be done and that quickly. A few thousand savages cannot be allowed to impede the great work. We understand that Col. Viall has taken prompt action in this matter and has recommended to the Department that he be allowed to visit this hostile tribe and endeavor to induce them to remove to a tract of country between the 105° and 109° of west latitude and bounded north by the British Possessions and south by the Missouri River, a section where game is abundant, where no railroad will ever run, and where white men will never settle.[18] If the Indians can in this way be disposed of, it would be a most fortunate consummation. A bloody war by these means may be averted. Let pacific measures be first tried, and if found of no avail, then [Major] Baker must try his persuasion once more.

It is to be hoped that the Department at Washington may favor at once

---

[16]The newspaper meant the Indians had crossed to the western side of the Bozeman Pass or into the Missouri River basin.

[17]The "Gallatin valley" meant from the headwaters of the Gallatin River at Fort Ellis and adjacent Bozeman west.

[18]Jasper A. Viall (1830–1910), Montana superintendent of Indian affairs.

the plan as proposed by Colonel Viall for the solution of this question. It is practicable and promises to be the means of preventing bloodshed and pillage on our border. It is understood that the garrison at Fort Buford has been ordered to the valley of the Yellowstone for the protection of surveying parties of the Northern Pacific Road now en route to that section. We trust that the measures proposed by our Superintendent may be tried before the troops and Indians come in contact, for the bloody work of the bullet and saber, once called into acquisition, cannot be stopped except by the extermination of this hostile tribe.

Source: Helena Daily Herald, *August 21, 1871.*

The Indians of Montana Territory

Washington, Aug. 23—Governor Potts[19] of Montana Territory, under date of August 12, writes to the Secretary of the Interior as follows:

"The presence of large bodies of Sioux Indians on the Crow Reservation, near the Crow agency, at this time, with what appears to be hostile intent, has frightened people of Gallatin Valley to such a degree that I fear they will abandon their crops and flee with their loose property to places of safety. The assembling of so many hostile Indians so near a settlement, and so soon after making a successful raid, can mean nothing but mischief. Major F. D. Pease, [Crow Indian] agent, came in from the Crow agency on the 10th and says that the whole movement of the Sioux Indians points to a general Indian war on the settlements.

"The officers of the Indian Department are doing all they can to aid the military, but it is too weak to give protection to a [wide] valley forty or fifty miles long.

"I am organizing the settlers and arming them, but have no authority to pay or subsist them. I shall take no steps toward calling the militia into active service until I have undoubted authority from the War Department. Our greatest need here is more troops and I hope that General Sherman will send me the commander of the Second United States Cavalry [John Gibbon]. I will leave here [Helena] in the morning for Gallatin and the Yellowstone valley to see for myself and to give

[19]Benjamin Franklin Potts (1837–87), territorial governor of Montana (1870–83), was tough, combat hardened, and a brevetted major general. He fully supported Cooke and the Northern Pacific. Malone et al., *Dictionary of American Biography;* Warner, *Generals in Blue*; *National Cyclopedia of American Biography,* 11:79.

directions to our people. I shall report to you from time to time on the situation, as the matter is one that belongs to your department.

"I am [etc.]."

Source: Philadelphia Inquirer, *August 24, 1871.*

The Santee Sioux

From the *Washington Patriot* of August 19th, we learn that Col. Stanley, 22nd Infantry, commanding the Middle District of the Department of Dakota, has communicated to General Hancock explicit and reliable information concerning the Santee Sioux. The Colonel says:

"Both Santees and Yanktons (so called) make constant war on the Blackfeet, the Crows, and the Assiniboines, and their war parties are always out. Since I came to this country, the buffaloes have constantly moved westward and the Indians have followed them; and the several times I have heard from the Indians, they have stated that they intend to go wherever the buffaloes went. I do not think it possible to induce these Indians to rejoin their own bands. Placing them upon the same footing as the Assiniboines, as regards annuities, might pacify them, as it has in a manner Red Cloud and the Oglala. The military could only control them by a new military post somewhere about Milk River, a measure I should hesitate to recommend with the small number of troops disposable in the Department.

"When the Northern Pacific crosses the Missouri, the entire Sioux question will be brought to a head and, in my opinion, will only be solved by an Indian war of some magnitude. Until that time I would recommend that conciliatory measures be taken with the Indians that are the subject of this paper. . . . The Teton Sioux in the Yellowstone valley are the ones to be looked after."

Source: Helena Daily Herald, *August 29, 1871.*

Northern Pacific Survey

The surveying party, under Mr. Muhlenberg, which has been operating in this [Gallatin] valley the past month, passed [east] over the range Friday last, and are now in the valley of the Yellowstone. . . . Mr. Muhlenberg informs us that the line of the survey is the most practicable in the valley, and it will not be varied from five hundred feet, in his estimation, should this route be adopted, which there is every reason to believe it will. We understand that an escort of two companies of cavalry will be sent after the party as soon as they get to the Yellowstone, and that two other companies will soon follow. Capt. Ball, we learn, is in command of the first squadron, and that Col. Baker will go with the second, taking command of the whole. Fifteen Crow scouts will accompany Capt. Ball, and an efficient corps will be attached to the expedition.

Source: Bozeman Avant Courier, *September 13, 1871.*

Gallatin County Items

From the *Bozeman Avant Courier* of the 20th Inst.

The Crow Indians, both Mountain and River Crows, are nearly all at the agency.[20] The nation now numbers about 4,100. They have been receiving rations of flour, meat, coffee, sugar, etc. They are in every respect friendly to whites, and some of their soldiers accompany the Northern Pacific R.R. Surveying party down the Yellowstone.

Capt. Ball, in command of two companies of cavalry, left Fort Ellis on Saturday last for the Yellowstone, to accompany the surveying party. . . .

. . . Recently the Blackfeet Indians stole about a hundred horses from the Crows, who discovered the loss and pursued the Blackfeet so closely that they recovered half of their stock.

The Northern Pacific Surveying party has now reached the mouth of [the Shields River] and from that point they are to have a military escort. The company [is] in fine spirits and speaks favorably of the route surveyed.

Source: Helena Daily Herald, *September 22, 1871.*

Bannack Indians

From the *Bozeman Avant Courier* of the 20th Inst.:

The whole tribe of Bannack [and many Shoshone] Indians, numbering we should judge, by the length of time passing through town, one

[20]The U.S. government had split the Crow Indians into two reservations. The Mountain Crows' agency buildings were some 5 miles east of present-day Livingston, Montana, on a defensible hill adjacent to the Yellowstone River.

thousand, Chief Tendoy in command, arrived in Bozeman on Sunday and are now encamped near town.[21] Their dusky forms, some gaily bedecked with red flannels, red blankets, and numerous other fancy trappings, while occasionally could be seen a stolid old squaw with three or four of her progeny all mounted on one dilapidated kiyus [*sic*], presented quite a grotesque appearance passing through our streets. They had considerable loose stock, and, as a general thing, it looked well. From the number of papooses and young ones belonging to the tribe, we image the Bannacks are considerably on the increase. In a few days they will proceed to the Yellowstone and Snake River regions where they will spend the winter hunting.

Source: Helena Daily Herald, *September 22, 1871.*

Indian Affairs in Montana

From the *Washington* [D.C.] *Chronicle*

A letter from Governor Potts, of Montana Territory, has been received by the Secretary of the Interior, dated Virginia City, September 12, 1871, in which the governor says the people of Gallatin Valley now feel comparatively safe from Indian raids. He had succeeded in organizing and equipping a force of 200 men in the valley, which, with the aid of the troops, he thinks will be quite sufficient to secure peace. He apprehends trouble from the Sioux Indians in the spring [of 1872] unless some terms can be made with "Sitting Bull" and his band. He learns that a band of 5,000 Santee Sioux are on Milk River, near Fort Browning, where they are being fed by the Indian agent. They positively refuse to go on their reservation, saying they do not want to live near white men where there is no game. The governor says it has been clearly demonstrated that feeding these Indians is much better and cheaper than fighting them, for they have been thoroughly tractable ever since the feeding has commenced. He says he understands that "Sitting Bull" has declared war against the engineers of the Northern Pacific Railroad Company, and a large military force has been sent into the Valley of the Yellowstone

[21]Chief Tendoy or Tin Doi (ca. 1834–1907) was a Bannock-Shoshone chief able to keep his fast dwindling tribe and followers at peace with the whites. His taking his tribe peacefully through Bozeman was an annual trek that apparently continued until about 1875. Tendoy was a nephew or cousin of Sacajawea of Lewis and Clark fame. Wikipedia.

to protect the engineers. The Governor adds that nearly every band of Indians is accompanied by some white men, who are the worst characters in the West, and no raids, he says, are undertaken that are not led by these whites. He suggests that all white men should be prohibited from residing with Indians.

Source: Sioux City Daily Tribune, *September 29, 1871.*

More Indians

The advance of the Flathead Indian tribe, en route to the Yellowstone valley for an extensive buffalo hunt, passed through Bozeman a few days since. The Bannacks and Crows have been on the hunt during the past three weeks and have been remarkably successful. The Flatheads will consequently find the buffalo rather scarce in the valley.

Source: Bozeman Avant Courier, *October 26, 1871.*

J. Gregory Smith (1818–91), president of the Northern Pacific Railroad and an able, farsighted, energetic, and natural leader and businessman. However, he was unaware of his limitations, preoccupied by his personally owned Vermont Central Railroad's financial problems, awarded Crédit Mobilier like contracts, and was seldom in Minnesota. During the winter of 1870–71, with construction behind schedule, Smith gave the disastrous instructions that resulted in construction over Minnesota's ice and snow. *Courtesy National Archives, Washington, D.C.*

Jay Cooke (1820–1905)
As America's leading banker and the "Financier of the Civil War," he had raised over a quarter of the North's money. He believed that he had been chosen by God to save the Union and later to build the Northern Pacific. As an operational manager, however, Cooke's skills were questionable, and his decision not to visit Minnesota vastly reduced his influence over Northern Pacific construction. *Courtesy National Archives, Washington, D.C.*

W. Milnor Roberts (1810–81) became the Northern Pacific's engineer in chief in October 1870. A Philadelphia Quaker, he was honest, able, and considered one of America's leading railroad engineers. Smith opposed his hiring but, after being forced to do so by the Northern Pacific's Board of Directors, he was mostly able to keep Roberts out of Minnesota—where corruption was greatest—in 1871. *Courtesy Burlingame Special Collections Library, Montana State University, Bozeman.*

Ira Spaulding and Tom Rosser, ca. 1871

Bvt. Brig. Gen. Ira Spaulding (1818–75; standing, top row, fourth from left), a wartime combat engineer, and Maj. Gen. Thomas Rosser (1836–1910; seated below Spaulding, in light-colored hat) led the Northern Pacific's surveyors in Minnesota and on the eastern Yellowstone survey. *Courtesy Small Special Collections Library, University of Virginia, Charlottesville.*

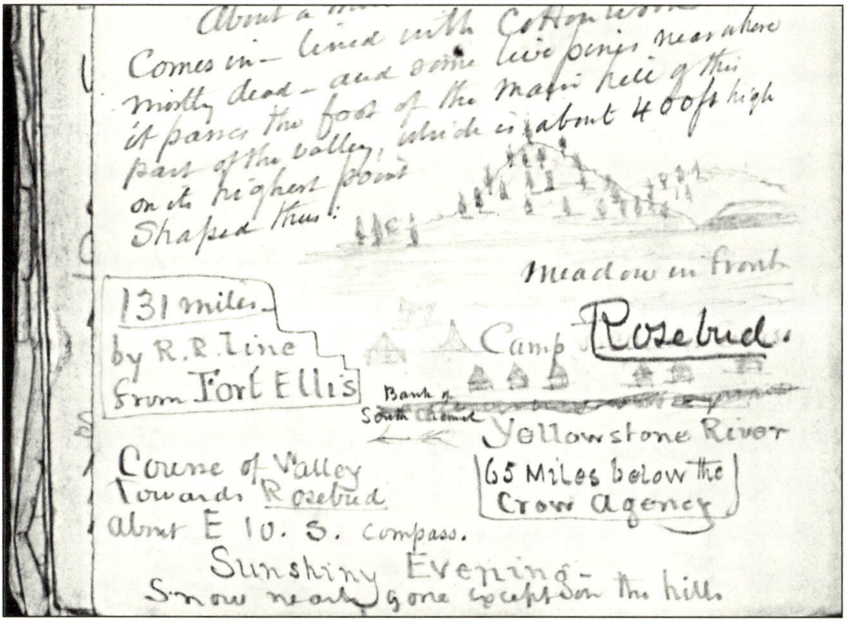

Two sketches made by Roberts in November 1871

He was forever writing, taking notes, often while riding. His reports, letters, and diary form the backbone of our knowledge of the western Yellowstone surveying expedition. *Courtesy Burlingame Special Collections Library, Montana State University, Bozeman.*

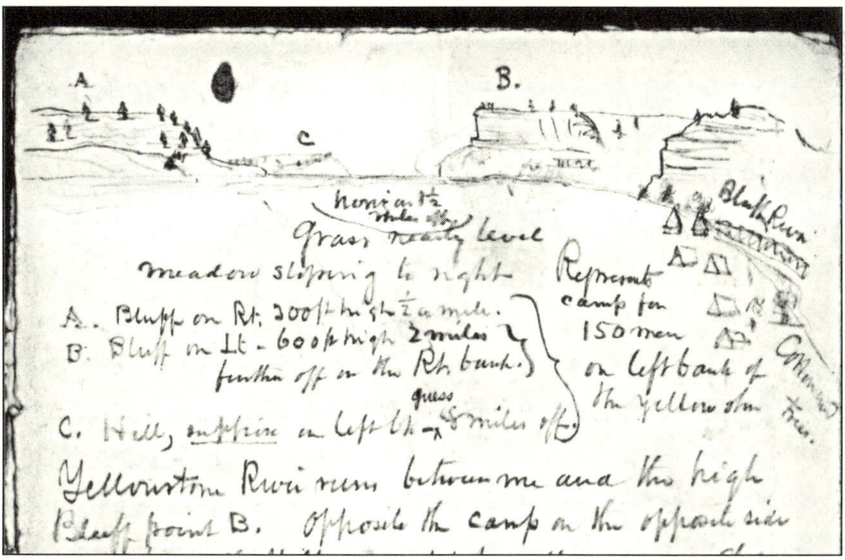

Maj. Joseph N. G. Whistler (1822–99)
A breveted brigadier general who saw little wartime combat, the unlucky Whistler was stationed in Texas in 1861 and then captured. Finally exchanged, he was badly wounded in the 1864 Richmond campaign. By 1871 his wife and children had moved back east and he had become a dysfunctional alcoholic, unable to read a compass. *Courtesy U.S. Army Military History Institute, Carlisle, Penn.*

Capt. Javan B. Irvine (1831–1904)
As marginally competent as he was idealistic, Irvine literally blundered into a Confederate colonel at Bull Run, capturing the highest ranking officer of the day. His diaries and letters offer a fascinating account of the eastern surveying expedition. The following year he was shot through the head by an Indian, somehow survived, but continued in the army (understandably becoming somewhat "odd") until his retirement. *Courtesy South Dakota State Historical Society, Pierre.*

Basil Clement (1824–1910)
lead scout on the 1871 eastern Yellowstone survey. Despite Clement's impressive trapping and scouting "résumé," Rosser didn't trust him, and his skills were marginal for railroad surveying. He was either unfamiliar with the country, drinking, or both. *Courtesy South Dakota State Historical Society, Pierre.*

Maj. Eugene M. Baker (ca. 1836–84)
The commander of Fort Ellis, Baker had caught Phil Sheridan's eye during the 1864 Shenandoah River valley campaign. For years he had done the army's dirty work with "recalcitrant" Indians, including being responsible for the infamous Marias River Massacre. Another alcoholic, he escorted Milnor Roberts down the Yellowstone valley, at one point "jokingly" shooting at Roberts. This is the only known full-faced photo of him, taken ca. 1858. *Courtesy U.S. Military Academy, West Point, N.Y.*

Lt. Lovell H. Jerome (1849–1935)
Jerome, who came from one of New York's financially leading families, was a prototype West Point graduate on his first frontier posting at Fort Ellis. Six years later he achieved an unfortunate degree of notoriety by being captured by the Nez Perce and then exchanged for Chief Joseph himself. Additionally, he was the close first cousin (the two families lived in adjacent townhouses) of Jennie Jerome Churchill, the mother of Winston. *Courtesy U.S. Military Academy, West Point, N.Y.*

Early 1830s locomotive
Without the rapid development of the locomotive, the Northern Pacific would never have existed in 1870. This early 1830s locomotive was state of the art when trains could climb only the gentlest of hills, made only gradual turns, and carried only passengers and their luggage. *Author's collection.*

Lt. Edward J. McClernand (1849–1926) was the son of Maj. Gen. John McClernand, who was fired by Grant during the Vicksburg campaign. The undistinguished looking lieutenant was awarded the Medal of Honor following the Nez Perce campaign, was a combatant in the Cuba and Philippines campaigns, and retired as a brigadier general. Nevertheless, his posthumously published *With the Indians and Buffalo in Montana* sadly contains little but fantasy concerning his 1871 role on the western survey. *Courtesy U.S. Military Academy, West Point, N.Y.*

Brainerd train wreck/bridge collapse
The nasty winter of 1870–71 resulted in this 1875 disaster over the Mississippi River. *Courtesy Small Special Collections Library, University of Virginia, Charlottesville.*

Lake Superior & Mississippi locomotive in Duluth
By 1871 the Northern Pacific had taken control of two other strategic Minnesota railroads: the Lake Superior & Mississippi (pictured above) and the St. Paul & Pacific. *Courtesy of Minnesota Historical Society, St. Paul.*

DULUTH IN MAY 1870

Until Cooke and the Northern Pacific chose Duluth, Minnesota, as its eastern terminus, the town had a population in the low hundreds and was many times smaller than neighboring Superior, Wisconsin. The towns were just a few miles apart and separated by St. Louis Bay. By choosing Duluth, Northern Pacific "insiders" made huge profits in Duluth real estate. However, the price was high: the originally supportive Wisconsin congressional delegation in Washington became the railroad's bitterest enemies. By the 1920s, despite the fact that the Lake Superior port was iced in five months a year, Duluth was America's second busiest port, shipping enormous amounts of grain and minerals. *Author's collection.*

Steamer passing under partially constructed Fargo-Moorhead Bridge

Taken in the spring of 1872, this shows the small 100-ton capacity steamer Selkirk, passing what would become the Northern Pacific's bridge over the Red River. This river was too shallow, narrow, and twisting to permit larger shipping to and from Canada. *Minnesota Historical Society.*

THE ROAD TO YELLOWSTONE NATIONAL PARK

Southwest of present-day Livingston, Montana, the Yellowstone River makes a sharp right turn toward the east on its journey toward the Missouri. From this bend the Northern Pacific would follow the river for some fifty-five miles until it reached the park. As Jay Cooke had foreseen, the only easy way to reach the newly created national park was via the railroad, its Livingston-to-Yellowstone spur completed in 1883. *Courtesy Library of Congress, Washington, D.C.*

Little Missouri River
The success of the eastern survey was almost entirely due to Rosser's finding a passage through the Badlands of the Little Missouri valley. This photo, taken some five miles south of present-day Medora, North Dakota, illustrates some of the problems in finding an acceptable crossing. *Author's photo.*

Yellowstone River near Greycliff, Montana

In central Montana the Northern Pacific did everything possible to respect the 1868 treaty with Crow Indians and stay on the northern side of the Yellowstone. While the north bank (on the right) was surveyed, the results clearly showed that construction would be required where today's tracks exist. Unlike so many other examples of confiscated Indian land, the Northern Pacific actually paid for the land, albeit a modest amount in today's dollars. *Author's photo.*

FORT ELLIS SITE TODAY

This ideal camping site, on the headwaters of the Gallatin River, was used in 1806 by William Clark on his return (Meriwether Lewis followed the Missouri) from Oregon. In 1866 the site was selected by the army for a post astride the Bozeman Pass and guarding both Bozeman and west-central Montana from large-scale Indian attacks. *Author's photo.*

CHAPTER 6

The Eastern Survey to the Yellowstone

September 20 to October 4

That summer and early fall throughout Dakota, western Illinois, Iowa, central Michigan, Minnesota, eastern Montana, and Wisconsin, weather conditions were particularly dry. Multiple forest fires roared through parts of these states, trapping and killing thousands, far surpassing the estimated three hundred deaths in the Great Chicago Fire.

Somewhere near Gladstone, North Dakota, the prairie fire that had been moving east, but on the south side of the Heart, leaped over the tiny stream. In a worst case scenario, the expedition might have been overrun by fire: officers mostly escaping, enlisted men leaping on wagons pulled by panicked horses that predictably ran over fleeing infantry, crashed into each other, on fire, careening wildly until overturning, or as exhausted infantrymen were individually overtaken by leaping flames. Fortunately, as Whistler and Irvine describe, there was no worst case.

In Dakota, without millions of buffalo roaming across open prairie, the grass grew uneaten, then withered under the hot summer sun, susceptible to the slightest spark. Before they left Fort Rice, the surveying expedition had been warned—likely incorrectly—that the Indians were firing the grass. Regardless of the cause, it was a huge potential problem of which everyone was aware. Thus on September 23, as the fire leaped the Heart, all the survey's participants were about to be tested as never before. For perhaps the only time, Whistler would do his duty.

Days later the survey entered the Badlands, first seeing them from where today a rest stop on Interstate 94 greets awed travelers. The views in 1871, seen by so few whites until Sully's 1864 campaign, while expected, were nevertheless overwhelming. Campbell, Irvine, Rosser, and Whistler all tried to put to paper what they saw and heard.

If the Badlands were beautiful, of greater importance was finding a practical route through them. In this, the survey was a success, Rosser and Basil Clement finding a route that required only modest construction through the valley of the Little Missouri.

The chapter continues until the Yellowstone was reached. However, less than half of the expedition actually would see the river. Whistler's report dances around the fact that he himself didn't go. The reason given, that the trail was too rough to take the entire train—as Irvine wrote to his wife (see chapter 8)—was ridiculous. Whistler's issue seems to have involved his lack of willpower with drinking without the responsibility of command. Riding in a makeshift ambulance because of "piles," Rosser reached the river; Whistler did not. Even if the route was too rough for wagons—and driving today's dirt backroads paralleling I-94/Glendive Creek causes disagreement—as the C.O., Whistler could and should have ridden. End of discussion and, as it turned out, end of Whistler's career.

Whistler's Report

Report of the Expedition Accompanying the Engineers of the Northern Pacific Railroad from Fort Rice D.T. to the Yellowstone River and Return, during the Months of September and October 1871

September 20. Left camp about 7 a.m. After going back on our road for a short distance we struck into the valley. Just south of where we were in camp, there is quite a large tributary which empties into the Heart River, and after we had traversed the valley by about a mile we came across Capt. Inman A.Q.M. at work fixing a crossing over a stream that the guides called "Young Men's Creek." The crossing was soon completed and the train quickly across. This stream seems to have coal cropping all along its banks and in some places the bed of the Creek is all coal. As soon as we crossed we found evidences of Genl. Sully's camp spoken of before. Our route now took up along a high ridge dividing the Heart

River and Young Men's Creek, in an almost due west course. The road was very fine, there being no steep places to go up or down. We were in sight of the river most of the time during the day whilst we approached the Creek several times. About 1 P.M. a guide came to us to say that Lt. Turnock in charge of the Scouts had found a camp. After travelling some distance we found we were getting into some broken country and we were compelled to change our course very materially to get to the river. We were soon in sight of the horses of the Scouts down in the bottom, and a few minutes later the command was in camp.

The Engineers came into camp very late having failed to run up the line by about 6 miles. Distance travelled over 18 miles.

SEPTEMBER 21. Started from camp about 8 A.M., passed over a small bottom in a northwest direction, passed a coulee where the pioneers had been doing some work. After which we struck for the high ground which we reached without any trouble. The train was closed up in four lines in which order we moved for about 3 miles when we struck rough ground. It was found impossible to get down to the river without a great deal of trouble, so the train was put in corral on a high bluff overlooking the bottom. The river is very crooked and has but little water and that standing in pools. There seems to be plenty of good coal along the river, some of the specimens looking like cannel coal. The day was very hot, but the march was light, with the exception of the company with the Engineers who had to march about 25 miles. Distance travelled 5½ miles.

All day the smoke rising in the west gave us to understand we were in the immediate vicinity of prairie fires. Towards night the impressions were strengthened by seeing it gradually coming towards us and by taps the whole heavens were lit up and reflected on the clouds formed by the vast conflagration. The wind coming up soon after nightfall drove the flames towards us with great speed, so that by 10 o'clock the hills southwest of us and across the Heart River were one vast ocean of flame rolling on like some troubled sea. The flames would shoot towards the heavens in angry columns only to be levelled to the ground again, but far in advance of where they shot onward.

SEPTEMBER 22. Morning broke still and quiet, with smoke hanging around, the effects of last night's fire. By 7 o'clock we were off passing almost northeast for a short distance to avoid some broken ground in the direction of our march. We now changed to the proper direction of our march, over country similar to that passed over before. After going some four miles it was evident that the fire had succeeded in crossing the river and that we would have to pass through it, which was strengthened very soon by seeing the fire coming towards us. No time was to be lost as it was almost upon us. The train was hastened across a deep ravine in double time, so as to gain some high ground, for being caught in the ravine would have been disastrous as the grass was very tall. It was evident that even the mules were excited, judging from the way they brought the wagons across the dangerous place. Men were now set to work burning the grass while others armed with gunny sacks stood by to keep it in proper bounds. We soon had a vast conflagration of our own, burning the grass off in a short while, so that the teams moved on to it as a harbor and were safe. Then came hard travelling, the wind blowing fearfully, carrying ashes, cinders, and smoke into our eyes, ears, and nostrils, but there was no help for it, as the prairie was one black mass. On we went until we met the guides who informed us we were to get to the river, along the banks of which we found patches which had not been burned. We finally reached the river, which had to be crossed, and at a point where as usual we found quicksand, but which did not interfere very much with crossing.

Near where we crossed a large tributary, [Green River] comes into the Heart River from the northwest. It is quite large, with plenty of wood and water. After crossing the river, a high hill had to be driven up, which was finally accomplished, but not until one of the Engineers' wagons, horses, and all had rolled to the bottom, but as no serious injury happened to horses or wagon, the damage was soon repaired. After we came up the hill, we went into camp, where we found grass for the stock. We had hardly formed camp before fire was communicated to the grass, and it seemed for a while as if the whole left of the corral would be burned, but the men worked splendidly and conquered it. The fire drove the antelope almost frantic; they would run parallel with the flame and then make a dart and escape. Distance travelled 11¼ miles.

September 23. Prairie fires raging all around making a panorama for which many would pay well to see. The fires would run up the valleys resembling long streets lit up with gas. This was especially so after the first flame had passed, the smoke from the fires hanging like a pall over the whole country. Reveille very early and we were off by 7 A.M. taking almost a southwest direction and running to keep as near General Sully's trail as possible.

We found a large outcrop of sandstone on which were several names (of Co. C, 6th Iowa Cavalry), evidently men of Genl. Sully's command. The trail is almost obliterated, but we managed to strike one of his camps on Heart River where we went into camp. The country passed through was rolling prairie. As we could see for a great distance, the impression was that we were getting near the "Mauvaises Terres" or "Bad Lands." All around us the grass is burned, which adds twofold to the lovely condition one feels in this country. We found a small spot to encamp on which there was plenty of good grass. The Heart River is rapidly assuming the appearance of a small brook. We still found plenty of water, but it was in pools and plenty of alkali in it. The timber is small and everything indicates that we are getting to the source of the Heart River. Game plentiful. Distance travelled a little over 17 miles.

SEPTEMBER 24TH. Left camp at 7 A.M. and at once struck the burned prairie over which the march was made most of the day. The direction was west passing near the river. The fire had swept everything in its course, almost all the timber in the valley being consumed.

We had to cross a small stream which puts in from the west, but after this we had easy going. Indian signs were observed in several places today and very fresh. The Engineers now abandoned the river and ran their line almost west. We passed a butte early this morning resembling some old castle, very beautiful to look upon but an indication that we were very near the "bad lands." We managed to get a camp where we had a little grass and water, but very scarce. Near the camp was an outcrop of coal which appears to have been ignited by the late prairie fire. The coal appears to be of good quality, burning rapidly, and giving off smoke resembling the bituminous coal of Indiana and Illinois. About 2 miles from camp, we crossed a tributary of the Heart. This was as large as any one in sight and may be the principal branch. Distance travelled over 10 miles.

SEPTEMBER 25. The train was put in motion about 6 A.M., having to cross a deep gully near camp, and by a little after 7 the last passed over. We now started in a due west direction leaving the waters of the Heart River for those of the "Little Missouri." Our road was very good for about 6 miles (the grass and soil being poor) when all at once we came in sight of the celebrated "Bad Lands" of which we had heard so much. The sight was magnificent beyond anything we had yet seen or that we hoped to see. Far off to the north ran a stream, bordered on each side with timber and under wood, and extending back from this for half a mile was a fine grassy valley. From this valley rose walls almost perpendicular, which were cut through by cross canyons, giving the valley the appearance of a grand street on whose sides were magnificent buildings. There are to be seen detached mounds resembling all kinds of houses, fine public buildings with immense domes, old castles, the pictures of which ornament all the old histories. Elegant residences, railroad depots, in fact anything and any style of architecture could be seen from the point where we first caught sight of this wonderful valley.

The sides of the steep hills are of a diversified nature, red, gray, white, brown, all in the same and running in stratas. The most of this wonderful country seems to have been subjected to a very high heat, the rooks in some places resembling molten iron, and in others glass. But our business was not to look upon this beautiful scene. We were to get into the valley and then to the "Little Missouri River" of which the creek was a tributary. The guides returned to the train in a short time with the information that they had found a way down. We started and reached the valley in a short time, which we found more beautiful to look up to than when we were standing above it. It so resembled a street that the men were calling the different points after large hotels which were familiar to them. Some vast dome-shaped hills rose out of the valley resembling Mosques; others looked like gasometers do.[1] We found a road leading down the valley, at least nature made one. The grass was very good, the fire not having reached it. After crossing one or two deep gullies, we went into camp. The valley appeared to be getting narrower and the chances are that we will have to get to the Little Missouri down it. We found water plenty but strongly alkali, but by digging into the sand it was much better.

The camp was completely surrounded by very steep hills, and the notes of the bugle were re-echoed from one to another until you could hear it half a dozen times, the effect of which was truly grand. The Scouts reported having seen very fresh Indian signs not over 24 hours old. The Engineers are pleased with finding so easy an approach to the river as this valley affords. Distance travelled 14½ miles.

SEPTEMBER 26. We found our course was down the valley of the little stream on which we camped last night, and the prospect being so good

[1]A gasometer was a tank for storing and measuring gas.

for plenty of trouble in getting along, an extra pioneer corps of 75 men was detailed. We left camp about 8 A.M., having been detained while a crossing could be made. We were soon on our way, and a very rough one we found it, as we had to make seven crossings of the creek, besides fiscing some gullies.[2] The hills on each side are of the wildest kind, towering to an immense height and perfectly bare of any kind of vegetation.

From the time we entered this valley until we left it at the Little Missouri, there are but few places where we could get out even with a horse. In the valley is a luxuriant growth of grass and some timber, while evidence of coal can be seen on every hand. A man was missing from Capt. Clarke's Company 17th Infantry last night, and a fire was kept burning on the highest point above the camp for a guide for him, but he did not return until today, having had a rough experience with the wolves, who insisted on having two deer which he had killed. He kept them off for some time, but was finally obliged to give them up and retreat. Four scouts were sent out to hunt this man, but he joined the command before they returned.

Found evidences of bears, but did not see any. Passed several old Indian encampments. Reached the Little Missouri River about 4 P.M. and went into camp in a most beautiful spot. The bottom is wide and covered with a thick growth of cottonwood timber, much of which had been killed by fire. The water is slightly alkaline, but not sufficient to make it unpleasant to the taste. We found that our camp was in the same place where Genl. Sully camped. About 5 P.M. Genl. Rosser and Lieut. Turnock returned from a reconnaissance with the information that they had found Genl. Sully's trail on the opposite side of the river. Our course was nearly west today.

Great quantities of gypsum [are] found near our camp. Distance travelled a little over 9 miles.

SEPTEMBER 27. The first thing we did this morning was to cross the river on a brush bridge which had been constructed by a detail of 80 men, which was accomplished by 9 A.M. The train was soon across and started to gain the high ground through a deep gorge, which I suppose is a creek in the spring of the year. We soon passed out of this into some very broken country, having to pass down places that looked as it if was

[2]Here the writer appears to be using a word that meant creating a solid fill of wood, gravel, rocks, brush, and sand—in short, anything that could create a temporary bridge strong enough to support the wagons.

impossible for wagons to travel. While resting about noon, a mountain sheep came to look at us from an almost inaccessible peak. We found coal everywhere. And the Scouts report it on fire near our route and say from appearances it has been on fire for several years. We passed some very high buttes, all of which looked as if they were standing as monuments to a past age. We were compelled to stop and go into camp on account of a deep gorge.

The camp was on the spot where Genl. Sully had a fight with the Indians [at the battle of the Badlands]. A twelve pounder shot and other evidences of the fight were found.

The Engineers on leaving camp this morning went down the river about 4 miles where they found a small stream coming in from the west up which they propose to run their line. They came into camp very tired, having had to walk some distance after quitting work. The grass from the river to this point is very good in the valleys, and plenty of wood can be found. The wind blew very hard, making it a cold and unpleasant day. Distance travelled 9 miles.

September 28. Wind blew fearful all night, which rendered sleeping out of the question. We were up at the usual time and off by 7 A.M., but made a very zig-zag course. The first thing done was sending the guides to hunt water. When about 3 miles from camp one of the guides came to the train with the information that he had found water, but that it was almost in our rear, started, but were soon told by another that there was water in our front, which we went for. This carried us a long way out of our line of march. We finally struck the water where the animals were all watered and the kegs filled. After this we started almost south to gain our original track, but we soon found we were far ahead of the Engineers and made camp. The grass was burned, but there were many spots which had escaped and on one of these the camp was pitched. Near camp signs of water were discovered, the pioneers were set to work and at the depth of about 2 feet struck water, which came out in large quantities.

Capt. Inman set his men to work, and in a short time they had a large trench dug which filled with water. This water is strongly impregnated with sulphur, but is very good compared with some we had to use. The country seems almost deserted by all kinds of animals, which is attributed to two causes. The Indians hunting before the fire, and the fire which destroyed all the grass. Timber was seen in most all the valleys during the day, and up to late in the summer there must have been plenty of water.

The timber away from the large streams is principally elm, scrub oak, and box elder, and a great deal of it is dead from the effects of prairie fires.

Outcrops of coal can be seen on any of the streams and ravines. Fresh Indian signs were observed today, but in small parties. Distance travelled a little over 12 miles.

SEPTEMBER 29. The Engineers on coming into camp last evening stated that they had run their line up the wrong branch of the creek from the river; consequently, today they started almost north to commence a new line, intending to correct it with the old one further back towards the Little Missouri River.

We left camp about the usual hour this morning in a northwest course and in about 3 miles found a spring where the animals were watered and the kegs filled, water not very good. The Engineers now came up, and we all started due west over a good road. The grass was burned excepting a few small patches. Near the spring is a very high butte which can be seen a great distance. We passed some detached buttes for the first 5 miles, but after that we were out of the "bad lands." After travelling for some time, we found we were diverging from the Engineers and had to make quite a turn to get on their track. Night was coming, and the guides and Scouts were sent to hunt water. They returned and reported it ahead about 11 miles, but the command being tired and having found a little water, went into camp. Had some good grass, but no wood, and had to use buffalo chips, which was found to be not a success; we encamped on a tributary of the Beaver [or Inman],[3] a creek running almost north and emptying into the Little Missouri. Distance travelled 20 miles.

SEPTEMBER 30. Started from camp in an almost west direction, down a valley where there had been good grass before the fire. After a march of about 4 miles we came to a very beautiful stream of water which from the size of the bed affords a great deal of water in the spring. It is supposed to be "Beaver Creek." The animals were all watered and the kegs filled, as it was very uncertain where we would find water again. As soon as we had crossed this stream we found that the grass had not been burned, which was very pleasant to contemplate after having travelled many days over that which had been burned.

Our general direction was still west, and as the country was up and down gentle slopes we could keep very near the Engineers. When about

[3]Rosser and others frequently refer to it as Inman's Creek.

9 miles from camp we came into sight of a very rough country which every one believed to be bordering on the Yellowstone. We struck a little valley which carried us in the direction we wished to go, and while in it and about 12 miles from our morning camp, we struck most delicious water where the animals were again watered. We now found we had very great difficulties to overcome before we reached the point indicated by the Chief Engineer as the place he would be able to make by night.

It was impossible to go down the valley, so we had to make a wide detour, travelling to all points of the compass in so doing. From a point where we watered the last time, a beautiful view could be had of the surrounding country. Here could be seen nature in all its wildness, crags, peaks, high points that might be extinct volcanoes, all calculated to impress one with the grandeur of the scene. It looked almost impossible to get through on foot, much less to take our immense train through. We wound our way down valleys, around hills, over divides, across deep ravines too until at last we brought up safely in camp on the banks of the stream we had left several miles below. We were very much surprised, however, to find that it had no water in it. Timber was in great abundance, some of which is very large. Grass very good. Just before we came into camp we came across four buffalo, three of which were killed by the Scouts. Distance travelled 19 miles.

OCTOBER 1. Did not leave camp this morning but sent the guides and Scouts ahead to look for the Yellowstone River and a passable road to it. Towards night they returned, having been to the river and reported it to be about 20 miles, and from their report it would take several days to make the river with the heavy train. Given the impassable state of the roads, the horses of the Citizen train being pretty well used up, and no Indians being reported along the river, I concluded to go no further with the whole Command and accordingly made a detail of the following companies and detachments under the command of Captain J. C. Bates, 20th Infantry to escort the Engineers to the Yellowstone River and return:

Company B, 20th Infantry, Capt. J. C. Bates [See chapter 8 for Bates's report.]
Company A, 22nd Infantry, Capt. J. B. Irvine
Company H, 17th Infantry, Lieut. Henry Marcott
Eighteen Indian Scouts under Lieut. E. Turnock, 20th Infantry
One Gatling Gun under Lieut. L. E. Campbell, 22nd Infantry

Actg. Asst. Surgeon E. L. Shirley accompanied the detachment
Some lightly loaded wagons were furnished each Company as transportation.

OCTOBER 2. The detachment under the Command of Capt. Bates started at 8 A.M. to escort the Engineers to the Yellowstone River and return.

The main command fell back to where wood and water was more convenient and there awaited the return of the detachment. Passed back over our old road and encamped on the same Creek which from the maps is supposed to be "Glendive." We went into camp about half a mile from where we crossed it going down. Water and grass plenty and at a short distance there is plenty of wood.

The men took advantage of the delay and washed and put their clothing in serviceable order. Distance travelled 8½ miles.

OCTOBER 3. Morning cool, the night having been frosty. The men were still employed fixing themselves for the homeward trip.[4] Wind blew terribly.

Source: Records of the War Department, Records of U.S. Army Commands, 751 MDM 1871, National Archives.

Capt. Javan B. Irvine's Diary

SEPTEMBER 20. Marched 18 miles. Broke camp about 7 o'clock A.M. Marched out on same trail by which the train entered camp day before yesterday. Saw some large cactus this morning, the first I have observed since leaving the Missouri. After a march of three miles we crossed a small stream emptying into Heart Creek and camped upon the camp of Genl. Sully's made against the Indians. Boxes, sticks, and books were scattered about. Followed Sully's trail for some distance. Crossed a beautiful bottom selected day before yesterday for our camp but rejected by this Major Commanding. . . . Saw numerous herds of antelopes, many of which ran so close to us as to tempt the men to fire on them in violation of orders. Then the antelope ran within another twenty yards of my company, and the men—some of them in the excitement of the

[4]In contrast, Irvine's diary, more likely correct, states that nothing was done.

moment—fired but missed. These continued running down the line when the skirmishers opened up on them but without effect. There was so much firing that it resembled a skirmish, and the Major was very much enraged at this breach of discipline, although he was out in front all day neglecting the train and main column not having [been] with it since morning. The manner in which he conducts the affairs and marches the command, the maledictions which are daily and hourly showered upon him by all, both officers and men. He has been constantly hunting in advance of the column and has given so little attention to his command and exhibited so little judgment and good sense in the management and conduct of affairs as to cause general remarks. We arrived in camp about 4:30 P.M., encamped in a bottom near the river covered with fine grass for the animals and close to wood and water. . . . But little of the water was fit to use. Much of the pieces of laminated stone which we picked up as petrified wood is in my opinion a species of rock which has been thrown to the surface by volcanic action and whose layers represent all the appearance of layers of wood. After we arrived in camp, the C.O. brought in three men belonging to Co. I who he had caught shooting antelope on the flanks of the command while entering camp. He endeavored to foster them on to my company, alleging that they belonged to it, which they instantly denied and [he] claimed I was their C.O. [Ends abruptly here.]

SEPTEMBER 21. Marched 5½ miles today. Mild, cloudy morning, reveille at 4 A.M. After breakfast Sgt. McClary of K Co., 17th Infantry, the largest soldier in the escort got [into a fight with two others]. During the melee something was said or done to the sergeant when he pulled off his coat and shirt and raved and danced and pranced about like a madman. He evidently [was] spoiling for a fight and emphatically [stated] that he was as good as any other man. Soon as a non-commissioned officer of the guard and a file of men made their appearance for the purpose of arresting him, he was as [meek as a lamb]. Co. A is designated as rear guard today. One of my hunters from the front brought in an antelope, one of the largest that roams the prairie. The Major has shot only two since we left Fort Rice, rather a small number for an excellent shot and such an experienced hunter.[5] We camped six miles ahead of the engineers today. We went into camp about 10 A.M. About 11 A.M. the engineers came along surveying the river bottom and passing us west or four miles

[5]Another indication of Whistler's drinking.

in advance of our camp. We all suffered from the heat exceedingly. Some hunters were detailed from each company today, and as many as fifteen or twenty antelope were brought in. We had guard duty for my company today. A hot wind blew from the west most of the day, and the prairies were observed burning in that direction this evening. The whole heavens are lighted up by the flames to the west and south of us, though no flames are yet in sight. But little timber lives in back of the train; in fact, there is nothing but brushwood observable now. A heavy sparking and some mares fearful of a conflagration. All the camp fires were covered, but during the night Dr. Shirley came to our tent evidently alarmed at the [fire's] appearance and thought the C.O. ought to be notified. Found the sentinels less vigilant last night than usual.

SEPTEMBER 22. Marched 11 miles today. Broke camp this morning at 7 A.M. Two wagons broke a wheel each and delayed the column in march. After we had proceeded about four miles, the enemy appeared on our front and flank moving towards us in heavy columns of black smoke. Soon the flames appeared leaping from hill to hollow, driving large herds of antelope before them. After progressing a mile or more, heavy columns of smoke appeared immediately in front and the flames on our right approached gradually nearer. The C.O. with a party of mounted escorts and officers rode in advance to reconnoiter; shortly they were seen riding rapidly toward the train, which had then arrived in a ravine opposite some cliffs; the train was halted and back fires were kindled and the train at once moved up to the top of the opposite bluff. We succeeded in moving the train on to burned ground after undergoing much excitement [after] passing through a cordon of fire. One of Rosser's teams stopped short at a critical point and [began] backing down, and before the man could seize hold of the wagon, they backed over the steep bluff and went pell-mell to the bottom. The wagon and horses turning over repeatedly in their descent; fortunately the animals and driver escaped uninjured and the wagon was not broken. After marching about twelve miles, we came to Heart Creek where we observed the engineers just ahead of us moving up the creek. We crossed the creek to go into camp, but Mr. Rosser was anxious that we should proceed as far as the engineers, so we attempted to ascend the hill on the opposite side, which was very steep. . . . Another [accident] of a more serious nature occurred [in the evening when] the cook of "K" Co., 17th Reg., built a fire for cooking purposes, but the [fire spread, causing extensive damage].

SEPTEMBER 23. Marched 17 miles today. Cloudy calm morning. Clement the guide told me this morning that had [we] gone on Sully's Trail as he advised we would have had to have marched no further than we did and have been six miles further up the river, but the Maj. Commanding thought we would go another day on that side of the river. Last night the spectacle of burning prairie was magnificent. Fires were burning on the opposite side of the creek as far as one could see. Yesterday the wind blew strong from the southwest, the first windy day we have had.

The fire in camp yesterday from K Co.'s kitchen came near being serious; it was only through great exertion that it was grounded. The animals began to show signs of stampeding; the loss of blankets and clothing is a serious one for the men. Broke camp at 6:30 A.M. . . . After making about four miles we came to a sandstone butte where we found relics of Sully's expedition, initials of the men being cut in the stone such as "BEN," "A.B.D.," et cetera.

Capt. Inman broke off some specimens of the rock in one of which was the impression of a leaf very clear and distinct; he has made quite a collection of curious specimens and petrifications. . . . Numerous herds of antelope approach on our front and flanks. Two antelope ran between the main command and wagon train. The men are not allowed to fire on the game for fear of accident. We marched today over burned prairie for the distance of eighteen miles. Passed "Three Rain" Butte where Sully fought the Indians for two days. Our road has been over undulating prairie, and the march was made with but a single ordered halt. We marched ten miles and only halted then in order to allow the Commanding Major to eat his lunch; after lunch we proceeded to Heart Creek where we found a fine bottom with grass abundant with sufficient brushwood to answer for cooking purposes; excellent water in abundance from the beaver dams, which were numerous. We encamped on the same ground [as] Sully's expedition in 1864. I found pieces of hard tack, tent pins [and] an iron chest handle. The guides inform me that a Travois trail two or three days old was found going in the same direction that we are traveling.[6] The country presents the same barren aspect; the soil sandy and unproductive white clay can be seen along the route.

SUNDAY, September 24. Reveille at 3 o'clock A.M. Cloudy and calm. We leave the creek today and strike for the Yellowstone. We left camp

[6]In short, Indians were close by.

at 6:30 A.M. prepared to camp without wood or water. When about 6 miles out from camp, came in sight of White Earth Butte, one very singular appearing. One man observed that it resembled . . . a suspension bridge. It might well be called Suspension Bridge Butte. Saw a gray fox this A.M., being the second one we have seen on this trip. Saw numbers of antelope and some deer, one of which was killed by hunters; a porcupine was also killed by the soldiers. Our route today led along the creek up which the surveyors are running their line, and we saw them in the distance frequently. We marched sixteen miles today, and the engineers chained fifteen. We encamped on Heart Creek an hour before sundown. Having reached its headwaters, it is the intention of the engineers to leave this creek and strike due west for the headwaters of the Little Missouri. The soil has a reddish appearance, and the banks of the gullies are more red than white as formerly: our train moved along nicely today but were near being misled by Maj. Whistler, who affirmed we were marching in the wrong direction and stopped the train and had the pioneer corps commence cutting down the bank of the stream with the view of crossing the train to go another four or five miles out to another branch outright, when just as the road was nearly completed for crossing, the engineers were seen coming up the branch we had prepared to cross. We then turned and proceeded in the same direction that we were going when the C.O. stopped me; he endeavored to lie out of his blunder by saying that the engineers were up another branch and had just crossed over to the one following the country over which we are traveling has been over. . . .

The flames driving off most of the game. Vast groves of scrubby trees and underbrush have been consumed, and from appearances has been done recently. Some think it has been fired by the Indians with a view of impeding the progress of the expedition, etc. Scouts we used have no apprehension of any trouble from the Indians while [we are] in this burned district, for there is no grass for their ponies or game for themselves to subsist on.

SEPTEMBER 25. BAD LANDS. Cold and frosty last night and ditto this morning but clear and calm. Broke camp at 7:00 A.M. Marched about six miles when we came to a canyon on the opposite side of which the Bad Lands came into full view presenting a grand spectacle of broken bluffs taking on the most fantastic forms imaginable. Cone, pyramidal, flat, and other. A branch of the Little Missouri rose in the canyon descending gently toward the west. We descended the canyon a hundred feet to the valley below and followed down the stream encamping thereon about 4 o'clock P.M. having marched 14 miles and the Engineers chaining 12 miles. We went into camp by order of the Adj., and our wagons were nearly unloaded and we had commenced pitching our tents when the Major Commanding ordered us to cross the creek as he intended to cross the whole train before dark. . . .

Our troops crossed in quick-time being first in camp and on the best ground adjoining wood and water. A soldier brought me a fine specimen of petrified wood which he took from a log with the butt of his gun. Just as we went into camp, the engineers passed us and continued their survey a few miles further. Our hunting party did not get any game today, the antelopes being too wild. They saw a large panther or mountain lion, however, but did not get a shot at it. Signs of Indians were seen today, not over three or four days old. We are now assembled . . . in a very dangerous position. The space we occupy is very contracted, cut up with ravines and precipitous bluffs hemming us in on front and rear, and only the narrow valley of the creek bottom on our right and left, and that cut up by the deep channel of the dry creek.

Should the Indians attack us here, there is some reason to fear disaster. If they are as wise as they are cunning, they will attack now, for we are in a trap: we should have kept on the high lands and not descended to the creek bottom at all. If we pass through these dangerous locations unharmed, it will be through [good luck] and not through any precautions or preparations made by the Major Commanding, for he has given no thought to the subject but directed his whole mind to antelope hunting. Several deer have been found burned to death by the fierce fires in the bottoms of the Heart. The fire did not cross onto this creek bottom.

SEPTEMBER 26. Marched 8 miles. Sign of bears seen a day or two ago, and yesterday their feces were seen in this creek bottom. We overturned a six-mule wagon just as we were coming into camp last night. The country on this side of the crossing there not being sufficient vegetation in the canyon to feed the flames. The bluffs and hills are all [made] with reddish clay and in the distance present a picturesque appearance. Cedar grows on the side of the Mauves Terres. Saw and tasted Juniper berries the first time yesterday. This morning it was quite cold and frosty, "long johns" being necessary to make the men comfortable. . . . [Frost] perceptible on the grass, passed a small pool which was covered with ice, the first I have seen this autumn. Found buffalo feces a month old, also bear feces. The bluffs on either side of the stream we are following are very precipitous and broken; the channel of the creek is very deep and [rocky].[7] This is well named the Bad Lands; one cannot well conceive worse. I write these words sitting on the highest point of land at the mouth of the stream down which we have been surveying this morning. This butte is on the banks of the Little Missouri about 250 feet above it and gives a magnificent view of about ten miles up and down the river: the river bottom is thickly timbered but very [filled with watery sand]. I found a painted Buffalo on top of the Butte. I struck my sword in the ground and [used] the handle of my sword for the engineers to sight with their instruments, they being five miles behind. . . . The scouts killed a black tailed deer out of [a group] of five and sold [?] it to Chief Rosser. Chief Rosser fired at a couple of Big Horn or mountain sheep. . . . The engineers arrived at the Little Missouri about 11 A.M. having chained six miles. The train crossed the creek seven or eight times and with road filling arrived at the Little Missouri at 3:30 P.M. when we went into camp on the same ground occupied by Sully in 1864.

SEPTEMBER 27. Marched 7½ miles. Cold chilly morning, wind flowing from the north, cloudy in the west. We cross the Little Missouri here and follow Sully's trail to the Yellowstone. The pioneers are now constructing a corduroy bridge across the river which will be completed about 9 A.M. when we cross over on our meandering way to the Yellowstone which we ought to reach in four days. Mountain Sheep or Big Horn appeared on the bluffs south of camp this morning. . . . Some men of my company went out to shoot it but were unsuccessful. One found a very large pair of elk horns but they were too heavy for him to carry in. Should we return this way we will endeavor to secure them. Day before yesterday a soldier by the name of Smith of Company D, 17th Infantry went hunting and got lost. He laid out all night and suffered very much from the cold. He saw our campfires but did not suppose anyone but an idiot would [employ] such a plan, so he did not come in until yesterday as we went into camp. Our road after we crossed the river fell through a

[7]Tom Rosser named this creek for the surveyor, Henry Chandler Davis (1849–12/15/1910). In 1872 Davis was almost trapped by Gall's Hunkpapa Sioux while hunting for agates. Later he was given credit for driving the first spike of the NP (1870), and he definitely was one of those driving the last spike in 1883. See *National Cyclopedia of American Biography*, 16:299, *New York Times* obituary, and Lubetkin, *Before Custer* (2015).

very broken country and we halted to dig down some steep places and fill in some gullies besides descending and ascending some very steep hills. We did not get the train [on to] the table lands until about 3 P.M. Our line of march following Sully's trail, we found the debris of his camp and scattering fragments of wagons, cracker boxes, etc. Lt. Marcotte found an unexploded six pound shell which the Indians had unloaded by cutting a hole in the side of it. . . . Marched over the battleground and saw the remains of the campfires. The country presents a very rough broken, rugged appearance and the grade made by the Engineers averages 100 feet to the mile. We marched about nine miles and would have gone farther but the guides missed the road . . . and went into camp where there was plenty of dry wood but no water. The country seems to have been devastated by fire a year or two ago; the timbers [have all] died. We have now come to a standstill on account of the guides not being familiar with the routes or country. The C.O. instead of going out and endeavoring to look out about engaged Lt. Fisher in a game of poker and thus passed the whole evening.

SEPTEMBER 28. Marched twelve miles and gained four. Cold, windy morning, strong wind blowing from the north and blew all night. Struck tents at six and left camp at 7 A.M. Major Commanding . . . favored us with additional duty by sending a citizen teamster for us to take charge of alleging that the teamster had threatened his life. The facts of the case are these: This man had his team harnessed up and was sitting by a fire with others eating his breakfast. The Major Commanding went into the corral and seeing some teams yet unharnessed commenced to curse the teamsters calling them, "You drunk lazy sons of bitches. Why haven't you got these teams harnessed?"[8] Just at this moment one of the men carelessly stepped into the fire, and this man Arbuckle, seeing it, laughed or shouted. The Major reached up and said, "You shout at me, will you?" and seizing hold of him said, "You come with me!" Arbuckle jerked away from him and said, "No, I won't come with you, and you can't take me." The Major then said he would send someone who could take him and, calling a guard, arrested him and turned him over to the rear guard.

This is the coldest morning we have experienced, and overcoats are in demand. We marched a couple of miles and crossed a dry creek, probably the one on which the engineers are at work. We then marched three or

[8] Quotation marks and punctuation have been added as the diary is so explicit.

four miles to some mud holes which Sully dubbed "Tadpole holes" but found no water there fit to drink. Chief Rosser, observing where we were going, came up at this moment and notified the C.O. that we were going in the wrong direction and had already traveled five miles out of our way. We then turned to strike across to get on the right course, and after going about two miles came to excellent grass, water, and wood. Inman begged the C.O. to go into camp there, but he refused to do so, and we went on three miles further and camped about 4 P.M. where we had neither wood nor water and very little grass. The wind has blown hard all day, and it was very dusty. We came to some burned prairie about 12 o'clock and are now traveling on it. . . . A number of pieces of [artillery] shells and other relics of Sully's campaign were picked up on the camping ground we occupied last night.

SEPTEMBER 29. Marched 19¾ miles. After arriving in camp last evening the men dug a well and trench at the base of a hill where there were abundant indications of water from the swampy nature of the ground. The water flowed forth like a spring, but is strongly impregnated with sulphur and soda. There is sufficient [water] for man and beast and with the wood which we gathered at a distance we are very comfortable thanks to Lt. Daugherty who selected the camp ground.

Since we crossed the Little Missouri and several days before no Indian Scouts have been sent out ahead or on the flanks for what reason I am unable to say. Three march in a body in advance with the major commanding apparently in the capacity of guard personal. We are getting very careless it seems to me just in the spot where we should exercise the most vigilance. Our train gets very much strung out and scattered on the march and we are unable to cover it with one company of flankers. The other two companies of the main command should be deployed under such circumstances as additional skirmishers so as to cover the flanks. Chief Rosser returns from reconnoitering the position.

SEPTEMBER 30. [Total] distance marched 267 miles. Jamie's fourteenth birthday. God bless him! May he enjoy many and many happy returns of it. Yesterday we did not make such a good march as I expected, for after we left the Engineers the C.O. managed to lead us eight miles north out of the direct line and we were compelled to turn and come back again, gaining the ground lost. By marching diagonally he was not aware that he was out of the way until [name illegible] came up and told him. Yet at the same time he had his compass before him and was endeavoring to make a scientific run. The animals are almost famished for water, which we could have reached in a march of four or five miles that we could have easily made had we not been led so much out of our way. Last night it sprinkled a little and this morning it is cloudy and calm. . . .

Broke camp around 7 A.M. and marched about three miles to the north branch of the Little Missouri where we found an abundance of wood, grass, and good water: this is the ground on which we should have camped last night. . . . [T]he water is very good and there appears to be sufficient wood on the stream for camping purposes. This is the north fork of the Little Missouri called by some Beaver Creek. We crossed the creek and marched about eight miles when we found a fine stream of water where we watered the stock and rested a short time. I saw several Antelope and some fresh Buffalo tracks. About 3 P.M. we entered rough, broken lands again and pitched our camp for the remainder of the day over very bad land going west. Passed through two [prairie] dog towns, one very large. Just before we entered camp, the Scouts, C.O., and Adjt. 20th Infantry saw four Buffalo and succeeded in killing two. We arrived in camp at sunset and it was dark before the last team was corralled. . . .

We camped without water on very broken ground. The Engineers left their line two miles out of camp. Chief Rosser is not well, suffering from fever, piles, etc. Five horses in the train hauling the engineers' property gave out today, and one that could not eat was shot. One mule also gave out and is very sick. The country presents the same rugged, barren appearance characteristic of Dakota. The land is not fertile, but sterility is a predominant feature. Many singular specimens of curious stones and petrifications have been found.

SUNDAY, October 1. Commenced raining last night about 11 o'clock and continued raining this morning. The portion of the country not covered with grass is soft and slippery and until it dries up will be very difficult for our transportation to transverse it without exhausting the animals. Guides Clement and Isaiah [Dorman] with six Indian scouts were sent out to the Yellowstone River early this morning for the purpose of ascertaining the route there and its practicality.[9] Tis not raining hard but drizzling, our infantry pickets are posted on the adjoining peaks from a half to three-quarters of a mile from camp, too far for their safety in case of an Indian attack. Their position should be occupied by the

[9] Does Irvine really mean Isaiah Dorman? If so, this is the only reference to him after mid-September in any known source.

Indian scouts who are mounted and readily retire and give the alarm on the approach of an enemy, but the latter are allowed to loaf in camp and gorge themselves with buffalo meat while the infantry are placed as pickets on the most exposed positions. We rest today, not on principal but because Chief Engineer Rosser is sick, our animals are exhausted, and the rain (though slight) has rendered traveling impassable for the train. We are enjoying our rest. . . . We have found water about two miles distant and have sent our teams with kegs to bring in water for the troops and the animals were sent out to water though I was fearful they would be lost should Indians endeavor to stampede them as the ground was entirely inadequate for their protection going such a distance for water in an Indian country. . . .

Two guides were sent out late in the P.M. to hunt around, and about sunset the party sent out to the Yellowstone returned reporting it twenty-five miles distant and the route there impracticable for our train in the frequent exhausted condition of the animals. . . . The train [will] return seven miles to a good camping ground that we passed yesterday and where we should have stopped instead of going into this broken region and there go into camp and await the completion of the survey by the engineers and return of the escort. It cleared off about noon and was quite pleasant in the P.M. Country quite rough, broken [and] similar to the Bad Lands [and] in fact are the Bad Lands of the Yellowstone. . . . [E]ncamped on Glendive Creek.

OCTOBER 2. Marched 11¼ miles. Bright, frosty morning. Co. A designated as escort for engineers on the route of their survey today. We left camp at 6:45 A.M. and proceeded back up Glendive Creek about three miles and took up the line where the surveyors left off September 30. Returning down the creek we arrived opposite our old camp where we halted until the engineers came up with their line and observed the rear of the train just moving out of camp going back seven miles . . . there to go into camp and await our return from the Yellowstone. Saw a covey of fifteen or twenty sage hens or prairie chickens as we went up the creek this morning. Here made a fine day's work running a line thirteen miles and reaching camp just at sundown. The valley we surveyed today is beautiful, and the engineers deem it the best adopted for railroad of any that they have [seen] on the trip. It gradually widens to one-half or three-quarters of a mile. . . . The table level of the valley presents every appearance of having been the bed of an ancient ocean of bygone ages, the ground gradually declining towards the center. The contour of the surrounding bluffs is broken and marked in all conceivable shapes, and where not totally [devoid] of vegetation is covered with a growth of cedar whose dark green foliage standing out in bold [contrast] against the broken, barren cliffs gives to the whole scene a grandeur and pictures seldom witnessed by the tourist or traveler. [The bluffs] lifts their jagged peaks assuming all conceivable shapes and contours and the imagination pictures to itself castles, fortresses, cathedrals, and mausoleums. The rain on Sunday gave us quite a stream of muddy, running water which is [an] entirely new feature of the landscape—running water not being characteristic of this region—much of the water in pools is black from the [mud] beds which line the banks . . . of the stream. . . . The valley of the creek has but a slight growth of trees, cottonwood trees of scrubby growth being observed here and there dotting the landscape and no undergrowth being observable. Passed two large prairie dog towns whose inhabitants greeted us with their melancholy barking.

OCTOBER 3. REACH THE YELLOWSTONE RIVER! The battle is fought, the victory won today, we see the Yellowstone. We march 7½ miles today. Clear frosty morning. Broke camp at 7 A.M. and continued our march down the valley of Glendive's Creek which we crossed and recrossed several times before reaching the mouth thereof: the road is quite practicable for lightly loaded wagons; quicksand troubled us, one wagon sinking to the hub and being extricated with difficulty. The left hand bluffs of Glendive Creek are filled with perfectly round stones composed of iron and sand. The stones have the appearance of grape shot and cannon balls. Our train to the Yellowstone amounts to seventeen wagons and one ambulance. At about 10 o'clock A.M. we debouched on the beautiful bottom of the Yellowstone where we found the largest prairie dog town I have yet to see; it is more than a mile long and of nearly equal width. Numerous trails cross the plain evidently made by buffalo, but none were observable nor were there any recent signs of any. No game of any description today. We arrived on the banks of the Yellowstone about 11 o'clock A.M. and were pleased so much as surprised at the appearance of the river. The stream is about one-quarter mile wide and about three feet deep, clear and cold, with an abundance of fish, the bottom is pebbly. . . . There are three beautiful islands opposite the plateau on which we are encamped. The islands have a dense growth of beautiful cottonwood trees growing with the lustiness of youth. [Illegible for 75 or so words.]

The engineers completed their survey around 12:30 P.M. Having made the distance from the Missouri over fine [and] easy grades for a road as have ever been secured for so long and continuous a route. Surveyors Eastman and Meigs with two scouts forded the river opposite and sketched the plateau on which we were encamped and the adjoining bluffs. The foliage of the trees is a uniform deep yellow. Everyone who could partook of the luxury of a bath in the waters of the river: this is more of the character of our eastern rivers than any stream I have observed in the west.

OCTOBER 4. Such sights as we have seen one would hardly believe and today we [re]join the Army of the Glendive.[10] Marched 28 miles today. Rained slightly last night but is pleasant this morning [and] slightly breezy. Broke camp at 7 A.M. Took a last, long, lingering look at the beautiful Yellowstone and turned our faces homeward. The scouts left some peculiar [picto]graphic signs for their Indian brethren to read. [It] was a long pole set upright which had sixteen shadings cut in one side and on the smooth part of the pole from which the shaving was peeled four horse shoes or marks representing horses' feet were made showing the number of scouts accompanying the expedition. Then there was a long, serpentine line of sticks stuck in the ground pointing westward and terminating at two yellow stones on each side of which a stick was stuck showing that our expedition terminated. Then, in front of the stones was a long stick on which there was a white piece of paper indicating that our visit was a peaceful one. At the rear of the line of sticks was a long one covered with black marks representing that a larger part of our forces were left behind a short distance.

A few miles from the river Capt. Inman again found the remains of two mastodons[11] which he reports of uncommon proportion measuring forty feet in length. He secured some portion of them for the scientific associations which he represents. . . . The wind sprang up about 9 A.M. and blew all day from the west becoming quite cold towards night. At 11 A.M. we halted . . . for lunch. We then struck out again and made

[10]Irvine is sarcastic when speaking of the "Army of the Glendive." During the war Union armies were named after important rivers, thus the Army of the Potomac, Army of the Ohio, and the James, Tennessee, Cumberland, etc. "Naming" their two hundred man force after a virtually dry creek likely seemed both amusing and symbolic.

[11]Inman had found dinosaurs, not Ice Age mammals. Today this dramatic, gorgeous area is protected in Makoshika State Park with ongoing "digs" by Montana State University–Bozeman.

such time that Capt. Bates concluded to [return] into the camp of the Army of the Glendive. When we came to the vicinity of our old camp we found the ground quite broken and the road in some places so steep that we apprehended difficulty on [the] part of the teams in ascending them, but they came right along and reached camp about 5 o'clock P.M., two days sooner than was anticipated by those left in camp. We have gazed at the Yellowstone River and its beautiful bottoms, having traveled a [great] distance in twenty-five days through a hostile Indian country unmolested by the savages; in fact, without obtaining a glimpse of the noble creature. Not a man has been injured nor has an accident of [importance] occurred to anyone.

Source: Javan Irvine Papers, State Archives, South Dakota State Historical Center, Pierre.

Rosser's Diary

SEPTEMBER 20. Went out with the Indian scouts, found a good camp. The engineers did not get within 6 miles of camp. I will be with them tomorrow and will have camp moved only 6 miles and the engineers will work up [to it].

SEPTEMBER 21. Ran 11½ miles. Got into camp about 4 P.M. I went out with QM and guides to look up the road and for tomorrow found it all right. The country continues to improve. But large fires appear in the west and in a day or two we will have no grass.

SEPTEMBER 22. Left camp at 6 A.M. as usual. The fire had approached to within a few miles and the smoke was so dense that but short sights could be taken. Ran 8½ miles. Detained by wagon trains which suffered an accident. The country greatly improved.

SEPTEMBER 23. Ran through a beautiful country. Coal thicker and more abundant. Made 14½ miles and could have run 4 miles further had the Commanding Officer not gone into camp at 4 o'clock. All the grass burnt off and traveling is very disagreeable.

SUNDAY, SEPTEMBER 24. Made a good day's run. Wagons were very fortunate in having a good road and got into camp at 4:30 P.M. Plenty of wood and water which was better than we anticipated. If I have luck will reach the Little Missouri in two days. All are very anxious.

SEPTEMBER 25. Encamped at the headwaters of the Heart River. Left at 6 A.M. and ran due west for 6 miles. Then came suddenly on the Bad Lands at our [front]. A grand sight! Descended into the valley and found a stream which we have been following. Camped at 3:30 P.M.

SEPTEMBER 26. Reached the Little Missouri River at 11:45 A.M. by a good line. Not knowing what course to peruse, halted and went on a scout [and] discovered Sully's Trail and a creek by which I hope to leave this river. The night and morning cold.

SEPTEMBER 27. Ran down the Little Missouri 5 miles thence west via a small creek which as far as followed answers my purpose very well. Saw no game. No signs of Indians. Camped on the ground without water. Cold and windy. Very dusty and as disagreeable as one can imagine.

SEPTEMBER 28. This has been one of the most disagreeable days I ever spent. The wind is blowing a perfect gale and our line has been bad, terminated in the bluffs and had to be abandoned. Will go to the north tomorrow. Piles very bad.

SEPTEMBER 29. Found the creek on the north a good one and ran from it out on the rolling prairie on easy grades. Ran 15 miles. The bad lands passed and the country quite level and soil fair. Grass burnt off by the Indians. Suffering greatly of piles.

SEPTEMBER 30. Sick.

SUNDAY, OCTOBER 1. Sick.

OCTOBER 2. Sick.

OCTOBER 3. Have been very sick since Saturday of violent inflammation and ulceration of the rectum. Sunday I was confined to my bed and command had to halt. Yesterday and today I have been resting in an ambulance and I will not be able to take my saddle again on the trip. Reached the Yellowstone at 12:15 P.M. today.

OCTOBER 4. Spent the P.M. of yesterday and last night on the Yellowstone. This morning turned our faces homeward. Marched via same route. Am anxious to be reunited with the precious ones at home—far away. I am still sick and in ambulance.

Source: Rosser Papers, Collection 1173-g-h-j, box 1, Small Special Collections Library, University of Virginia, Charlottesville.

Rosser's Report to Smith

The country about the headwaters of the Heart River is quite level, and the grade, leaving the valley, is light and ascends, for a few miles, to the top of a well-defined ridge, which is the divide between the waters of Heart and the Little Missouri Rivers. Upon rising this ridge, the "Mauvaises Terres" come so suddenly into view as to shock the vision of the beholder by their strange and wild grandeur! The prairie is cut short off at your feet, and dropped two hundred feet below the plain on which you stand!

The crumbling walls of this immense abyss are almost vertical, but at their feet a beautiful valley spreads out before you, as far as the eye can see, and studded all over with fantastic mounds, pyramids, towers, &c., formed by erosion of the friable material composing the "Mauvaises Terres." At first sight I thought I had met an insurmountable obstacle, but upon making a careful examination, I found a watercourse in the valley, and but a short distance south of the point where the "Mauvaises Terres" were first seen, I discovered a fork of it, by which a very easy descent into the valley can be made. After the valley of this watercourse is reached, there are no engineering difficulties encountered in following it, although it washes from one side of its valley to the other, and my profile shows frequent crossings. The work of changing its channel is so light as to make it of small consequence. There was found in this valley (I called the stream Davis' Creek) a fine growth of Buffalo grass, and in the surrounding "Mauvaises Terres" there are great quantities of dwarf cedar; but, with the exception of the large quantities of coal found here, this portion of the country is worthless, except as a winter home for the mountain sheep and black-tail deer, which assemble here in great quantities in winter. I found the water of Davis' Creek in pools and strongly alkaline. The timber is principally cotton-wood, and very scattering, yet some of the trees are quite large.

From Davis' Creek we passed into the Valley of the Little Missouri. This valley is, of itself, insignificant, buried to the depth of five or six hundred feet below the surrounding hills, and as it is only about half a mile wide it can only be regarded as a large canyon. This narrow valley is entirely covered by a dense forest of cottonwood, and some of it is very large. The banks of the stream are low, and there is but little of the valley not liable to overflow. The main channel of the river is very crooked, being deflected by the hills from one side to the other, and at each point of contact it has washed away—the hills having vertical bluffs, which, in many instances, are several hundred feet high, exhibiting to the best advantage the peculiar geological formation of the "Mauvaises Terres," composed of horizontal strata of tinted clays mounted on a broad black base of lignite of fifteen feet in thickness.

To get out of this valley it was necessary to run down the stream some five miles to the mouth of Andrew's Creek. The valley and course of this creek I found to be eligible and the grade light, and was enabled to pass by means of it out of the "Mauvaises Terres" on to the rolling prairie beyond. The general character of this prairie is quite similar to that lying between the Sheyenne and James Rivers, which you have seen. The soil is fair and covered with a good growth of buffalo grass. From this high prairie we descend to Inman's Fork [Beaver Creek], which is one of the principal tributaries of the Little Missouri and is but little inferior to it in size. This stream possesses a good valley; some timber is scattered along its banks, generally oak. Its waters are fresh and pure. Beyond this the prairie had not been burnt, and the grass was abundant and good.

The profile shows rough country on approaching and leaving this stream, but I regard it as a very easy matter to make a good location across this valley, and am so sure of it that I did not deem it of sufficient importance to occupy the time of the party in making more than a hurried reconnaissance. A small stream flowing into Inman's Fork caused a sufficient depression in the high ground beyond to admit of the passage of the line, and this ridge turned out to be the divide between the waters of the Little Missouri and the Yellowstone.

Just opposite the point where I accidentally crossed this ridge I discovered the source of a stream, and as it was in the course I wished to run, I followed it, and soon ascertained that it would lead into the Yellowstone. The general course of this stream is good; its waters are pure, being fed by numerous springs. The nature of this stream, which I learned after reaching the Yellowstone, was Glendive's Creek is not unlike that described in the cases of Davis' and Andrew's Creeks. A little cottonwood and box elder are scattered along the stream, and its narrow valley, as a general thing, is of fair soil; but the surrounding country is very rough, and with the exception of the coal which it contains, is of little value until you reach its mouth, where it spreads out into a beautiful meadow, which expands to meet the lovely valley of the Yellowstone.

The Yellowstone, at this point, is about one thousand feet wide, and its waters cold and limpid. Its valley, which is about two miles wide, possesses a good soil, and bordering the stream is a heavy growth of cottonwood, box elder, and elm timber.

I reached the Yellowstone on the morning of the 3rd of October, and after examining the country as far as I could with safety, on the morning of the 4th we began to retrace our steps on a homeward march. As there were several points on the line that I wished to examine more closely than I had done going out, I deemed it most expedient to return by the same route I went out on, and this course was also necessary, inasmuch as we had a beaten trail with bridges constructed in our favor.

After making such corrections as I deemed necessary, I returned to the mouth of Heart River and completed the unfinished work which I left behind me.

I now submit to you a map and profile of the entire line, from the Missouri to the Yellowstone River via Heart River and Glendive's Creek route, a distance of 226.96 miles.

In conclusion, I will state that the thanks of the Company are due to General J. N. G. Whistler, and the officers and men of his command composing my escort, for their cheerful co-operation and support in the prosecution of this work, and to each member of my engineering party, for their energy and fidelity in the discharge of their duties. I am proud to state that all returned in health and safety, and that not a horse was injured or lost, nor a wagon left behind.

[Salutations, etc.]

Source: Roberts Papers, Collection 783, series 6, box 10, Burlingame Special Collections Library, Montana State University, Bozeman.

Lafayette Campbell's Diary

SEPTEMBER 20. We broke camp early and went down to a ravine where we were about two hours crossing as we were compelled to make a bridge of willows. Finally crossed all and got on all right for about 2 miles where we came to another bad ravine. Col. Inman was [nearby] with the [bridging equipment] so we made the crossing in short time. Then we came to the trail left by Genl. Sully. It is still quite distinct.

SEPTEMBER 21. A beautiful September morning. We broke camp at 7 and marched over a fine rolling country and we are ahead of the engineers. We go into camp on a hill close to the river. We find the weather very warm. Poole and I are lying around in the tent playing with Jim [a hunting dog], but it is too hot to think of doing anything much. The men kill plenty of antelope which is very fine. I am thinking of you.

September 22. A fine warm September morning. We broke camp at 7 o'clock and passed around a large butte and crossed into a valley where we discovered a large fire in the distance. Traveled on until we came to a large ravine about four miles from camp. We found that the fire was gaining upon us so rapidly that we would be compelled to [come up against] it. It was at once decided to set the grass on fire and clear a way for our train; this was soon done. We had a fine march on to the River which we crossed and went into camp.

September 23. A fine morning we broke camp early and started out over a burnt country. We got along finely, passed a huge sand stone on the right hand side of the road on which quite a number of Genl. Sully's men had carved their names. . . . Crossed a small fork of the river which goes to the south . . . went into camp on a fine grass plot found some of Sully Relics. I am thinking of you.

Sunday, September 24. A beautiful September morning. We broke camp at 7 and went on finely as we found a good road. The smoke became so dense that we could scarcely see. Passed a beautiful white clay butte to the left. It looked like an old castle. It reminded me of Sebastopol and the large butte in front was much like the [Russian's] Malakoff [fortifications]. I suggested it and it was so named.

September 25. A little cold. We broke camp and got along finely for about 7 miles when behold: we came to the famous Bad Lands of which we have heard so much. The view is perfectly graced and far excels anything I have ever seen. It is a perfect set of cones some quite small while others [leap] hundreds of feet in the air.

September 26 and 27. [No entries]

September 28. Wind blew fearfully all night and it kept us from getting our usual allowance of sleep. We start early; just before starting I found that one of my mules had escaped. I at once ran out and after some time found them just in time so as not to delay the command. We go on and get out of the Bad Lands. . . . Found a sulphur spring here, dug a trench and got water.

September 29. We have a fine morning and we go out almost a north-west course. Lt. Dougherty and I go ahead and killed two antelope. Brought one of them into the command. Traveled along parallel to the engineers and make a good march. We go into camp close to Beaver Creek. Found quite a nice little spring.

September 30. This morning we leave camp early and go on to Beaver Creek where we water all the stock, very fine water. Go on and soon strike the head of Glendive Creek which we follow down for 3 or 4 miles where we go into camp. Here we found 5 huge buffalo; killed three of them. I had the good fortune to kill one of them with my revolver. We found a rough road down to the Creek.

Sunday, October 1. Today we lay over on Glendive Creek. Rains some in the forenoon but clears off and we have quite a fine day. We are all looking over our [papers] and talking of the incidents of the [expedition]. We send a courier with the guides to the Yellowstone to find how far it is and the rest of us take a good rest. The men return and report the Yellowstone 26 miles distant, so we start for that tomorrow. Got to sleep and get a good rest.

October 2. This morning I have an order to go on the Yellowstone. I take one guide. Col. Bates goes in command. We moved out at 8. . . . We find the road quite rough and in some places are compelled to go down the Creek bottom. The Bad Lands are far more grand here than on the Little Missouri. One hill on our right looks like the ruins of an Abbey. While to the left the hills rise in majestic grandeur almost kissing the skies topped with cedar. The sight is perfectly grand.

October 3. We broke camp early and once started down the valley of the creek which we follow. The Yellowstone [turned out] to be further than we had anticipated. On looking at the bluffs last evening passed quite high and steep, Bad Lands on each side of us. At 11 A.M. we arrived at the long looked-for river and went into camp. We find the water beautiful and clear and the bed of the river feels of all kinds of rare stones, fungus, moss, algae.

Source: Collection 10435, American Heritage Center, University of Wyoming, Laramie.

CHAPTER 7

The Western Survey's Return to Fort Ellis and the Blizzard

Although the western survey had no prairie fire to battle, it was to face something equally dangerous: a powerful late November blizzard, the full force of its winds blasting through the Bozeman Pass. The Pass acts as a year-round natural funnel and would be a surefire investment for today's wind farm investors—other than destroying the view, of course. However, in 1871, as the reader will see, soldiers and surveyors only wanted to survive after they waited far too long to return to Fort Ellis. Here Captain Ball's report gives an understated but nevertheless dramatic and—one feels—entirely accurate depiction of events.

And how bad was the blizzard? Newspaper accounts make clear that the monster storm was not limited to the Bozeman Pass. To the north, a company of the infantry was also caught in the open (VII-E), its suffering far greater.

As for Milnor Roberts and Colonel Baker, they had fortuitously left days earlier, and Roberts was in Helena when the storm hit. However, their return would prove to be far from uneventful. The obvious mutual animosity came to a head when Baker began to shoot at a distant Roberts (VII-D), later lamely claiming it was only a joke. Roberts was too much of a gentleman to report Baker. However, the consequences of his remaining silent were seen in 1872 when Baker's drinking resulted in his disastrous leadership of that year's western survey.

Chapter 7 concludes with a detailed story from the *Helena Herald* which explains what Sitting Bull was doing as both surveying expeditions were entering the Yellowstone valley.

Captain Ball's Report

At this point [November 15] it appeared very conclusively that winter had set in and that it would be unwise to attempt to extend the survey any further this winter.

I accordingly made preparations to start back on the morning of the 16th November but owing to a severe snow storm that came up on the evening of the 15th lasting until the morning of the 17th, I did not get off until the morning of the latter day when I broke camp and started on my homeward march, reaching the Crow Agency on the evening of the 25th, a march of 110 miles in nine days through snow from six to ten inches deep and snow storms seven days out of nine.

On arriving at the Crow Agency, a number of the men had their hands, noses, faces, ears, and feet badly frozen and our grain was exhausted, not having taken but ⅓rd rations with us, which was at the time deemed sufficient and would have been had it not been for the severe snow storms, something that the oldest settlers of the country have never known before at that season and our horses showing signs of weakness, they having had but little grass for ten days on account of the great depth of snow and would have suffered materially before reaching [Fort Ellis] had it not been for the kindness shown by Mr. Pease, Agent of the Crow Indians, and Mr. Charles H. Hoffman, their trader, who furnished us with almost every pound of hay and grain they had on hand, leaving their large stock of animals almost destitute and that in the midst of one of the most severe snow storms ever known in the country and at a time when they had at least twelve inches of snow on the ground.

On the evening of the 20th November, I satisfied myself that unless grain should reach me at some point near the Crow Agency, a number of horses would not be able to reach the post. I accordingly turned over the command to Captain Tyler and with a detachment of seven men and started for Fort Ellis and after making a night march I reached the Crow Agency at 8 P.M. of the 21st having marched through a severe snow storm. Here I rested for the night, leaving early next morning [22nd] for the post, the snow still falling fast, and at 3 P.M. of the 23rd reached the post having traveled a good portion of two days and one night a distance of 32 miles through snow from two to four feet deep.

On arriving at Fort Ellis I reported the condition of my command and the roads to the Commanding Officer, who immediately made provisions for sending out grain the following day, but owing to the severe storm which still raged, nothing could be done until the morning of the 25th when companies "L" and "G" 2nd Cavalry with shovels and all their horses were turned out for the purpose of breaking the road across the divides [Bozeman Pass].

These companies with great energy and exertion succeeded in breaking the road across the first divide, a distance of nine miles, returning to the post late in the evening. This left five [downhill] miles of a road to be broken over a second divide, and on the morning 26th of November I left the post for my command with Lt. McClernand and a detachment of twenty-eight men from companies "G" and "L" 2nd Cavalry and twenty-six pack horses (cavalry horses, the snow being too deep for mules) with grain and at dark on the evening of the 27th. I met Capt. Tyler with the command twenty miles from this Post, he having been compelled to leave the wagons at the Crow Agency and push on with very limited amount of bedding that could be carried on the horses in their exhausted condition.[1]

After reaching Capt. Tyler I turned about and marched six miles homeward when we went into camp about 9 P.M.[2] The storm still raged furiously and [we had] no tents for the command.

Next morning [the] 28th I resumed the march arriving at this post at 3 P.M. [the] same day. On my arrival at the post and on an examination of the men it was found that thirty-three of the escort and twenty-four of the detachment from "G" and "L" Companies taking grain to the escort had their faces, hands, feet, ears, and noses painfully frozen, though not seriously, I believe.

The day following my arrival at the post Lt. Jerome was detached with a pack train to the Crow Agency ladened with grain for the train which accompanied me down the Yellowstone and [with] a further purpose of

[1]In contrasting the differences with Ball's report and McClernand's account (*With the Indian and the Buffalo in Montana,* 26–28), no two paragraphs are more important than this and the previous one. There are major differences: Ball states that after clearing nine miles of snow Saturday the men turned back and spent the night at Fort Ellis, not at the top of the Bozeman Pass as McClernand states; two companies of men, not just McClernand's rescue force, cleared a path through nine miles of snow; McClernand, serving under Ball, was never in "temporary command" (26) leading the rescuers; and Tyler's men (and the surveyors) were met late in the afternoon on Monday, November 27, west of the Crow Agency, not at 2 P.M. on Friday, November 24, some fifteen miles east of the Crow Agency, just before the storm engulfed them.

[2]This would have put them just west of present-day Livingston on the eastern side of the Bozeman Pass.

bringing in the bedding of the escort and on his return to the post was again detached to the same point with more grain to the train and for the purpose of bringing it in which duty he performed admirably and to the satisfaction of all concerned arriving at the post on the 5th inst.

The transportation of the escort consisted of nine six-mule teams and one [illegible] belonging to the freight contractor, two government four-horse wagons with cavalry horses, and one spring wagon (two-horse) with the private horses of an officer of the command.

The grazing for animals from the day of our leaving the post with the exception of four days while in the buffalo country up to the 15th November was excellent and with the scythes provided us we procured during the same period all the good hay necessary for the feeding of our stock at night (excepting the four days in buffalo country) which was invariably tied to picket lines until the snow became too deep to cut hay, when it was turned loose and herded under a strong guard.

The country, so far as traveled by the command, is well supplied with white and black tailed deer, elk, and antelope, and the Yellowstone River with the finest trout with which the command kept themselves well supplied.

I saw no hostile Indians, though at many points on the south side of the river I saw fresh pony tracks supposed to be scouts from the Sioux tribes.

The transportation company lost four mules on the trip—three died and one gave out and was abandoned. The Cavalry lost seven horses—two died, one from injuries by falling on rocks and one from general debility, one froze to death, and four gave out and were abandoned. The distance traveled by the command was two hundred and eighty-six miles, while the daily travel by the guards in protecting the working parties on the line amounted to about four miles and though not hard duty, yet it was very trying on the horses as a greater portion of the time the camps had unnecessarily to be pitched on the opposite side of the river to which the parties were at work, which made it necessary for the guards to cross twice a day and many of the crossings being quite deep and rocky, and the water growing colder every day, told very materially on them. In closing my report permit me to acknowledge the uniform good behavior of the Officers and men of the command during the entire expedition.

Under the most trying circumstances in the midst of severe snow storms when they were without tents, bedding, and only a scanty allowance of clothing and at a time when the mercury was many degrees below zero, their obedience to orders and cheerfulness with which they performed their several duties could only be equaled by the true soldier who subjected himself to strict military discipline.

To Capt. George L. Tyler I am under many obligations for his strict attention to duty while commanding the guards with working parties on the line, and the good judgment exercised by him in guarding against surprises by hostile Indians had they been lurking through the country in which we were operating.

Very respectfully [etc.]

Major Baker's Comments

Baker's comments appear to be as much as he ever wrote concerning the western Yellowstone survey. See his formal annual report to Hancock. Punctuation has been added as necessary, and most abbreviations completely spelled.

Sir:

. . . On the 16th of September Captain Ed. Ball, 2nd Cavalry, with companies "F" and "H" 2nd Cavalry consisting of five officers and ninety-one enlisted men left the Crow Agency, Montana Territory, from which point he escorted the surveying party of the Northern Pacific Railroad under Mr. Muhlenberg down the Yellowstone River and returned in compliance with telegraphic instruction from Headquarters Department of Dakota dated August 5th, 1871. The party returned on the 28th of November having marched 290 miles.

. . . On the 2nd of November I left the post [Fort Ellis] with one officer and twenty-five men for the purpose of escorting Mr. W. Milnor Roberts, Chief Engineer of the Northern Pacific, on a trip of observation down the Yellowstone. On reaching the camp of the surveying party and escort I took three officers and ninety men and marched about fifty miles below Capt. Ball's camp. Mr. Roberts, not wishing to go any further, we returned to camp. I then took my original party and returned to the post arriving on the 17th of November 1871.

Source: Both Ball (December 10, 1871) and Baker (December 31, 1871) Reports, microfilm MF-339, reel 1, Montana Historical Society, Helena.

Milnor Roberts's Published Letters

CROW AGENCY ON THE YELLOWSTONE RIVER,
Evening of Nov. 16th, 1871

I returned this evening from my trip down the Yellowstone, having reached a point about 170 miles from Fort Ellis, whence we had a good view of the valley for twenty miles farther, to Pompey's Pillar.

We left the surveying party and Captain Ball's escort about fifty miles this side of our lowest point, and Col. Baker took about ninety cavalry (without tents), and we pushed on two days' journey, sleeping the second night in a snow storm, where there was very little grass for our animals. We would have gone two days' journey beyond but for the fact that the grass was gone. Large numbers of buffalo had been ranging through that part of the valley, and many Indian horses had been feeding there. One day's journey further down would have been of little service, as we could see an open wide plain nearly that far. Without grain or grass, in cold, snowy weather, I could not ask the Colonel to proceed.

After leaving Capt. Ball, we soon reached a portion of the Valley that is much wider than any portion we had passed through the upper and middle portion, having good grass, the lower portion little or none—that is, no good grass. This stretch of the Valley, say for twenty-five miles in length, is from five to nine miles wide, averaging about seven miles of good arable land.

We then came to a narrow place where the bluffs approach within a mile of each other; but a few miles below, the valley again widens out to a width of five to ten miles of good soil, but at present without grass, having been ranged over by buffaloes, antelope, and deer and horses, besides not being as good naturally as some of the points above for grazing.

We saw a great many herds of antelopes—some of them with more than one hundred in them, many deer, one band of twenty-three elks, and a number of bands of buffalo. The elk were on the opposite side of the Yellowstone, where there was no ford. We killed a number of antelopes and deer and two buffaloes, also a couple of wild geese. We passed many rabbits and thousands of prairie dogs and wolves. We had plenty of game meat all the time. In fact, I never have been in a country where the game is so abundant. Capt. Ball told me that he had brought three beef cattle with him from the fort, but that he intended taking them back with him.

On returning to Capt. Ball's escort, we spent an evening with [lists names]. . . . Dr. Whitefoot tells me that Mr. Muhlenberg has worked most industriously and faithfully since he left the Fort, but that the survey has had a good many difficulties, owing to its being confined to the north side of the river. Most of the way the encampments had to be on the south side, and at times the crossing and re-crossing were troublesome. The north side has much more bluffs and is more difficult to survey than on the south side, although there are some bluffs, of course, on the south side. On the whole route as far as surveyed, there are only a few miles where there is no flat on either side.

Generally, the valley is from two to three miles wide till we get down below, as mentioned, [and] there are sloping rolling grasslands on one side or the other, and much of the way on both sides of the valley, beyond the flat portions.

Generally at frequent intervals along the river, there are forests of cottonwood; sometimes there are only thinly scattered trees, and then there are intervals without trees. In many places the side hills are pretty well covered with pine trees, sometimes amounting to real forests, but were frequently rather scattered; but enough pine trees to afford a great many thousand cross-ties without very long hauling. But the main valley, as far as we went, is comparatively bare of timber, the prevailing character being prairie.

At frequent intervals there are lovely spots for farms, with rich bottomlands a mile or two wide and much wider uplands interspersed with pines. The pine trees are usually from fifty to sixty feet and sometimes seventy to ninety feet—from one foot to two feet or more in diameter.

Capt. Ball said to me that he had often been out hunting four or six miles out from the flat portion of the valley and found very fine grass and good soil on the uplands, and in the valleys of the side streams. . . .

The width of the river between its banks is about 600 feet where the line first strikes it above Shields' River, and 150 miles down, it is from 700 to 800 feet—in many places wider. There are many islands, with two or more channels, making the whole width 1,500 feet or more.

Although the low flats are often not more than 10 feet above low water, there is no appearance of their having been flooded. . . . The bottom of the river consists of clean gravel boulders everywhere as far down as the Big Horn, varying in size in different localities. We forded the river eight times going down. Some of the fords were rather deep and the water very swift [and] clear as crystal. The best fords or the safest are at islands where the stream is divided.

I should think that wheat can be raised along the Yellowstone valley in many places without irrigation; but if irrigation should be necessary, the circumstances are peculiarly favorable for irrigating, as there is an abundance of water, and plenty of fall in the main stream, and in its tributaries, and the floods are of the moderate height stated.

I defer entering at present upon the method of finally locating a railroad line along this valley any further than to say that the *shortest* and cheapest line per mile to *grade* would obviously be one making a number of river crossings, with much of the route through the Crow Reservation. With our survey map and profile, Mr. Muhlenberg's notes, and my own full notes, we will have a very complete view of the valley. . . . Below that there is a canyon from 20 to 25 miles with pretty high banks, which none of us have seen. Below the Big Horn to the Powder River, according to the best information I have yet obtained, the country is quite as favorable as that we have passed over.

In parting with Capt. Ball and Mr. Muhlenberg I left the matter of proceeding further down the valley entirely optional with Capt. Ball. The survey was then going about five to six miles a day.

Last night we had a rain, and this morning at six o'clock it changed to a severe snow storm and snowed all day. If this extended down as far as the survey party, I think they will start back. There is much more snow than usual this early in the season.

* * *

HELENA, MONTANA,
Nov. 21, 1871.

I arrived last night from Fort Ellis, having been absent just twenty-two days, during which I have photographed on my mind 275 miles, going to within sight of Pompey's Pillar, leaving, as nearly as I can make it out, about 140 miles between Rosser's westerly and my easterly point.[3]

Of that 140 miles there are probably about twenty-five of canyons, about the mouth of the Big Horn, as described by Pierre Chène and Mitch Boyer, guides, said to be familiar with the Yellowstone valley. They refer to the valley below the Big Horn, and thence to the Powder River, as open and without canyons. If so, the valley of the Yellowstone as a whole . . . must be pronounced very favorable for the Company's purposes.

There are quite a number of fords of the Yellowstone to be made, and should severe weather set in, it would be very difficult crossing on

---

[3]Actually closer to 195 railroad miles.

account of ice, although generally the ice is not very heavy, but it is in some seasons. Not much snow in the Yellowstone valley at any time. On the Bozeman Divide for a few miles, the snow is sometimes several feet deep. There has been more snow this season up to this date throughout Montana than ever before known, yet there is not a particle left on the road crossing the valley into Helena for many miles back. It falls a few inches at a time and disappears in a day or two. It seems to dry away.

Source: Roberts Papers, Collection no. 783, series 6, box 10, Burlingame Special Collections Library, Montana State University, Bozeman.

Roberts's Formal Report to President Smith

Distances from mouth of Heart River to bend of Yellowstone at Shields' River (where the line begins to grade up from the Yellowstone valley) chiefly from surveyed routes: Mouth of Heart River to Shields' River, 514 miles, thence to initial point, at head of Missouri 62 miles.

[Discussion of optional Missouri River route omitted.]

There is another alternate route connected with the Yellowstone line which I have not had time or opportunity to explore and which does not affect the line along the lower portion of the Yellowstone or the point of departure at the Missouri River crossing. It is a proposed line leaving the Yellowstone valley about a hundred miles below the Bozeman Divide, passing over the comparatively low dividing ridge separating the Yellowstone and Musselshell, thence up the Musselshell valley to a divide farther north than Bozeman's, in the Belt range, and down into the Gallatin Valley *via* the Flathead Pass, or still farther north and down into the Valley of the Missouri via "Sixteen Mile Creek."[4]

Should the Yellowstone valley be adopted as the general route, there would be time to examine these next season, without delaying the extension of the road westward of the Missouri River. I am not impressed with the idea that any such alternate route will be equal to the general line we have surveyed; nevertheless, it may be advisable to have a reliable reconnaissance in the direction indicated.

My impression is that the dividing ground between the Yellowstone

[4]Thirty-five years later this route would be built by the Chicago, Milwaukee & St. Paul Railroad.

and the Musselshell is higher than unprofessional parties generally assume; that the advantages of the Musselshell Valley for construction of railroad are not likely to be superior to those on the Yellowstone; and the passage of the Belt range, at any point north of Bozeman's, will be less favorable, if practicable at all; but this is only my impression, not founded on any personal examination of the country referred to excepting such views as I had of the Belt range and of the position and magnitude of the "Crazy Mountain," whilst pursuing my investigations of the Yellowstone and Gallatin Valleys.

[Discussion of Salmon River route in Idaho omitted]

There is a long stretch of the Missouri River extending from Heart River to Fort Benton, which I have had no opportunity of examining; but from the best information attainable, the impression in my mind is that it is not at all favorable, as an agricultural region is devoid of valuable timber, and that it would be a more costly route on which to construct a railroad than the valley along the Yellowstone *above the Powder River.*

The country between the Missouri River crossing and the Powder River may be no more favorable than the general valley of the Missouri above Heart River; but if the Yellowstone valley be regarded as desirable, the route up Heart River seems to be the natural way to approach it from the Red River crossing.

I am disappointed in regard to the Yellowstone valley in one respect—I mean its immediate bottom valley between the foot-slopes of the river hills. It is not so wide as I had hoped to find it; yet it is a lovely valley, varying in width, exclusive of the grass hills, from two to four miles in places, and in other parts from five to ten miles.

The abundance of the never-failing flow of water in the Yellowstone and its larger tributaries, with their rapid fall and moderate height of floods, will afford immense water powers at frequent intervals, while there is little doubt that coal will be worked in a number of places. I had no time to devote to an examination of the coal measures. Only in one place I saw, across the river, an appearance of thick veins of coal, or lignite.

Cost

Respecting the probable cost of construction along the Yellowstone, I am satisfied that my estimate of $28,000 per mile, on an average, as given in my report of 1869 to Messrs. Jay Cooke & Co., should cover it.

I cannot judge, without further information in regard to the country between the crossing of the Missouri River and the point where the recent surveys touched the Yellowstone, said to be two hundred and twenty-six miles, what that portion of the route may cost.

. . . There are some thirty miles along the Bozeman Divide that will cost considerably more than the average per mile then estimated, but there are miles enough of moderate work to more than compensate for it. The line along the Jefferson River Valley, as a whole, will cost less than I then assumed. When finally located, it will be on much more favorable ground than where our survey this summer was traced.

The time and money consumed in making thorough final surveys and careful location constitute a most profitable investment for railroad companies.

Very respectfully [etc.]

Source: Roberts Papers, Collection no. 783, series 6, box 10, Montana State University, Bozeman.

Roberts's Letters to His Wife

Camp Milnora, Monday Morning, Nov. 13, 1871

Dearest O and Darling O,

After an excellent breakfast in Capt. Ball's tent—I am ready for a start homeward—towards Fort Ellis—this morning. It snowed a little last night, but not so much as we had the night before. We start from Camp Milnora, with the same escort that brought us from Fort Ellis, and will bid adieu to our more numerous friends, whom we leave hoping they may have some pleasant days yet; although ice is running in the river today and stands along the edges and ¼ inch thick in our tent. I think that when Capt. Ball gets his horses down about 30 miles further he will feel like returning—that will take them only about a week of good work [by] the survey. They do not on Sundays—only work in the tents. Good-bye Camp Milnora—9:50 A.M. Nov. 13.

* * *

Camp Linch Pin—Evening Nov. 13, 1871

Dearest O and Darling O,

It has been another favorable day for us; although we had a late start we have made a good day's march—26 miles! Our wagons are lighter—and getting lighter daily. We killed five antelope [and] two deer today en route. "Blackfoot" and "Wolfbow" are with us. The other Indians remained.

Good night, dearest O and darling O.

* * *

Camp Linch Pin, Nov. 14th 1871. On left bank of Yellowstone
26 miles above camp MILNORA, Tuesday Morning, 6 A.M.
Addie

Dearest O and Darling O,

Good Morning. I have had a good night's rest—a storm was promised by Col. Baker, but it did not come. Frank Kneass, who is returning homeward, travels now in the ambulance with me, and he slept night before last and last night in my tent. He is quite a companionable young man, and I regret that he and Muhlenberg do not suit each other.

The thermometer is 31°—not very cold—barely freezing—and the day looks promising. Although it is not time for Sunrise, I see the rosy clouds in the east tinged with his shining rays.

"*Breakfast is ready, Col*"! These are pleasant words to one who only eats two meals a day and no lunch, and who has a magnificent appetite for any meal and plenty of good things to satisfy it. We are aiming at an early start, [hoping] to reach the "Agency"—75 miles or so above here in two days. Breakfast is over, and we will start directly.

* * *

28 miles from Camp *Linchpin.* Camp *Addie* opposite
Mount Addie on the south and Tyler's Ford on the north
6 P.M. Tuesday Night, November 14, 1871

Dearest and Darling,

We arrived at this lovely camp, with the nicest *grass,* and surrounded by beautiful scenery, a little after 3 this afternoon. We took a new route to day, marking a new road, by which we avoided two fordings of the river and found a better ford for one of those we had to make. We also crossed the *Rosebud* creek, which has a strong flow over big boulders. It did not begin to thaw much till past noon, so that our road was better than when we passed down the valley. All of the snow has entirely disappeared in the valley and from the river's hills. The thermometer was 48° today and this evening it was still 46°—and a clear sunset at 3½ P.M. in the valley.

I have named this Camp "Addie," after one I love. I have named the ford just opposite here "Tyler" because I heard that he came near getting wet while crossing it some time ago. We do not have to cross it. Directly opposite the camp, on the same side of the river, is a pretty Mount, which I have named Mount "Addie," and soon after we stopped I took my pistol, barometer, and thermometer and started across the beautiful natural meadow to its foot, and ascended to the top, which I figured to be 400 feet above the plain.

It took me 8 minutes of rapid walk to reach the foot and 25 minutes, slower gait, to ascend to the top, where I had a fine view of the valley for many miles up and like distance down—the windings of the river and its islands opened out like a map before me. As soon as I reached it I fired my pistol, while standing on the highest peak of rock. Soon after I heard a ball whiz and strike the rock about 20 feet below me, and a little while after another ball whizzed and struck the rocks not far below me. I called out to the party to stop firing at me. It was, as I learned when I returned, their [belief that the] rifles would not carry that far, while it was very clear to me that they did. Col. Baker had fired the first shot, but none of them had believed that the ball struck so high up. One reason for this belief was that we had all overestimated the width of the plain and the height of the mount.[5]

From the peak of Mount Addie I had a good view across the river, where there are high rolling grassy plains interspersed with pines, and back of them a few miles another, higher range well covered with dark pines. Here and there were remaining patches of snow—and beyond the valley hills [and] the mountains, entirely snow covered for the season. On the south side behind Mount Addie, there are also growing bunch grass and pines here and there, altogether making picturesque scenery, and at the same satisfying me of the value of the hills for pasturage and the valleys for farming.

Along near the apex of a portion of Mount Addie it is all rock, not much more than two to three feet wide, very steep. . . . On the very apex

[5]What would they have done if they had wounded or killed Roberts? Talk about cover-ups!

the rock has crumbled sufficiently to make a small rounded summit as big as a parlor, on which the Rocky Mountain bunch grass is growing. I observed here as I observed elsewhere, where the mountains are composed of volcanic rock, that as soon as the rocks deteriorate from frost, snow, or rain into small particles, the bunch-grass springs up—even on the highest parts of the chain of the Rocky Mountains. I descended, along a steeper part of the Mountain . . . [reaching] the summit to the base in 5 minutes, and in 8 minutes more I was in the camp. There is a large cottonwood grove just below, and a small one about an eighth of a mile above, and in the clear spaces between the best grass we have had at any time. We have given up the idea of reaching the Agency tomorrow night—as we are about fifty miles below it.

We had an elegant supper this evening: oyster stew, buffalo meat, antelope, and breakfast bacon, with excellent potatoes, grown in this valley at the Agency, and canned tomatoes. New moon tonight—stars bright—not very cold—Good night darlings.

* * *

Camp Addie, Wednesday morning,
November 15, 1871

Good morning, Dearest O and darling O,

Magnificent sunrise! Gorgeous clouds! . . . We are to have another fine day. We cannot reach the Agency tonight, but we will have a good start after an excellent starlight night and a good sleep. It froze very gently last night and there is new ice forming in the river. Thermometer now . . . 33° or one degree above freezing. I am writing in the open air, with my hand for a desk, and without gloves. I believe we will have no food to cook today, keeping on the right bank of the river all the way.

* * *

Camp "Upset" Wed. night
Nov. 15, 1871

Dearest O and Darling O,

We had the best start this morning of any day during the expedition . . . a light breeze blowing in our faces all day. We kept on the right side of the river all day, but about one o'clock we crossed the "Boulder," about a mile above where we encamped when we went down. It is a wide stream about 2 feet deep, clear & swift, and full of large and small boulders, making it very [illegible] for horses and wagons, although each individual stone is quite smooth and slippery. There was [an] encampment of Indians, said to be Shoshones, a short distance above where we camped, but we did not visit them. When we went down the valley there were a few other Indians encamped there—"Bannocks," I believe. Two of the Shoshones came out on colored horses looking like fantastical [illegible], then they returned.

[Page and letters ends abruptly here]

Source: Roberts Papers, Correspondence, 1871–1874, series 2, box 2, folders 4–5, Burlingame Special Collections Library, Montana State University, Bozeman.

Newspaper Coverage

Arrival of the NPRR Surveying Party
Terrible Suffering—Forty Soldiers and
One Citizen Severely Frozen

We received a call yesterday morning from G. D. Chenoweth,[6] assistant engineer of the N.P.R.R. party on the Yellowstone, who arrived at this place Tuesday evening, having left Mr. Muhlenberg and the balance of the surveying party at the Crow Agency. Capt. Ball and the escort also returned to Fort Ellis Tuesday evening. Mr. Chenoweth reports terrible suffering among the whole party by cold. They had broken camp and were on the march when the severe storm of Friday came upon them in all its fury, the blinding snow coming in [like] a hurricane drifting to the depth of many feet in their line of march, and the party getting scattered and the greatest suffering prevailed. Twenty-three soldiers were frozen badly, and about forty were more or less frosted. They would tumble off their horses perfectly benumbed, and it required the greatest exertion of those not so badly affected to rouse them from the stupor that was fast coming on them. One man connected with the surveying party, having become detached from the main body, was out all night and had his feet so badly frozen that amputation will probably be necessary. The survey of Mr. Muhlenberg's party extended about one hundred and forty miles down the Yellowstone valley, and Mr. Chenoweth is highly pleased with

---

[6]Nothing is known about Chenoweth other than he was able. Milnor Roberts was sympathetic to his problems working for Muhlenberg, but could do nothing to rectify the situation.

the country, and is satisfied that the line surveyed on the north side of the river is the most practicable route that could be adopted, which brings the road directly through the Bozeman Pass.

The party saw no hostile Indians on the trip, although fresh signs were visible every day. The Sioux were undoubtedly watching the movements of the surveyors every day. About one hundred and fifty lodges of Sioux were ascertained by the party as being camped on the Big Horn. The Crows were with the surveying party a portion of the time, making several sorties, capturing stock from the Sioux, which showed them to be in close proximity. Some of the stock belonging to the outfit perished from the cold and hunger.

Source: Bozeman Avant Courier, *November 30, 1871.*

From the Yellowstone

We had a call yesterday from Mr. C. W. Hoffman and Mr. Harry Williams, who came in from the Agency with Capt. Ball and his command of three companies of cavalry, returning from their trip as escort to the surveying party.[7] . . . From [the two] we learn additional facts of the fearsome storm and the terrible suffering of the entire party in making the trip from the [Crow] Agency to Fort Ellis and the effects of the storm in the Yellowstone valley. The Yellowstone River was frozen almost completely over, the whole command crossing on the ice, with the exception of a small space where the rapids prevented freezing.

Elk in large herds are abandoning the mountains and canyons and coming into the valley. Livestock of all kinds are suffering terribly, and the result will be a heavy loss to some of our stockman. The [surveying] party left the agency on Monday morning, shoveling their way through the drifts, which in some instances exceeded eight feet. Their horses were almost famished for want of food, and many dropped by the wayside from cold and exhaustion.[8] They were met between Ellis and the agency by a party of soldiers with grain and shovels, who dug a trail over the ranges, and the whole command reached Ellis after two days' travel, fraught with suffering and danger, the entire distance being thirty-two

[7]C. W. Hoffman was an entrepreneur, businessman, bank director, and horse breeder known to be alive in 1905 and residing in Bozeman. Wikipedia. No available information concerning Harry Williams.

[8]The Crow Indian Agency had virtually no grain because Indian ponies didn't eat it.

miles. About two-thirds of the command were slightly frozen, none being dangerous. All of the party highly commended the commanding officer, Capt. Ball, for his humanity, courage, and foresight, under circumstances of the most trying nature.

Source: Bozeman Avant Courier, *November 30, 1871.*

Montana
Soldiers Badly Frozen

HELENA, NOV. 25.—Fort Shaw [MT]. A special dispatch of to-day says that two companies of the Seventh Infantry, Major [H. B.] Freeman commander, returning from Fort Browning, were caught in yesterday's fearful storm, and now camped twelve miles from here with a number of men badly frozen.

Later—Ten of the frozen men have been brought to the hospital. The worst cases still are being brought in as fast as possible. They are frozen generally about the feet, and some will lose their feet. The thermometer this morning was 30 degrees below freezing point.

Helena 8 P.M. The thermometer is fifteen degrees below freezing point. No stages have arrived from any direction for thirty-six hours.

Source: Philadelphia Inquirer, *November 27, 1871.*

Down among the Sioux: Interesting Report of Special Indian Agent Simmons

Special Indian Agent A. J. Simmons who recently returned from the Lower Missouri country, whither he was dispatched some time since to interview the Teton Sioux, with orders to propitiate, if possible, that powerful and hostile confederation of Indians to a peace footing with the Government, [and he] has filed in the Indian office an elaborate and highly interesting report of his journey and the result of his undertaking.[9]

[9]A. J. Simmons (1834–1920). Born in New York State; in the California gold fields at nineteen, and later a member of the Nevada Territorial Legislature. He was appointed by Grant to be a special Indian agent to assist in getting rights of ways for the Northern Pacific. By the late 1870s he had married, moving to Deadwood and then to Rapid City, South Dakota, where he spent most of his life in mining ventures. His report is that of a calm, intelligent, and inherently honest man. Wikipedia.

Through the courtesy of Superintendent Viall, access to the Agent's report has been allowed us, and we have taken some pains to transcribe for publication the larger part of this eminently trustworthy and unusually readable document for the benefit of the public. Mr. Simmons, in addressing the Indian Office says:

FOR BROWNING, MILK RIVER AGENCY,
DECEMBER 5, 1871

Pursuant to your instructions directing me to visit the bands of the Teton Sioux, roaming between the Missouri and Yellowstone Rivers, with the object of obtaining full information in regard to them, their disposition for peace, etc., to enable the Department to take such steps as might be proper in the premises, and to ascertain whether a delegation of said Chiefs could be induced to visit Washington for the purpose of concluding a treaty, I have the honor to report that I arrived at Fort Peck, on the Missouri River near the mouth of Milk River, on the night of the 4th of November, and found the Tetons encamped from twenty to sixty miles south of that place. There I met the head chief and orator of the Hunkpapa or Teton nation, Black Moon (We-Sapa) and five other chiefs, viz. Iron Dog, Long Dog, Little Wound, Sitting Eagle, and Bear's Rib, besides a great many head men and about 200 lodges of the people.[10] I remained twenty-one days, during which time I held fifteen interviews of from one to ten hours duration each.

Before proceeding further, and in order that you may have a full understanding of the matter, I will state a few facts and circumstances concerning the visits of Sitting Bull and other Tetons to Fort Peck prior to my arrival.

[10]There were three chiefs named Black Moon all living at the same time and all at the Little Big Horn. The one who takes the lead in this account was a Hunkpapa cousin of Sitting Bull and was likely "Old" Black Moon, not his son, "Young" Black Moon. Logic says it was the older/wiser father who represented Sitting Bull, and there is later specific reference to his using his son as a messenger. One of the two witnessed a solar eclipse and gave himself the name "Black Sun," further confusing matters. The younger was killed in the earliest phases of the Little Big Horn, but his father survived, living at least another five years. The third Black Moon (ca. 1821–93) was a Miniconjou at the Little Big Horn who fled to Canada with Sitting Bull, returned, but was not placed in captivity (likely because of his age), and he survived long enough to see most of his family killed at Wounded Knee. See Malone, *Dictionary of American Biography*; Utley, *Lance and the Shield*; specialized histories and biographies of Teton/Lakota Sioux, and Thrapp, *Encyclopedia of Frontier Biography*.

These people have been hostile to the whites for many years, having made war upon all the posts of the Upper Missouri and committed numberless depredations and murders. They have refused all friendly intercourse with the whites, not even having been at peace with the white traders on the borders of their country, but have procured ammunition and necessary articles of traffic from half-breeds of the north and friendly Indians. From their standpoint, all whites found in or traveling through their country are regarded as enemies intruding upon their hunting grounds and interfering with their game, but their hostilities have not been confined to these, as they have made frequent incursions out of their country into white settlements and committed depredations [there].

Fort Peck was established five years ago as a trading post for tribes who have since moved further west, and the Tetons have come to the vicinity, so that the post may now be regarded as a convenient point for them to trade. The trader at this post has frequent messengers to them with presents of tobacco, inviting them to come in and make peace with the post for purposes of trade, which have been unheeded on the part of the Indians until the 8th day of September last, when Sitting Bull, the head war chief of the nation, with a small party came to the post after night and called out his name, stating he came as a friend and for peace. He was treated well by the trader, with whom he established a truce and arranged for his people to trade, after which small trading parties continued to come in, and on the 12th day of October following, Sitting Bull again visited the post. At this visit, I am informed he expressed a desire to see an agent of the Government, said the Tetons would make peace, and would not allow any more war parties to go out of the camp, which declaration was verified a short time afterwards in the following manner.

A war party had organized and was about starting out upon a foray up the river against other tribes and whites. The "soldiers" of the camp, headed by Sitting Bull, prevented its going at the cost however of a fight in which some eight men and twenty horses were killed and the lodges of the refractory persons were cut to pieces by the "soldiers." I was not disposed to credit this statement at first, but it came to me from so many different sources and in such a reliable manner that I became convinced of its truthfulness.

Like most other bands of Sioux, the Tetons have an organization for the government of the camp, called "soldiers," who are composed of leading and influential men. Their authority is supreme and their mandates are arbitrary and must be obeyed, otherwise severe penalties are inflicted, such as cutting lodges to pieces, killing horses, and sometimes inflicting the death penalty upon malefactors.

On my arrival at Fort Peck, I found it wholly impracticable to visit the Teton camp. I therefore sent messengers with presents of tobacco, inviting the chiefs and head men to come in, employing as messengers Hunkpapas and the trustworthy Indians who accompanied me. My first messenger was kindly received, but while he was smoking in a lodge and delivering my message, the horse I had loaned him to ride was spirited away by some evil disposed person, and as his dignity and outraged feelings would not allow him to accept another, which was proffered by Sitting Bull, he returned on foot, a distance of sixty miles. Sitting Bull, however, immediately dispatched a messenger to me deploring the loss of the horse and stated he would find it and bring it in when he came.

Communication was kept up with the camp, and small parties continued to arrive daily until the 14th of November, when Black Moon and the chiefs before named and an encampment of two hundred lodges arrived. I was then informed that the "soldiers" had refused to let Sitting Bull leave the camp on account of apprehended disturbances among the people resulting from the conflict above referred to. He sent word he could not come to see me at that time but that he desired Black Moon and his brother-in-law (Shunka-haska) to speak for him.

Interviews were now held with Black Moon and party during the following ten days. Much information was elicited, and an agreement was entered into whereby a truce was established. Notes were taken of all important conferences, and I herewith present all the main points in as brief and condensed a form as possible.

I told them I came as a messenger from the president to learn their disposition, whether they would make peace or were going to continue their warfare against the whites. The president was anxious to live on friendly terms with them. Peace would be beneficial to them. Their brethren, the Oglala, had made peace a short time ago, and a delegation, headed by Red Cloud, had visited the president and returned to their homes in safety. The Santees and Yanktoni, [living] on the other side of them, had entered into peaceful arrangements last summer with the whites, with whom they were now living on friendly terms. The Tetons were now hemmed in and almost surrounded by whites and Indian tribes who were their friends. All the tribes around them were contented and did not live in constant fear of white soldiers and were getting along better than the Tetons, because they were friends to the whites and listened to the words of the Great White Father and his agents. Game, upon which they depended for subsistence, was fast disappearing; if they continued their warfare they would also disappear—would perish with the buffalo. If they made peace and were faithful to it, they would live, and the president would help them, as he did all friendly tribes. I told them I had no authority to make a treaty, but urged a delegation of chiefs to visit Washington and arrange terms with the Great White Chief, who had sent for them. I would accompany them to where the superintendent lived and guarantee to them a safe journey.

Black Moon declared himself emphatically in favor of peace, and stated that Sitting Bull agreed with him and would stand by him; that most of their head men and men of sense wanted peace with the whites. Whatever he said he would do, he would make it so; when he talked in camp all the people listened; was afraid of no Indian, and spoke what he believed to be good and right. He had the power to make good his words. He would now tell me if he wished to have peace, what the President must do. He must stop the railroad (meaning the Northern Pacific); it was going through their country and would destroy the game. The white soldiers and citizens must be kept out of their country. The Tetons would not make peace with the soldiers. Fort Buford, below, and the Musselshell trading post, above, must be abandoned.[11] If the Great Father would do those things, it would satisfy all, and they would have peace; demanded of me to tell him whether [the Great Father] would do it. They would smoke over the proposition of visiting the President when [Black Moon] returned to camp.

Others spoke, generally endorsing what Black Moon had said. The Railroad was being built through their country without their consent. How could they live when the game was gone? They would die, and would rather choose to die like brave men fighting. One person declared they would make war upon the railroad to the last.

I replied that the railroad would be built, that they might as well try to stop the Missouri River from flowing down stream as to stop the road. They had already seen one railroad built across the plains and over the mountains. The Sioux declared at the time they would prevent that, but events had shown they were powerless to do it. The road now transported presents and provisions from the President to the Indians in that vicinity;

[11]The Musselshell River trading post was where the river (really a stream) entered the Missouri.

it would be the same with this road; if they made peace it would be a great benefit to them. The Great Father would help them to live if they ceased their warfare. He was strong and powerful; his white children were as numerous as the trees in the mountains. He could exterminate the Tetons if he so desired; they were but a handful with arms inferior to all the friendly tribes around them. The Great Father's heart was good; he took pity upon them because they were weak and inferior. He had seven great and good men who made it their business, without pay, to labor for the improvement of the Indians.[12] The Tetons must do as all the tribes around them had already done: cease their hostilities, make peace, learn the way to live as the whites do, and accept the civilization that was surrounding them. Otherwise they would perish. If they had men who would throw their lives away fighting rather than accept peace, I would tell them, if they were brave men, they would think of their women and children and not subject them to the sacrifice of war and starvation. Brave men who had sense in their hearts would not do that.

In regard to the country they occupied and through which the railroad would pass, I would tell them that it belonged to the whites; the Crows and the Gros Ventre had ceded it by treaty to the President. The Tetons had no right to it and could only occupy it by permission of the President. In regard to Fort Buford and the Musselshell trading post, they were outside the country that the Tetons occupied. They had waged ineffectual war on both. Fort Buford stood between them and the tribes below, with whom they were at war, but who were friends of the whites, and [the] Musselshell was in their way; it interfered with their war parties against the Upper tribes. Hence their desire to have these posts abandoned. If they kept away from these posts they would do them no harm. The Great Father was in the habit of sending his soldiers wherever it was necessary to protect his people and their property. If the Tetons ceased this hostility and made peace, there would probably be no occasion for soldiers coming into their country.

They had made war on the whites for several years; had committed many outrages; charged them with having made a raid into the Gallatin Valley last July, when they killed two unoffending citizens and drove off a large number of horses, and that some of them now said they would

[12]This is likely a reference to Quaker and other Indian agent volunteers who Grant had hoped would be able to treat the Indians with respect and honesty. It was a well-meaning experiment that failed, partially due to the construction of the Northern Pacific.

make war on the construction of the railroad. [I] Would tell them plainly I did not believe the Great White Father would submit any longer to such conduct; that if they began a war on the railroad, he would send soldiers enough here to punish them severely. They could not now carry on warfare against white soldiers, like they had in former times in the lower country. Then game was abundant; now, if the white soldiers route their camp and keep them moving for thirty days, they would starve to death. I had just traveled one hundred and fifty miles without seeing a buffalo. I came as their friend to tell them the truth; urged them to consider well my words; talk and smoke over them in camp—smoke the tobacco the Great White Chief had sent them, and make up their minds whether they would make peace and live, or continue the hostilities and die like the wolves.[13] I urged a party of chiefs to go and see the President who was anxious to shake hands with them and agree with them on terms of peace. Black Moon denied that they were going to fight the railroad. They had not all made up their minds what they were going to do about that. Whoever said he would fight it spoke for himself alone. He would tell his people present that a few days ago the chiefs and soldiers in camp did not let a war party go out, and their camp was in mourning in consequence. He wanted to know if this man was writing down his words for me to take to the Great Father. I told him such was the case. He said: "Then tell him this"—(He repeated the circumstances of the conflict among his people: the "soldiering" of a war party in which eight men and twenty horses were killed and the lodges cut up).

"Tell the Great Father this was done for peace; that those who have some sense and think as I do did that, and that we will make things go our way. There were many brave men among them who would throw their lives away fighting the white settlers; they were fools and would not listen to reason."

He said he would talk and counsel for peace with his people; if they refused to listen, he would take those who would follow and leave the camp; he would go to the north side of the Missouri. Many of the people would follow him; he was not afraid of the white soldiers; he deprecated war with them and was alarmed and trembled for his people; as for

---

[13]Here Simmons is referring to the scores of trappers (called "wolvers") who were flooding Montana at that time looking for wolf pelts and focused on killing wolves with poisoned bait, a slow painful death for the animal. The problem was that the bait attracted the Indians' dogs, killing them, too. See E. S. Topping's *Chronicles of the Yellowstone* (1884).

himself, he would have peace. He then shook hands with the eight white men present. He said it was the Arapahos who made the raid into the Gallatin Valley and declared that none of his people joined in it. He said in their way the country belonged to them; they had fought for it and driven the Crows and Gros Ventres back. The whites settled in and drove them out of the country below, and they were compelled to come here where they could get game. They crossed the Yellowstone six years ago. They had fought for the country they occupied, and it would be difficult to restrain their people from fighting again. He pledged his best efforts for peace and would labor with his people. At the lower agencies they tied up the Indian children and whipped them into trying to teach them as white children are taught. The Tetons did not want any civilization, but wanted something to eat. The railroad would fill the country with whites and whites' houses, and their game would be destroyed. He made a strong appeal for provisions to be furnished them as a basis for peace and in consideration of their giving up their country to the railroad.

Several others talked, concurring with Black Moon. They represented the destitution of their people and urged that supplies be furnished them. I replied to them that if they made peace and lived up to it, they would receive assistance.

On the 15th of November, runners arrived from the main camp reporting that scouts had come in, giving information of a party of soldiers on the Yellowstone [Colonel Baker's]. Also, an expedition [Whistler's] had been discovered lower down that river a short time before, accompanied they said by a party of Indians dressed in soldier uniforms; that they had many wagons and horses; and there was much excitement and talk and some preparation for fighting.[14] They wanted to know the object of these soldiers; if they were coming to fight them? I explained to them that they were escorting the engineers looking [for a] route for the railroad; that they would not harm them unless the Tetons attacked them. I demanded of Black Moon to make good his words of yesterday; if he was sincere in his expressions for peace and wished the President to regard him as a big chief, now was the time to act, to prevent a conflict which would bring on a war that would be terrible in its results to his people.

[14]Why it took Sitting Bull and Black Moon's followers so long to discover the eastern survey is unknown. In fact, Whistler's column had returned to Fort Rice a month earlier. As for the western survey, it is doubtful that they could have been intercepted given the date that the information arrived.

After consultation among themselves, messengers were sent to camp, headed by Black Moon's son advising them to keep away from those expeditions and not to begin any war. I furnished tobacco and feasts to take to the soldiers' lodge and dispatched one of my Indians with the party. In other interviews with Black Moon and party, the following terms were definitely agreed upon:

No war parties to go out of the Teton camp, and no further hostilities to be engaged in on their part against the whites pending negotiations for peace, I agreeing to report to the Department Black Moon's words, the disposition for peace, and to ask the Great Father to provide them with food, and to visit them again as soon as practicable, bringing the words of the President.

In the meantime, Black Moon goes to his people to talk and council with them for peace, and urge a delegation to visit the President. He solemnly declares he will have peace for himself and his band proper, and if others decide upon war, he will leave them and take with him all who want peace.

A few days after this I received a message from Sitting Bull, stating that he had found the horse lost by my messenger; that it was not good for him to leave camp then, but as soon as he could do so he would bring the horse to Fort Peck, and that he and Black Moon would visit me at Fort Browning during the winter.

Becoming convinced that no opposition to the expeditions on the Yellowstone, escorting the railroad engineers, and believing that Black Moon and the others were sincere in their expressions and desire for peace, upon their urgent demand I purchased a small amount of flour, sugar, and coffee from the trader at Fort Peck and gave it to them, and sent some presents to the soldiers' lodges, with words of encouragement and advice. As little expense as possible was incurred under the circumstances, and the little given them was absolutely necessary in furtherance of the object of my visit. The accounts for the same will be forwarded at an early date.

I was disappointed in not being able to meet the chiefs Four Horns, Red Horn, and Sitting Bull. However, I am of the opinion that three of those met—Black Moon, Iron Dog, and Long Dog—are as influential and as great as any others in the tribe.

It was impossible, from the conflicting statements of the Indians, to ascertain anything like a correct statement of their numbers; but I am convinced that the various bands composing the Teton nation, now in proximity to Fort Peck, will not fall short of one thousand four hundred lodges. Estimating eight souls to the lodge, this would make a population of eleven thousand two hundred [some 2,250 warriors].[15]

That a portion of the Teton Sioux are not only willing but anxious to make peace with the Government is certain; and if the steps already taken are promptly followed up by rendering them assistance, it may lead to a reconciliation of the whole tribe.

Many of the chief's and leading men fully understand their situation and the results that will follow the opening up of their country to civilization by the Northern Pacific Railroad: the game will disappear, that they will be surrounded and overwhelmed by the whites, and will perish by starvation, cold, and warfare unless they make peace and obtain assistance from the Government.

They have a wholesome fear of the power of the Government and its military, which will prove the most influential motive in inducing them to accept peace.

That all further depredations can be prevented and a thorough peace be maintained with this powerful and aggressive band, through friendly negotiations, is, from the very nature of things, uncertain and improbable. However, the surrounding circumstances place them in a most favorable condition for receiving peaceful overtures at the present time, and it is certain that much good can be accomplished. I would therefore earnestly call your intention to the importance of the department rendering prompt and substantial aid to the peace party, headed by Chief Black Moon, believing that if this is done before conflicts shall arise with the people of the Northern Pacific Railroad, and the Indians are made to feel that they will receive assistance from the Government, a general war with the tribe, which would be expensive, terrible, and sanguinary in its results, may be averted.

Source: Helena Daily Herald, *December 23, 1871.*

[15]Warriors are estimated at about 20 percent of the total. Not included in Simmons's numbers were thousands of Teton/Lakota Sioux living on Dakota reservations.

CHAPTER 8

The Eastern Survey's Return

The surveyors having reached the Yellowstone, everybody wanted to return to Fort Rice—and as fast as possible. However, the march back would prove no cakewalk. The weather quickly turned cold and ugly. Snow, sleet, freezing rain, and strong winds were the bane of infantrymen marching with heavy rifles and cheap shoes (brogans). Literally adding to the weight of the infantryman's marching discomfort was the necessity of wearing heavy buffalo hide overcoats.

Additionally, Whistler's drinking continued if not actually increasing on the return. The result was more unnecessary miles and wasted time, infuriating all. This situation finally exploded when, near the great southern bend of the Heart River and closing in on Fort Rice, Rosser gleefully countered Whistler's incorrect marching orders for the day. Suddenly the officers in the main column, equally fed up and disobeying orders, followed Rosser, a civilian and former Confederate officer! On returning to camp, the humiliated Whistler could do nothing, for the camp was demonstrably closer to Fort Rice. He couldn't very well make them march further away, could he? Equally mortifying, the thin-skinned C.O., as he had proven with teamsters earlier, must have been fully aware of the whispers and giggles behind his back.

However, that evening the parties agreed to split up—Rosser to examine more thoroughly the mouth of the Heart River and Whistler to take a straight line to Fort Rice. After Rosser's return, and as etiquette demanded, he sent a public letter of thanks profusely praising Whistler, a letter which led to some of Javan Irvine's angriest comments. The reader will also note Campbell's insightful diary comment about Irvine, leaving us with far more questions than answers regarding Irvine's personality.

But Rosser had not yet finished with Whistler. Soon he leaked the story of Whistler's drinking to the *St. Paul Press*, and the article circulated around the country. As for Whistler's not going to the Yellowstone, I could find no specific published reference to it, but one can be sure that army gossipers (especially Irvine) passed the story on and, as the current idiom goes, at warp speed.

Whistler's Report

Report of the Expedition accompanying the Engineers of the Northern Pacific Railroad from Fort Rice D.T. to the Yellowstone River and return, during the months of September and October 1871

October 4. Wind continued all night and after daylight blew a perfect gale which continued all day. During the day most of the tents were blown down, which rendered the men very uncomfortable. Wagon sheets flapped, which music was anything but pleasant to hear. About 2 P.M. three of the Engineers came in and reported that the detachment would be in this evening, they having left the Yellowstone River this morning. They arrived about 5 P.M. Having travelled 28 miles, all seemed very tired. The evening was still cold and raw and the wind blowing so hard that it was almost impossible to get the tents up.

October 5. Left camp at 8 A.M. to go over to Beaver Creek, we travelled our old route. Camped on Beaver Creek and in the afternoon prepared the train for the return trip. Distance travelled 6½ miles.

October 6. Left camp this morning feeling very good, air cool and bracing, everyone, even the mules and horses, seeming to realize that we were homeward bound, followed our old trail most of the day and after travelling 22 miles went into Camp, wood, water, and grass plenty. This morning two mules were missing, were searched for, but no signs of them could be found.

October 7. Started from Camp at 7 A.M. and followed our old trail for a short distance when we struck off to the left reaching the road again about two miles ahead saving quite a distance by the cut off. We had a great deal of trouble getting up a hill about 2 miles from the Little

Missouri. Finally got the train up and encamped on the Little Missouri on our old camping ground. Distance travelled 17 miles.

SUNDAY, OCTOBER 8. Left camp this morning having to pass the Bad Lands which all were anxious to get by before the bad weather sets in. Morning very fine, air cold and bracing. The Engineers did a little work but did not detain the command. Travelled over the old route. Made camp about 5 P.M. on the Heart River, wood and water plenty, but grass scant, being mostly burned. Distance travelled 20 miles.

OCTOBER 9. This morning being very cold—sleeting and raining—which made it very disagreeable, I concluded to remain in camp. Two Citizens belonging to the train were found missing, which probably accounts for the loss of the Mules.[1] These men I understand were suspected of being deserters by some of the men and probably were from the fact of their leaving the train.

OCTOBER 10. Train under way by 7 A.M. The air very bracing. Followed our old trail, passing the last camp we made on Heart River in about 1½ miles made a cut off and camped on a stream passed on the 23rd near one of Genl. Sully's old camps. Plenty of water and grass, wood source. Distance travelled 20 miles.

OCTOBER 11. Started from Camp in an easterly direction which we kept for some time, struck the old trail in about 4 miles, and about the same distance from the river. Reached the river in about 15 miles crossed the river and following our old trail and went into camp about two miles from our 10th camp on Heart River. This was the worst camp yet made having neither wood, water, nor grass except what was carried in the train. Distance travelled 24 miles.

OCTOBER 12. Left camp about the usual time our course was to the left of our old trail, struck our old trail about 9 miles from where we started and travelled along it until we reached "Sully's Corral" near which we camped on our way out. Watered all the stock, kegs filled, and plenty of wood gathered as the prospect was good for another dry camp. The wagons being now light, one-half of the Command was allowed to ride so as to make better time.

---

[1]The men were teamsters who had likely joined the surveying expedition to safely pan for gold in the "Yellow-stone" River.

Being in sight of "Heart Butte" and having made almost 25 miles, we went into camp. Had some snow this morning, weather very cold.

October 13. Left camp about the usual hour, marched about a mile when we crossed a nice Stream where there was plenty of water and wood could be procured at a short distance from the road. Started directly for "Heart Butte" intending to cross Spring Creek at the same place we crossed it going out. About two miles from the Creek we crossed our old trail. We passed very near Heart Butte.

This is quite a landmark, as it can be seen for many miles. The summit appears to be covered with a sandstone formation about 20 feet high and almost perpendicular. Reached Spring Creek about 12 P.M. After crossing the Creek we were in a strip of country that had not been burned, kept our old trail, and made camp just opposite camp No. 8, wood, water, and grass plenty. Distance travelled 21 miles. Shortly after coming into camp, two of the Scouts brought in two Indian ponies they had captured whilst hunting.

October 14. Left camp about the usual time, followed our old trail most of the day, had to make a circuitous route of about 5 miles in consequence of the Engineers wishing to leave the train at the mouth of the "Little Muddy." Distance travelled 24¾ miles.

Sunday, October 15. Finding it was but a short distance in a direct line to Fort Rice from this point, and I could save several days travel for the train, I came to the conclusion after consulting with Genl. Rosser to detach one company to escort the Engineers to the mouth of Heart River where he had some work to do. I accordingly detached Company "D" 17th Infantry Capt. C. E. Clarke, with the wagons belonging to Fort Rice to escort them to the mouth of Heart River. They started across the country so as to make our first camp on Heart River in a direct line. The main command left camp at 7 A.M. and struck across the bluffs in a south east direction. After gaining the level we struck our trail of the day previous but did not follow it, keeping further to the right over a very splendid road. At the distance of about 9 miles we saw Heart River, which is the nearest point to Fort Rice from here. We made a due east course passing over some of the finest country we had seen since leaving the Missouri River. We passed several places where there was plenty of water but little wood. Two men belonging to Lieut. Fisher's Company "C" 22nd Infantry were reported missing having gone hunting. Two scouts were sent out to look for them, but returned after an unsuccessful search, and the opinion was, finding themselves lost, they would strike for Fort Rice. After travelling 25 miles, we encamped where there was good grass, wood, and water we carried in the train.

October 16. Everything in a bustle as this was to be our last day of march. Started from camp briskly and measured the ground rapidly. Passed over several ridges and from the top of one could see the Missouri River. Wound around some hills and finally came in sight of Fort Rice. We were met and welcomed by Col. Crittenden and Officers of the Post. Found the two missing men had made the post this morning. Made camp near where our old camp was. Everyone seemed much pleased at the result of the trip and rejoiced that so little trouble had been encountered. Having made the trip to the Yellowstone River and return without the loss of a single man and very little stock and material. Distance travelled 21 miles. Distance from Fort Rice to the Yellowstone by odometer 295 miles. Return trip 255 miles.

Losses—Four Government Mules died with colic and two strayed—7 Government wagons broken. Contractor's train—4 horses died or abandoned.

As far as I am individually concerned I was agreeably disappointed [*sic*] in the country over which the expedition passed. That it was much better than I had reason to anticipate from reports I had received. There are portions of the country in the valleys and on the table lands susceptible of cultivation and well adapted to grazing purposes, being covered with a luxuriant growth of buffalo grass, well watered and good protection for animals from winds and storms by the deep valleys and broken country. From indications seen the whole country is underlaid with anthro-lignite coal and outcrops could be seen in every valley and ravine we passed.

The expedition was brought to a much more speedy terminus than we had any reason to anticipate, which was in a great measure due to the efficiency of the Officers, and the cheerfulness and energy in which the men performed their duty together with the good feeling existing between the Command and the Engineers.

The Report is made from notes taken by 1st Lieut. W. W. Daugherty, 22nd Infantry Acting Adjutant.

J. N. G. Whistler, Major 22nd Infantry
Commanding Escort

Capt. J. C. Bates's Report to Whistler

October 5, 1871

Sir:

I have the honor to report that in obedience to Special orders . . . I proceeded with the following troops viz:

Company "B," 20th Infantry, Capt. J. C. Bates, 20th Infantry and 2nd Lieut. O. M. Smith, 22nd Infantry attached.

Company "A," 22nd Infantry, Capt. J. B. Irvin and 2nd Lieut. J. E. Macklin, Co. "H," 17th Infantry 1st Lieut. Henry Marcott and 2nd Lieut. J. M. Burns.

Eighteen (18) Indian Scouts under 2nd Lieut. Edwin Turnock

One Gatling Gun and 11 enlisted men under 1st Lieut. L. E. Campbell, 22nd Infantry

Capt. Henry Inman, A.Q.M. in charge of transportation and Acting Asst. Surgeon E. L. Shirley U.S.A. as Escort to Mr. T. L. Rosser's party of Engineers to the Yellowstone River a distance of 21 miles from on Glendive Creek, which stream I followed to its mouth arriving at the Yellowstone at 12 o'clock P.M. on the 3rd instant.

The road followed lies along the valley of this creek and for a great distance along its bed and owing to the numerous crossings and quicksand bottom would be almost impassable for heavy trains. Owing to a recent rain there was water in the Creek, but strongly alkali.

The Yellowstone River is a rapid stream of very clear and good water, with a depth of about 4 feet in the channel and the cottonwood and timber upon either side.

I broke camp on the Yellowstone at 6:30 A.M. on the 4th. . . . [A]rrived at camp the same day having marched 28 miles. The country on either side of the narrow valley of Glendive Creek is of a wild and broken character and utterly impassable, being just such bad lands as are found on the Little Missouri River. No Indians were seen, but the fresh trail of a small mounted party was discovered at the crossing of the Yellowstone River, opposite my camp.

I have the honor [etc.]

Dr. Charles E. Goddard's Report to Whistler

November 26, 1871[2]

Sir:

I have the honor . . . to state that during the trip from Fort Rice, D.T., to the Yellowstone valley and returning, the health of the Command was excellent. The only cases of sickness were those arising from excessive use of alkaline water and cases of Rheumatism with syphilitic complications the foundation for which had been laid months and in some cases years before. The route may be travelled at any time so far as water is concerned if care be taken in the use of such water as contained salts of Alum and Soda.

Very respectfully [etc.]

Source: Records of the War Department, Records of the U.S. Army Command, 751-MDM 1871, National Archives.

Capt. Javan B. Irvine's Diary

OCTOBER 5. Marched 5½ miles today. After passing a cold night . . . awoke refreshed and find that the wind has subsided leaving the temperature very much milder than we had anticipated. We broke camp at 8 A.M. and marched two hours and went into camp on the North Fork of the Little Missouri River [Beaver Creek]. Here we rest today to enable the troops to wash their clothes and . . . to reload or equalize their loads in the train—nothing of the kind having been done during the three days we were absent at the Yellowstone, the time of the Major Commanding too fully occupied hunting and playing poker for him to give attention for something so unimportant affairs as preparing the train and command for the return. . . . Day sunny but chilly. We traveled twenty-eight miles yesterday and today. About one o'clock P.M. Headquarters tents caught fire from a Sibley stove which ignited the surrounding grass . . . in [unclear] ran up the sides of the tents destroying two of them. No damage was done to the contents. Both the Major Commanding and Adjutant were both out from camp hunting at this time. . . . Chief

[2]Charles E. Goddard, M.D., a major in active service, died at Fort Yates, D.T., in January 1886. He had entered the Civil War as a surgeon, so he was likely born in the 1830s. See Powell, *List of Officers*. Not to be confused with enlistee of the same name in Wikipedia.

Engineer Rosser and [I] had a conversation concerning the costs of the road surveyed by him from the Missouri to the Yellowstone from all the information he could gather from official reports and persons who had visited this country.

OCTOBER 6. Marched 22 miles today. Cloudy and calm this morning. Mr. Bigler breakfasted with us this morning and messed with us during our trip to and from the Yellowstone to Glendive camp. Broke camp about 7 A.M., crossed Beaver Creek and entered the burned district extending from the west fork of the Little Missouri to the east fork thereof. We marched at the rate of three miles per hour and rested ten minutes every hour's march. . . . We encamped at 4 P.M. on the creek where we should have camped coming out when we went to [the] spring. The country we have traversed today is the best for marching that there is on the entire route being rolling, gentle undulating prairie. We camp in sight of the Bad Lands which we enter tomorrow morning. . . . The whole country is one mass of hills, resembling bubbles on a boiling pot with scarcely a space intervening between them. The tops of the hills are red and in many instances is covered with scorched [illegible] or lava, great masses of lava have been projected to the surface and stand out in bold relief on many points taking on many fantastic and erratic [erotic?] forms. The clay soil is burned to a red tinge and the rocks are broken and fire cracked from the intense heat to which this whole region has been subjected. Mr. Dickinson discovered a smoldering fire burning beneath the ground while passing through the Bad Lands.

I can truly say that the land I have seen is not worth one mill per acre and I do not believe that it will yield enough to subsist [*sic*] one antelope per acre the year round. No mineralogical appearances crop out on the surface that would indicate the existence of any wealth of that nature. Lignite [coal] exists to a limited extent but is of such a worthless nature as to preclude the possibility of its being used with any success as an article of fuel. No stone for building purposes can be found. The principal rock being sandstone which is all broken and fire cracked by the intense heat to which this whole country has been subjected.

OCTOBER 7. Marched 17 miles today. A high wind sprang up last night and continues blowing this morning with clouds obscuring the heavens. [W]e marched very lively to the [Little] Missouri. . . . Passed two of our old camp grounds yesterday and one today. Passed the carcass of a horse yesterday and that of a mule today. There must be an abundance of wolves in this country judging from the manner . . . with which the carcasses of the animals we have lost have been devoured. . . . About one P.M. the wonderful sight of the Mauves Terre of the Little Missouri burst upon us right through a gap in the hills that we were threading our way through. We soon entered the defile leading to the most difficult pass of the Mauves Terre through which we debouched on the Little Missouri: this narrow defile where the road descends and ascends very steep declivities delayed our progress 2½ hours where we proceeded to the river which we crossed and went into camp on our old camping ground. . . . The engineers took up their line which they surveyed going out and made some corrections. Herein they joined us [at] two o'clock P.M. While we were passing through, Lt. Poole, who accompanied the Engineers, found an unexploded bombshell in a ravine which was probably thrown at the Indians by General Sully in 1864.[3] Some petrified wood was found by the men, both stone and wood clinging together. We found less water in the Little Missouri than when we crossed Sept. 27th. We could have cut off several miles and reached our camp an hour or two earlier had the C.O. sent out guides yesterday to have examined the route instead of allowing them to loaf in camp. Mr. Dickinson rode out to the right of our column to some very high buttes and found an extensive bed of lignite on fire and smoke and steam issuing from the fire in the earth. Have seen neither live Indians [nor] Buffalo on the entire trip to and from the Yellowstone.

SUNDAY, October 8. Marched 20 miles today. This is a day of rest in all civilized countries and should be with us, but the opinion of the powers that be demand that we pursue our main march homeward. We broke camp about 7 A.M. and immediately entered the valley of Rosser Creek[4] leading from the Little Missouri through the eastern division of the Bad Lands. This stream, whose bed is now dry, we crossed and recrossed nine times and then rose to an elevated valley terminating in the eastern bluffs of the Bad Lands. Our march was quite fatiguing for both men and animals: for the men on account of the long delay caused by stringing out the train at every crossing and for the animals on account of the difficult crossings and consequent hard pulling. The day has been quite cold and in the evening we had a slight rain. . . . We passed our

[3]DeWitt Clinton Poole (1828–1917) was actually a captain in the 22nd Infantry and commanded company H. He retired in 1892 and wrote *Among the Sioux in Dakota*.

[4]Likely today's Railroad Creek.

old gulch camp about noon and emerged from the Bad Lands about 3 P.M. Marched on about five miles and went into camp at 4:30 P.M. We camp five miles east of the [location] where there is both wood and water sufficient for camping purposes. We are [almost] 115 miles from Fort Rice and should be there in about six days. Saw some Antelope and the hunters killed four or five. The Executive Officers were on the hunt as well but killed nothing. The most difficult portion of our journey is now accomplished and from here to Rice we should make quick time. The prairie was accidentally set on fire by some marcher in the Bad Lands, and the column of smoke rising gives it a more gloomy and melancholy appearance than usually. The whole region is of the most desolated and entirely uninhabitable for the habitations of white men. Its rugged nature with its broken and ragged contours may render it a favorite resort for Brigands and Highwaymen.

OCTOBER 9. Raining and snowing. Commenced raining last night and rained gently and quietly all night continuing this morning mixed with flakes of snow here and there; tis not too cold for marching, so we break camp at 8 A.M. and march through the rain and snow. The ground is very slippery and it is doubtful whether we make much progress until the roads become settled. We made our preparations for the march, but when the designated [time] arrived, orders were issued to the effect that the command would not move until it stopped raining. Meanwhile, the Major Commanding got engaged in a game of poker. Orders were given not to move until tomorrow morning: it cleared off about 11 A.M. and the wind soon dried the ground sufficient to enable the command to march had they been directed to do so. I should have been glad had we been permitted to march as I have no doubt we could have made ten miles this afternoon and we would have been so much nearer home and the end of our trials under so imbecile a commander. Noted that water is only found in three or four pools in the creek bed and is strongly impregnated with salty alkali and soda. The animals are grazing at a distance of half or three-fourths of a mile without a mounted guard or herder near them. I observed that a large majority were without hobbles and not picketed, many dragging their picket ropes, and some only tied to each other. I counted only nine that had ropes on out of one hundred animals that I passed. I learn that Capt. Inman gave as a reason for his taking along so much forage in disobedience of orders that he would not have to guard his animals so carefully so he could feed forage out of his wagons. Mr. Dickinson is selling Officers stores to soldiers today when two months ago he was checking their supplies for fear of coming short. Yesterday some of the men shot an antelope which ran inside of the line of skirmishers after being wounded and confused; two of the men caught it and while drawing their knives to finish its career the antelope springs away from them and ran a short distance and fell exhausted from its gunshot wound. Went out and examined the remains of a petrified stump and brought in several fragments as specimens. The surface of the country seems covered with remnants of petrified wood scattered here and occasionally are in a stump [of a] fallen tree.

OCTOBER 10. Marched 19 miles today. Cold, clear, calm, frosty morning, ground frozen. The coldest day we have experienced on the trip.... After we had proceeded about seven or eight miles the C.O. concluded to make a cut off and we struck out across the country, but the change was not made until the advance companies had proceeded some distance and they were compelled to assume a direction of a half mile or more to join us. He was so busy talking he allowed the company to pass right by him [never] thinking of notifying them of the contemplated change of march. Saw several antelope today, the hunters of Company "A" killed two.... We passed "Suspension Bridge" Butte or the Malakoff as it is designated by some leaving it to our left about 12 o'clock; it is a singular formation of clay and lime, the ridge apparently rising from the center of the prairie: two large elm trees were growing in the vicinity of the ridge: no other trees... were growing in the vicinity. From this point the guides desired to conduct the command across the country by Sully's route to the corral formed by him on Heart River in 1864 and thereby cut off from ten to fifteen miles of travel. But the attempted cut off which we have already made having resulted in increasing our march a mile instead of shortening it, the Major Commanding refused to attempt any more and we clung to our old trail reaching our old camp of September 23 about noon. Here we watered our stock and took in a supply of wood and water with the view of camping on the prairie tonight, but the order for so doing was not imparted to the companies until some of their wagons were so far advanced... that it could only be got to them with great difficulty.

OCTOBER 11. Marched 24 miles today. Left camp at 7 A.M. The road ran over a rolling prairie and we made good time but we were not allowed to rest often enough, we only rested once during the forenoon and also in the afternoon. Saw some large herds of antelopes.... We reached our old camp on Heart Creek where we encamped September 22nd about 1 o'clock P.M. [Loaded] wood and water on the wagons preparatory to encamping on the prairie. We are now encamp . . . with only wood and water sufficient to last the night and tomorrow morning with every indication of a storm approaching. The guide tried to persuade the Major Commanding to take the trail made by General Sully and had we done so yesterday morning we could have reached Sully['s] Corral today about 4 P.M. We [could] have been at least ten miles further on our road to Fort Rice and in good camp with plenty of wood, grass, and water. At this camp the engineer's wagon returned and Company "H" 17th Infantry met with serious loss from an accidental fire. Yesterday the command was quite amused by a dog chasing a jack rabbit up and down our train right in among the mules, frightening them considerably. About 4:30 P.M. the train reached a small stream where there was plenty of good grass, water, and wood. . . . The Major Commanding being out antelope hunting, Capt. Bates, being senior officer with the main column, ordered a halt preparatory to going into camp. In the meantime, the Major Commanding, on the ground with bloody hands from his recent slaughter of an antelope, inquired who orders this. When told by Capt. Bates what he had done, he wanted to move back to our old camp of September 23rd, and . . . it was with some difficulty Capt. Bates and Lt. Turnock dissuaded him. Here we supped on bear steak and antelope and relished it exceedingly; the bear resembles pork in flavor and fattiness. Lignite crops out of the bank of the stream and we secured specimens from the trunk of a tree buried in the banks partially carbonized. We burned some on an open fire and from what we observed [we] think [that] it would burn well in a stove.

October 12. Marched 25 miles today. Snowing, blowing, raining, and sleeting. The men and animals suffered for [*sic*] water and wind. This morning broke camp at 7 A.M. and commenced our march through rain and snow. It was so cold that we were obliged to walk very fast to keep warm. We moved so rapidly that the rear guard and flankers had to move in double time. After we had marched an hour or more we struck our old trail and followed it the balance of the day; the sleet and snow . . . ceased about noon, but the wind blew exceedingly cold with piercing effect on the men . . . causing half of the men to ride in the forenoon and the other half in the afternoon. By this means we got along very comfortably arriving at Heart Creek at one o'clock P.M. where Sully corralled his train in 1864. Here we crossed the creek and out on wood and water preparing to make another dry camp on the prairie tonight. After the animals had been watered we pursued our march and about 5 P.M. encamped on the prairie where there was plenty of grass but no wood or water. Heart Butte can now be seen in the distance probably twelve or fifteen miles away. . . . After we crossed the creek, the Adjutant for Major Commanding started out after a herd of antelope which appeared on the bluff in the direction we were going [and] the train moved up to the top of the bluff and stopped, awaiting their return for directions as to when to move on and what course to pursue. Two wagons broke down today, one army wagon and one contract wagon. Some of the horses and mules also gave out from fatigue and exhaustion. We have lost four or six animals from hard work and short feed. Chief Rosser [had] turned out two or three of his [going] to the Yellowstone and found them on his return. . . . We camp on the prairie within a half mile of wood and water notwithstanding. The guide notified the Major Commanding to that effect. Chief Rosser, Capt. Inman, and Mr. Dickinson, who were at the water waiting for the train to come up were quite indignant at the C.O.'s capricious action.

OCTOBER 13. Marched twenty-one miles today. Yesterday was the coldest day we have yet experienced, and this morning it is colder still, but calm, hence we do not suffer as much as yesterday. The best team of horses that was assigned to Company "A" . . . died last night from overwork and irregularity of rations. It is a serious loss to the owner as they were a valuable pair of draught horses. Bright, calm morning cleared up, quite warm in forenoon but cold in P.M. After marching one-half mile came to find water, wood, and grass where we should have encamped last night. Through the idiocy and contrariness of the Commanding Major we encamped just short of it, and the men and animals suffered in consequence, though the guides informed him of the close proximity of the water and wood. Still he pugnaciously directed the camp to be made on the prairie. We left our old trail . . . and did not strike it again until we were within a mile of that noted landmark, Heart Butte, where we crossed the trail and marched close along the base of that wonderful elevation. Mr. Eastman, topographer for the engineers, sketched the noted formation from various points. Some officers and soldiers climbed to its summit from which an extensive view of the surrounding country is had. Numerous large bands of antelope came in view, and some of the mounted officers killed several. Chief Rosser brought in three at one load and Assistant Engineer Jordan brought in one. About 12 o'clock we came to the fine stream of water which I have designated Beaver Creek; the water is very pure. We stop there, eat our lunch, and fill our water kegs. After we had lunched and watered the stock, we proceeded to ascend the steep hill and when on the prairie looked back at Heart Butte standing out boldly from the surrounding prairie. Rode in the ambulance during the greater part of the afternoon. Arrived in camp on the banks of Heart Creek at 4:30 P.M. where there is plenty of wood, grass, and water. Mr. Bigler, clerk in General Hancock's office in St. Paul, Minnesota, and who is acquainted with many of my friends in that city, supped with us tonight.

OCTOBER 14. Marched 25 miles today. Cold and frosty wind blew some last night. On the 11th we passed a fine stream where there was wood and water where we should have camped and made the troops and animals comfortable, but we marched on three or four miles and camped on the prairie. On the 12th we marched within one-half mile of wood and water and stopped short of it: this mismanagement or rather want of management together with the fact that the Maj. Commanding declines to send couriers in to Rice to stop any steamboat that may be passing down condemns him as a man and officer of no capacity, judgment, or common sense whatever. Yesterday I found a bayonet where we watered and a man found a gun bayonet and a full set of equipment which had been lost by a man of Co. "I" on the outward trip.[5] These circumstances show conclusively to my mind that no Indians have been previously on our trail else they would have [kept them]. We left camp around 7 A.M. and crossed Heart Creek, the crossing being very steep [we] found the ordinance very hard pulling. . . . No guide or officer was present to direct us and we followed the old route again. . . . The Major Commanding, his Adjutant, and Chief of Artillery [Campbell] all off hunting. . . .

[Here Irvine, clearly agitated, is virtually impossible to decipher for he is writing often at high speed about orders and counter orders for the daily march. However, in Whistler's report, the incident is described as a "circuitous route."]

SUNDAY, October 15. Marched 27 miles today. Day before yesterday the scouts found two Indian travois running loose on the prairie which

[5]What difference Irvine was attempting to imply between "bayonet" and "gun bayonet" is not clear.

they succeeded in capturing and now have with them. It was understood between Capt. Clarke 17th Infantry, whose company is detailed to accompany the engineers to the mouth of Heart River for the purpose of completing their survey, [that] Chief Rosser and the Major Commanding [made] arrangements . . . so that the Engineering party and escort could withdraw from the main train and encamp at this point while we continued on to Fort Rice, but when the Chief went to see the C.O. this morning he declined to allow the train to depart, but said he would go into camp with them. There we arrived opposite the old camp [*illegible*] into camp continued right on, though his attention was called to the old camp as we passed Chief Rosser having reached camp about noon and seeing that the train was not coming in and learning that the C.O. desired going seven miles further to camp, mounted his horse, and hurriedly galloped to the train and in an excited manner turned out his own team from the train [and] drove them to the rear with a view of taking them back five miles to camp; he sent for the Major Commanding who immediately ordered the train back, thereby entailing an additional march of five miles on the already exhausted men and animals. It rained slightly last night and this morning also, but is [now] mild and calm. . . . A cook and two privates were detailed to report at Headquarters as guard. Broke camp at 7 A.M. Parting with the engineers, leaving them to complete their work while we pursue our winding way to Fort Rice. We took the back track going back at least five miles on our trail of yesterday which we crossed twice after making a mile detour to the northwest we struck out across.

[Remaining entry illegible.]

OCTOBER 16. We marched 21 miles today. BACK AT FORT RICE! Broke camp this morning at 7 A.M. The country over which we have marched is more broken than that traversed yesterday. Consequently our progress has not been so rapid. We came in sight of our trail leading out from Rice about 11 A.M. This morning our tent came near burning from the men carelessly removing the pieces from the canvas and allowing it to fall against the hot stones; while striking it, it caught fire and a small hole was burned in it. Two men of Company "C," 22nd Infantry got lost hunting day before yesterday and made their way into Fort Rice yesterday. They saw the party of nine who came in our camp yesterday, but did not join them for fear that they were Indians. The guide Clement, after being much annoyed by the Adjt. and Lt. commanding the scouts concerning the route to Rice they wishing to dictate or suggest as to its direction, finally brought us into Fort Rice by 4 P.M. This afternoon, when in sight of Fort Rice, the train was stopped and the whole command put in marching array; [C.O.] leading followed by artillery and infantry, the wagon train being escorted by a unit of skirmishers on each flank; the stars and stripes floating from the Headquarters wagon, Company "A" in the rear as guard: the Band, 17th Infantry met [us at the fort]. . . .

Our arrival was quite a surprise to all at Fort Rice, our arrival being twenty-two days ahead of time and marched to and from the Yellowstone having been accomplished in thirty-eight days instead of sixty as was at first contemplated. I learn that a courier started for the station this morning with dispatches announcing the safe return of the expedition. . . . [We] received the mail soon after entering camp, consisting of late papers, letters, et cetera, mine being one letter, good news, all well at home. Our camp is on the west side of the fort near our old grounds. . . . We now await the arrival of a boat to transport us to our proper stations. Learn that three boats are to transfer us to our proper stations, one of which is between here and Grand River. Col. Crittenden kindly invited me to take supper with him, but I excused myself on the grounds of rags and dirt. Many of the officers availed themselves of the proffered hospitalities. Maj. Whistler stopped at our tent for the first time in two weeks past.

OCTOBER 17. Beautiful calm clear morning remaining all day. It seems strange to rest in camp again without the oppression of not knowing what will occur next nor what a moment may bring forth. Busy writing to wife and son [a] letter for the courier Clement who crosses the river for Fort Sully this evening. Contractor Pettis is crossing his trains today over the Missouri preparatory to his return trip to Wadsworth and Abercrombie.[6] The dispatches for the courier were not completed till late this evening, so the courier leaves early tomorrow morning. It is reported that a steamboat is near here. . . . Some anxiety is exhibited by the troops of the Expedition relative to their probable march to Sully and Randolph. We all think we have had a surfeit of marching and are willing to wait for a boat. . . . Arrangements are approaching completion for the disbanding of the Expedition.

---

[6]G. D. Pettis or Pettus died on the 1872 Yellowstone survey, likely from tuberculosis. See *Before Custer*, 52.

OCTOBER 18. Lt. Smith and I rode down the river on horseback to ascertain the proximity of a steamboat. The morning was bright and beautiful and the atmosphere was fresh and invigorating. When near Cannon Ball Butte we started up a fox which soon ran off. After some delay searching for a crossing, we succeeded in passing over the Cannon Ball and proceeding five or six miles below it; scanned the river anxiously with our field glass to the distance of five or six miles down it, hoping to detect the smoke or steam of a boat, but our search was fruitless and we continued. Just as we entered camp, the Engineers and escort came marching up headed by the 17th Infantry Band, having completed their survey to the mouth of the creek. The escort marched to their quarters inside of Fort Rice while the Engineers crossed the Missouri and went into camp on the other side: thus ended the far famed Yellowstone Expedition.

Source: Javan Irvine Papers, South Dakota State Historical Society, Pierre.

Irvine's Letter to His Wife

Fort Rice, Dakota
Tuesday, October 17, 1871

My Dear Wife:

Availing myself of a courier who leaves with dispatches for Sully this evening, I have the pleasure of announcing our safe return to this post yesterday at 3:30 P.M. without the loss or injury of a man of the expedition or the serious loss of property or animals. We—that is to say, those who went there—have seen the Yellowstone, have drank of its refreshing waters, and bathed and sported in the limpid stream.

After we had overcome the greatest obstacles and chief difficulties in our way, we went into camp Sept. 30th on Glendive Creek, Montana Territory, 20 miles from the Yellowstone. The next day it rained slightly, sufficiently indeed to make it a little muddy in consequence of the rain, and not because it was Sunday, we remained in camp as the day was moist. It threw a damper over the Commanding Officer, and strange to say, his brave heart failed him; however, he sent out two guides and six Indian Scouts to the Yellowstone to ascertain the practicability of the route to the river, but strange to say—though not strange for him—he sent no officer with them. In the evening they returned and the rain having made the road somewhat slippery, they pronounced it impracticable to take the heavy train through. . . .

We left camp Monday, Oct. 2nd and arrived on the banks of the Yellowstone about 11 o'clock A.M. on the 3rd day of October. We went through with a train of 17 wagons without any difficulty whatever under command of Capt. Bates, completing the survey in a satisfactory manner. We went into camp on the bank of the river, remaining there until the morning of the 4th when the Engineers having made all the reconnaissance they desired, we turned our faces homewards and reached the camp of the "Army of the Glendive" about 5 o'clock P.M., having marched 28 miles.

The Engineers report a fine practicable route for a railroad, with very easy grades, the road will be shorter and more easily & cheaply constructed than by any other route that they have yet reconnoitered. They are much pleased to find so easy and practicable a route, with very many less difficulties than they were led to suppose existed. . . . I presume Chief Engineer Rosser will make a flaming report of the feasibility of the route, the fine grazing and agricultural district through which it runs, etc., etc., but if it contains as many lies as his letter of commendation to Maj. Whistler does, someone cognizant of the facts should enlighten the financial community on the points involved.[7] For agricultural, grazing, or any other purposes than that of building a railroad, the land is not worth one mill an acre, and no one who has seen it and is at all conversant with the climate would give that price for it. The soil is nothing but sand, no minerals exist save lignite or coal, but a little timber is growing on the river bottoms of a scrubby character, probably sufficient to supply the railroad employees while constructing the road, *not more.* A more forsaken, desolate region cannot be found on the globe; it is only fit for Indians, wolves, and rattlesnakes. From the fact that we have had no difficulties with the Indians, have found a good practicable railroad route, and executed the purposes of the expedition in a much shorter period than was contemplated, the expedition may be deemed a success, but so far as the administration of military affairs connected with it is concerned, it is a decided humbug and farce. It is conceded by every one that we owe it to a kind and watchful Providence that we are

[7] In 1874 a huge national dispute erupted over the value of the Northern Pacific's landholdings. See E. I. Stewart's *Penny-an-Acre Empire in the West.*

all safe back at Fort Rice, for if God had not been on our side and there had been any Indians, we never would have survived.

Maj. Whistler's administration, his whole mind was given to antelope hunting and playing poker; it seemed as if he never gave a serious thought to the expedition, and when he did attempt to give directions and orders, it only created confusion and more marching. The fact is he acted as if he was on a grand fall hunt and was away from his command most of the time for that purpose. He never rode with his main column where he should—one hour at a time during the whole trip—but was on the hunt all the time. Everybody is completely disgusted with his imbecility, incompetency, and mismanagement of his part of the expedition, yet notwithstanding Chief Rosser had repeatedly designated him an "old fool" and spirited him to warmer regions. He gave him a letter thanking him for the *ability, energy*, and *courtesy* with which he had conducted the escort. Such is the manner in which West Point whitewashes its imbecile graduates.

We did not see an Indian during the entire trip, nor did we see signs of more than 4 or 5 and this only once, near the Little Missouri. I account for this, only in this way, the Govt. officials have taken pains, through their agents, to impress the Indians with the idea that our force was four or five times larger than it really was, and advised them to keep away from it; again no buffalo ranges in the region traversed by us, and it is impracticable for Indians to exist in large numbers on the small game which roams over the country as it can only be killed with powder and ball, and this is a scarce article among them. We saw only four buffalo during the entire trip, two of which were killed by our scouts.

We are now encamped on the west side of the fort waiting for a boat to take us to Sully. We learn that the *Silver Lake* is between here and Sully, but Maj. Whistler is striving to make us march to Sully to gratify his childish vanity. We hope a boat may arrive in time to [ferry across] the train for Abercrombie and take us to Sully by Saturday night, but we may have to march it.

Love and kisses to all [etc.]

Source: Javan Irvine Papers, South Dakota State Historical Society, Pierre.

Rosser's Diary

OCTOBER 5. Drove 5 miles and went into camp on Inman's Fork, revised a portion of the line in this vicinity and spent the remainder of the day in camp. Took a bath. Feeling much better.

OCTOBER 6. Returning made some corrections in line near Inman's Fork. Thence camp on to Andrew's Creek. . . . Encamped opposite Sentinel Butte—quite well.

OCTOBER 7. Finished the reversed line to the Little Missouri. Got quite a good line then went up the river on a hunt but found nothing. Went into camp on the Little M where we camped on our way out.

SUNDAY, OCTOBER 8. Took up the line at the head of the badlands and ran it across to the head waters of Heart River. Somewhat improved the line but it is still bad. Found one of my lost horses. Party killed two antelopes. Cold, cloudy and threatening rain.

OCTOBER 9. Rained all night and all day till the afternoon then cleared off. Cold. The day so disagreeable that we did not move. Spent the day working up notes. As the time which separates me from my precious wife and children shortens I become very impatient and delay annoys me.

OCTOBER 10. Soon after leaving camp this A.M. we discovered a grizzly bear and I went in pursuit of it. We overtook it in two miles and had a desperate fight, killed it at last. The weather cold. Moved back [east] 20 miles.

OCTOBER 11. Marching down the Heart River. Cold and disagreeable. Went hunting but saw nothing. . . . Had good water and [wood,] beautiful camp.

OCTOBER 12. Still cold and disagreeable. [Remainder illegible.]

OCTOBER 13. Went out early in the A.M. and rode a short while. Killed 3 antelopes. Had difficulty getting them to the wagons. Party killed 3 others. Encamped on Heart River. Pretty camp. Was cold.

OCTOBER 14. A cold and disagreeable day. Rode down the river on a hunt and killed a large black tail Buck. The train went the wrong way and I turned it back, which threw the Command into quite a rage.[8]

---

[8]The location was likely just east of the "Big Bend" of the Heart River.

SUNDAY, OCTOBER 15. Separated from the command this A.M. Took one company and marched down the [Heart] river to finish some work near the Missouri. This is my 35th birthday and the eighth year of my marriage. Heaven help the future as the past.

OCTOBER 16. Resumed work at 10 A.M. I rode down the river and established camp. Killed one white tail deer and the finest antelope I ever saw. Will finish the survey tomorrow and proceed home.

OCTOBER 17. I finished work 10:30 A.M. and started for Rice. Encamped at Lost Man's Creek. Party had quite a walk. . . . Saw deer and elk but did not kill [any]. Had a good shot at one. At night mail came in. Got several letters, two from precious Lizzy.

OCTOBER 18. Left camp and got into Rice 1 or 2 P.M. and drove immediately to the ferry and by ferrying the men got over by 8 P.M. Had one wagon run off the boat and lost the load of grain. Had it replaced. All pleasant and [party] given me at the fort but I could not attend.

OCTOBER 19. Left the Missouri for home at 10 A.M. . . . Paid all bills at Fort Rice and marched 15 miles and camped on the dry prairie.

OCTOBER 20. Soon after leaving camp the men saw a suspicious horseman ride rapidly over the hills. Hope he will not trouble us. Found water at 7:30 P.M. and released the stock. Made a good march today and camped tonight without water.

OCTOBER 21. At 2 o'clock found a beautiful stream and watered. I am returning via a line 8 or 10 miles further south than Thome's line and the country is much better than his route.

SUNDAY, OCTOBER 22. Got a good start this morning thinking I would get to the James, but found good water in a spring 10 A.M. Thence drove to one of Thome's camps where I found water and grass and encamped at 3 P.M. Will reach the James tomorrow.

OCTOBER 23. A beautiful day, clear and cold. Left camp early and reached Pipestream [Creek] for dinner.[9] It is now a cold, clear sliver of fresh water. Reached the James at 3:20 P.M. Water abundant and good. Encamped for the night.

[9]As the Pipestream flows into the James at Jamestown, Rosser was where the present-day community is or just north of it.

October 24. Left camp early, and by driving very hard reached the Sheyenne at dark. Found things a little out of sorts [at the engineers' winter campsite] but will right them when I get matters in hand.

October 25. A cold, cloudy, disagreeable day. Drove from the Sheyenne to McClure's camp. There I found [Edwin] Johnson [Jr.] and endeavored to learn something of his work but he is so painfully stupid that but little could be learned.[10]

October 26. Took Johnson into Fargo and endeavored to communicate with Linsley and my precious wife, but could not. Took dinner then hired a team to Reno's camp to late supper. Very cold.

October 27. Left Reno's camp at 3:30 a.m. and drove to Oak Lake [Minnesota] by 10 a.m. Found the [telegraph] wire working east and sent dispatches to Mr. Linsley and my family. Left for Brainerd 1 p.m. but was detained at Grand River till 6:30. Thence to Brainerd by 2 a.m.

October 28. Found my door locked when I arrived at 2 a.m. this morning and after knocking violently at the door and failing to rouse my wife I busted the door down and found her sleeping soundly. All are well.

Sunday, October 29. At Brainerd. All pleasant and all quiet.

Source: Rosser Papers, Collection 1171-g-h-j, box 16, Small Special Collections Library, University of Virginia, Charlottesville.

Lafayette Campbell's Diary

October 6. We break camp early and leave Beaver Creek or Inman's fork as the engineers call it. We travel almost a true east course and cut off quite a distance from our former lines of march. We strike our old trail and go along finely. Pass the carcass of one of our dead horses from which the wolves had stripped all the flesh . . . and got into camp in good season.

October 7. We leave camp early and take our old trail over the Bad Lands pass Sully's old battle field . . . see nothing worthy of note except

[10] The son of "retired" NPRR chief engineer Edwin Johnson. He had been with Roberts in 1869.

the wonderful Bad Lands. They are one of the many curiosities of nature. . . . We camp on the Little Missouri.

SUNDAY, OCTOBER 8. We leave our camp on the Little Missouri this morning at an early hour. Col. Bates and I rode about 8 or 10 miles up the Little Missouri in order to strike the trail of a grizzly bear the scouts had seen the evening before. Found the tracks of an enormous bear but was unable to start him out of the almost impenetrable hills and brush. Go on over the worst country I ever saw and finally come out and to our joy see the train. Camp on the Heart River.

OCTOBER 9. We wake up this morning to hear a cold rain splattering on our tents. Get up and go to breakfast and fixed the old man in the notion of staying in camp all day. . . . He finally consents to remain so we all go to our tents and I go to sleep and try and while the lonely hours away. Rain ceases along towards noon and we have a fine clear sunset. I retire early.

OCTOBER 10. This morning was first quite cool [with] a big white frost. Leave camp at 7 and cross the hard waters of Heart River to travel on the east side of the river. We make quite a cut off on our former trail; pass the prominent and curious Butte called the Malakoff. I gave it the name. We strike the creek above an old camp and go into camp at quite a good place. 4 antelopes and one grizzly bear today.

OCTOBER 11. We leave camp early today and march straight for the hills on Heart River. Pass over a very poor and uninteresting country. It is all burnt off, which of course increases the barren aspects of the country. . . . Get wood and water and go on to our camp which we find in a cold barren place on the plains without anything to shelter us from the wind.

OCTOBER 12. We leave camp early in a snow storm and find it a miserably cold day. All the buffalo [over]coats appeared this morning. I am ahead today with Genl. Rosser. I find him to be a very agreeable companion, a fine engineer and the [illegible] stamp of the southern gentleman. . . . We can see the famous Heart Butte.

OCTOBER 13. I left camp early this morning with Genl. Rosser. We go down the creek to try and kill elk or black-tailed deer. [We] could find none of either, but found large quantities of antelope. Killed six of them and had a devil of a time in getting them into the train as my horse could only carry three. Rosser got three on his horse; we passed the beautiful Little Spring Creek, magnificent water.

OCTOBER 14. A fine morning. I go down Heart River with Lt. Dougherty and Genl. Rosser. We find a beautiful valley of considerable width with but little game and I hunted all day without finding anything more than some deer which did not give us a chance to get them. Our larder is well supplied with antelope. . . . Magnificent today.

SUNDAY, OCTOBER 15. This morning we leave Heart River and the Engineers and strike across the country for Rice. All anxious to get into the Post and of course they march right along. *Even Capt. Irvine pulls out at a fine gait* [emphasis added]. We cross a fine rolling prairie infinitely through back country.

OCTOBER 16. This morning we go on in good spirits knowing that we will get to Rice today. So all of us go to the limit of human endurance. Our guide Clement took us into Rice as straight as an arrow. Got to the Post about 4 P.M. and we are all very glad to see it! Go into camp just outside of the garrison.

Source: Collection no. 10435, American Heritage Center, University of Wyoming, Laramie.

Newspaper Coverage

THE NORTHERN PACIFIC RAILROAD IN THE YELLOWSTONE VALLEY

A telegram from Maj.-Gen. HANCOCK, dated at St. Paul, Minn., on the 24th of October, thus announces the rapid and successful survey from the West as far as the Powder River:[11]

"On the 16th inst. the expedition to the mouth of the Powder River was within one day of Fort Rice on its return. Country found much better than was expected. The engineer in charge of the surveying party is said to be delighted with the country for its railroad facilities, and considers his operations eminently successful. The party saw no Indians. Game was in great abundance. No men were lost. A few mules and horses worn out, and some wagons broken down. They struck the Yellowstone

[11]Note that even at this late date the assumption was that the surveying expedition would reach the Yellowstone at the Powder River, not Glendive Creek, which was some 40 miles to the north. This is a real comment on the faulty map everyone was using.

a short distance below the mouth of Powder River—distance about 280 miles.[12] The trip was made in twenty-three days."

Source: New York Times, *October 26, 1871.*

The Yellowstone Expedition
A Good Railroad Route Claimed to Have Been Found across the Bad Lands

Some of the members of the exploring expedition across the country from the Missouri to the Yellowstone, sent out by the Northern Pacific Railroad Company to survey a route for the road, have returned to this city [Saint Paul]. From David R. Livingston, connected with the citizens' train of this exploring party, the particulars are obtained which are given below.

General Rosser and his party of engineers left Fort Rice on the 9th day of September accompanied by seven companies of infantry and two Gatling guns under the command of General Whistler. [Businessmen] Messrs. N. P. Clark of St. Cloud and Mayall and Wilder of St. Paul furnished transportation for the expedition, having sixty-five men and about as many teams in their employ.

After leaving Fort Rice this expedition virtually followed General Sully's trail of 1864, shortening it in many places, and crossing and recrossing it many times before the Bad Lands were reached. . . .

General Rosser has not yet returned, but he is said to have given it as his opinion that the whole route is feasible for a railroad, and being a competent engineer, his judgment can be relied on.

The engineers, citizens, and soldiers all declare the trip to have been one of extreme hardship, and the number of anathemas hurled at that locality generally is said to have been innumerable as well as extremely strong in point of emphasis. General Whistler is said to have exhibited some considerable scarcity of piety, especially when he had no water for drinking purposes, considering his wants in this respect were limited.[13] Successful attempts were made in various places in boring for water.

[12] The 280 miles represent *odometer* or walking miles—including Whistler's misdirections—and not railroad miles from the mouth of Heart River.

[13] Although the writer's language is often difficult to follow, this sentence was not confusing to nineteenth-century readers and meant that Whistler was drinking heavily. The source of this "inside" information was Rosser, his way to even the score with Whistler.

The party was more fortunate than Sully's expedition in the matter of wood, the teamsters loading their empty wagons with fuel to be used in emergencies, thereby avoiding the necessity of using buffalo chips, which showed commendable foresight, for the combustible chips were unusually scarce on account of the prairie fires which have recently swept over the country. Forage was also scarce, and the horses were limited to seven pounds [of grain] a day which was severe on horse-flesh, and many animals died on the trip.

Mr. Livingston says that on the first of October, while the expedition was enjoying its Sunday's rest on the Cottonwood River,[14] about twenty-five miles east of the Yellowstone, a young man named Walters started out prospecting for gold, and when about three miles from camp he sunk a hole and after getting down about four feet, found splendid diggings and the gold quite coarse. Two days after, Mr. Livingston and John Crandall found gold-bearing quartz on the low bars of the Yellowstone.[15]

Mr. Livingston afterward procured a pick and a shovel, and found fine float gold in different places close to the water's edge. Livingston and Walters are both old miners. Col. Inman, who is a great favorite with the citizens, was very successful in securing a piece of gold-bearing quartz, as well as a great number of agates.

No Indians were seen during the whole time this party were on their journey, and as there were a number of old Indian hunters along with them, there is reason to believe they knew nothing of the movement of this expedition, as no signs whatever of their presence could be discovered. When the broad and fertile plateau that flanks the Yellowstone was reached, fresh Indian trails were seen, all pointing up the valley. There is a likelihood, therefore, that if any attempts were to be made by the savages to obstruct the passage of railroad engineers, it would be to throw themselves in the way of Col. Milnor Roberts' party, which is said to be on its way eastward over the Rocky Mountains. When Gen. Rosser started out on this survey it was with the presumption that he would form a Junction with Milnor Roberts on the Yellowstone, but he had probably not got along as rapidly through Montana as he had expected. At all events, nothing was seen or heard of him by Rosser's party.

---

[14]As there is no Cottonwood River today, the stream was likely Beaver Creek near Wibaux, Montana.

[15]Where "gold" stories came from is unknown. Certainly no other source mentions them. Was Inman the source for some reason?

General Rosser was quite sick for two days on this journey, near the close of the march to the westward, but he fortunately recovered sufficiently to enable him to make his preliminary surveys very complete and satisfactory.

Source: Saint Paul Weekly Press, *November 9, 1871.*

A special dispatch to the *Washington Chronicle* from Jay Cooke & Co. announces that the Northern Pacific surveying party, recently engaged in locating the line from the mouth of the Heart River, in Dakota, to the Yellowstone valley, has returned to Fort Rice. General Rosser, engineer in charge, reports that he has found an excellent and very direct line, striking the Yellowstone at the mouth of Glendive Creek. He reports finding coal in abundance along the surveyed line from the head of Heart River to the Yellowstone crossing; the valleys well timbered, well watered, and good soil. Work is now progressing on the Northern Pacific road, west of Red River.

Source: Army and Navy Journal, *November 4, 1871.*

PART III

Aftermath

CHAPTER 9

The Surveys Return
April through December

The successful return of both Yellowstone surveys had to have brought sighs of relief from Jay Cooke, Gregory Smith, the army hierarchy, the White House, and every Northern Pacific director, manager, and investor. There is little doubt that the company's decision makers and the army's top personnel had hesitated before undertaking the surveys. Concern over the possibility of triggering an Indian incident without having fielded sufficient forces and surveyors being killed horrified the army every bit as much as the railroad. No one had to be told that significant fighting, no matter the outcome, would scare off new investment.

In fact, rumors fanned by economic and geographical Northern Pacific opponents led to scare headlines, with the *Sioux City Daily Journal* being a prime example. Later it would be called "yellow journalism," but these rumors were reprinted around the country and, as journalists have always known, ax murders sell newspapers, not reports predicting good weather. Thus those supporting the Northern Pacific could only hold their breath and wait . . . and wait . . . and wait through October.

Even without Indians, the eastern survey's outcome could have been far worse had it been realized the degree to which existing maps were faulty. Many, including Colonel Stanley, thought that the survey would strike the Powder River. What if General Sully's lead scout, Little Black Foot, *had* been with the column when the survey reached Beaver Creek? And then let us assume he had taken them up, not across the stream. This route, to the Beaver-O'Fallon Creek divide and then the mouth of Powder River, would have taken at least a month or more under Whistler's leadership and Clement's "scouting."[1] Running low on supplies, the expedition would likely have limped into Fort Buford, a complete failure.[2] The 1872 eastern survey's experience in and adjacent to the O'Fallon Creek valley indicates the problems the 1871 survey would have faced taking this route. While this is hypothetical, ironically the eastern survey did exactly the right thing, although quite possibly for the wrong reason.

Regardless, the eastern survey did discover a route through the Badlands (still used today), Sitting Bull and his followers were not to be seen, and—a marvelous future bonus—the survey discovered huge coal deposits.

While there had been few questions regarding the western survey, it too was successful. The Yellowstone River was a known commodity. Which side of the river to build on, where bridges would be needed, the Yellowstone's actual drop per mile, and so forth were technical issues, at times difficult, but they had no strategic impact on future construction.

With the completion of the eastern survey, Minnesota construction began its final disastrous months. Routes were built that proved economically useless (to Breckinridge), the Sauk Rapids to Brainerd spur lay dormant, a route to Canada paralleling the Red River began construction with no possibility of immediate business, and the Thompson Junction–Brainerd/Staples route was shoddily *rebuilt*. In fact, this section was not finished (again) until late August 1872 when precious cash was in short supply.[3]

This brief chapter consists of newspaper stories that reflect the unwarranted optimism of management and then the realization that reaching the Red River would be—as the Duke of Wellington said after Waterloo—"a near thing," except that this "near thing" failed. A brief story concerning the Vermont Central nicely illustrates the scope of Gregory Smith's eastern management obligations and with only the tiniest of staffs. As for the quality of construction, a description of an accident and its causes involving high-level construction and NP personnel reveals the implications of shoddy work. Finally there is the short story of a grisly accident, which the squeamish reader can choose to avoid.

[1] In 1872 Rosser hired Pierre Bottineau as the railroad's and his personal scout, a clear reflection of his opinion of Clement's abilities. See *Before Custer*, 41.

[2] The 1872 eastern survey did go to the Powder River, looking for a shortcut from Bismarck to the Yellowstone, but was unable to find one. See Lubetkin, *Before Custer*, 196.

[3] The railroad's inability to reach Bismarck in 1872, as much as anything, was caused by this problem and overall substandard management. For details see *Before Custer*, 281.

Progress and Pipe Dreams

The Progress of Railroad Construction

An Army of Men at Work upon the Several Lines of the Road

The people of this state [Minnesota] will be pleased to learn that work upon the several great railroad lines is being pushed forward with wonderful rapidity and almost unparalleled energy. The forces engaged are of greater numerical strength than ever before, and more will be accomplished in the way of railroad building than in any former season. . . .

On the line of the Northern Pacific Railroad, between Thompson and Brainerd, some 3,500 men are employed in ballasting the track and putting it into the best of order.[4] Steam shovels are employed at all needed places on this portion of the line, and the track from point to point will be placed in excellent condition at the earliest date practicable.

The track has already been completed twenty-seven miles west of Brainerd and fully ready for the iron,[5] and from that point till Otter Tail Junction, 1,500 men are daily at work . . . and the junction with the St. Paul & Pacific and Otter Tail. This portion of the line will be graded and fully prepared for the reception of the superstructure by the first of August. About 800 men are also scattered along the line between Otter Tail Junction and Red River who are at present only partially employed on account of the recent determination by the Board of Directors to make additional surveys in the hope of finding a more feasible route than that heretofore adopted.[6]

St. Paul and Pacific under NP Control

While the Northern Pacific people are bending their energies to the accomplishment of the herculean task before them, and triumphing over all the varied natural obstacles in their way, the officers of the St. Paul and Pacific are running out the giant arm under their control with the speed which must demonstrate its ability to monopolize the traffic which is springing up between the great and comparatively unknown Northwest and this city [St. Paul], before the close of the current season.[7] Over 700

---

[4]In short, redoing the work from the just-ended winter.

[5]By "track being completed," the writer meant road bed, not track.

[6]The likely reason for the change was that the original line was too close to the St. Paul & Pacific to offer any chance of profitability for either, to say nothing of overlapping land grants.

[7]By the time this was written, the St. Paul & Pacific's decision making lay in an executive committee led by Moorhead.

men are employed between the present western terminus at Benson and the objective point on the Red River—a distance of eighty miles. The grading is complete on fifty miles . . . and track laying will begin next week. . . . [This] line will undoubtedly strike that stream at the mouth of the Bois des Sioux, which empties into the Red River at or near Breckinridge.[8] . . . The branch line of the St. Paul and Pacific road extending northwesterly from Sauk Rapids to Otter Tail Junction is receiving the attention which its importance deserves.[9] The grading will be finished between the points named by the first of July, and the road is expected to be in readiness for the operation of trains thereupon in three months' time.

Source: St. Paul Weekly Press, *June 1, 1871.*

From the Line of the Northern Pacific

Road Bed Graded to Detroit Lake

EIGHTEEN HUNDRED MEN AT WORK

ON THE LINE WEST OF OAK LAKE

To C. M. Loring . . . we are indebted for whatever interest our readers may find in the following: He informs us that Messrs. Norris and Murray are at present holding the outposts on the line of the Northern Pacific. They are at work with a force of 300 men, west of Buffalo River. Oak Lake lies about twenty miles east of Buffalo River. Between the two points 1,500 men are engaged, and the work is progressing favorably. From Buffalo River to the supposed crossing of Red River (where the Northwestern Construction Company's contract terminates), the distance is about thirty miles. The exact point at which the line will cross Red River is not yet definitely known. A party of engineers are now engaged in establishing the line between the Missouri and Red rivers, and as soon as their work is completed—as it will be within sixty days—the point of crossing will be fixed upon.[10]

---

[8]The Red River is formed by the merger of the Bois des Sioux and Otter Tail Rivers, Breckinridge's location. The 1870 population was in the low hundreds, the thousand population number not crossed until the 1890s. The reason: while historically ox-cart trade from Canada had come here, when paddle wheelers began serving Fargo-Moorhead, Breckinridge's trading collapsed. See WPA, *Minnesota,* and Wikipedia.

[9]In my opinion this construction was strategically wasteful. By putting this ahead of the Sauk Rapids–Brainerd route, the Northern Pacific forfeited its future.

[10]Charles Loring (1833–1922) was a Maine native, too sickly to follow his father to sea, who moved first to Chicago and then to the Minneapolis–St. Paul area. A merchant

The road bed is graded to Detroit Lake, within five miles of Oak Lake, and the iron is laid to the crossing of Crow Wing River, twenty-one miles west of Brainerd.[11]

Grasshoppers are reported in abundance throughout the entire section of country, and fears are entertained that crops will be seriously injured by them. In the vicinity of Fort Abercrombie [North Dakota], they are said to be devouring everything before them. Their course seems to be northerly.

Source: Saint Paul Pioneer, *July 19, 1871.*

Northern Pacific Regular Trains

Daily passenger trains will commence running from Duluth to Crow Wing River Crossing [approximately twenty miles west of Brainerd], September first [four and a half months following the spring thaw].[12] The time table is not out but will be published in due season. . . . Until the 1st prox., nothing but irregular iron trains will be run over the road.

Source: Duluth Minnesotian, *August 19, 1871.*

The Vermont Central Railroad

The *Springfield* (Mass.) *Republican* contains the following deserved complimentary allusions to this railway and its managers: Dying [1858], Mr. John Smith (one of the original projectors of the Vermont Central) left his property to his sons J. Gregory and Worthington C. Smith. . . .

This "Central," of which J. Gregory Smith is President, now operates with [743] miles of railroad. . . .[13] The car [manufacturing] department alone employs, exclusive of machinists, about 420 hands at $22,000 per month [$52.38]. The company has its main shops in St. Albans [Vermont], with branches or repair shops at Ogdensburg [New York], Rutland [Vermont], and Waterloo (Canada) . . . by the means of the Northern

businessman, his varied career included dry goods, railroad and telegraph interests, and later electrical power distribution. He cofounded and successfully operated one of Minneapolis's earliest mills, a company that decades later became General Mills. Wikipedia.

[11]The following year (1872) the Northern Pacific abandoned Oak Lake and instead selected present-day Audubon for a stop.

[12]Before the spring thaw in April, trains were running to just west of this point. In short, it had taken over four months to repair the tracks.

[13]The Vermont Central owned or controlled this actual number by year's end. Jones, *The Central Vermont Railway*, 1:83.

Transportation Co.'s boats [on the Great Lakes] and the Northern Pacific Railroad, [it] is extending its lines from shore to shore of the continent.

Source: Duluth Minnesotian, *August 26, 1871.*

Progress of the Great Northern Pacific Road

Messrs. JAY COOKE & CO., the financial agents of the Northern Pacific Railroad, furnish the following gratifying facts regarding the prosperous progress of this enterprise:

The track is now about completed across the State of Minnesota, 250 miles; the grade being wholly finished, and the track-layers approaching the Red River at a rate of three miles a day. Regular trains are running over the completed sections.

In the latter part of September contracts were let for the construction of the Dakota Division, extending 200 miles westward, from the crossing of the Red River to the crossing of the Missouri, in central Dakota. . . . In the meantime, a section of sixty-five miles is under construction between the Columbia River and Puget Sound, in the Washington Territory, where track-laying is rapidly progressing.

It will be remembered that the Northern Pacific last year purchased both the Main line and Branch of the St. Paul and Pacific Road. Within the last three months, the Main line has been completed, through a noble [agricultural] country, to the Red River at Breckinridge. Contracts were last week let for the construction of the Branch, from its present terminus at Watab [some five miles north of Sauk Rapids], on the Mississippi River, seventy miles northward to Brainerd, where it will join the trunk line of the Northern Pacific.[14] Finally, contracts have been let for the construction of a branch road from St. Cloud (seventy-five miles north of St. Paul) to Pembina on the British [border], a distance of 375 miles.[15] This line is

[14]This section was not built in 1872, a strategic disaster that triggered the Northern Pacific's legal default of the St. Paul & Pacific. One of the reasons that it was not built, I will speculate, is that "inside" investors thought it would diminish the value of their Duluth real estate. A decade later James J. Hill acquired control of the SP&P, making it the cornerstone of his Great Northern, the dominant northwestern railroad system in the twentieth century.

[15]Typifying William Moorhead's pigheadedness was his 1872 decision to pour cash into this unneeded extension, Red River paddle wheelers not being a strategic business threat. Moorhead's actions—and Cooke shares much of the blame for not questioning him early on—diverted monies from the Watab-Brainerd route and the Red to the Missouri Rivers. See *Before Custer*, 97n, 281.

to be completed within fifteen months of the present time. It will drain the richest portions of the Red River Valley, open direct communication with British settlements of Winnipeg and the rich Saskatchewan Basin. It will also serve as the southeastern arm of the Northern Pacific Road, reaching to St. Paul and Minneapolis, and thus connection with Chicago and the trunk lines to the east.

The completion of these contracts will give the Northern Pacific Company, at the close of next year, 900 miles of road . . . and will bring to the Northern Pacific the large and profitable traffic of Montana, and the Government transportation [to military posts and reservations] of the upper Missouri. It is anticipated that this business alone, without waiting for through trade [from the Pacific], will meet the interest of the cost of the finished portion of the Road. The Hudson's Bay Company has already leased docks and warehouses in Duluth, preparatory to doing the whole of its immense business over the Northern Pacific line.

Settlers are occupying the lands along the route with surprising and gratifying rapidity. About the 1st of January next [1872] nearly two million acres [from federal land grants] of the finest lands in Minnesota will be placed on the market.[16] . . . The Company's lands west of Minnesota, through Dakota, prove to be of superb character, and will speedily come onto the market.

Source: New York Times, *October 10, 1871.*

Saint Paul and Pacific

The formal opening of the completed main line of this railroad [the Saint Paul and Pacific] to Breckinridge [Minnesota], on the Red River of the North, took place on the 26th [of October]. The line from St. Paul to Breckinridge is 216 miles long. . . . The road is owned by the same parties who control the Northern Pacific, though the two organizations are yet entirely distinct, and one is not responsible for the debts of the other.

Source: Railroad Gazette, *November 11, 1871.*

[16]Ultimately only a tiny number of Minnesota acres went on sale in 1872. See *Before Custer,* 255–62.

Construction Problems

Private Letter to Jay Cooke, August 12, 1871

"One perplexing thing about the road east of Brainerd," [A. B. Nettleton] continued, "is this: portions of tracks over or near lakes continue to sink.[17] A sink occurred near Mud Lake on Thursday [August 10] and Linsley was forced to build half a mile of track round the break to enable the [Northern Pacific's] directors to get through."[18]

Source: Jay Cooke: Financier of the Civil War, *2:257.*

The Northern Pacific
King Winter Master of the Situation

Advices were received in the city [St. Paul] on Thursday evening, stating that snow and frost had overtaken the laborers on the Northern Pacific, and officially put a stop to further proceedings. There remains eleven miles of iron to be laid before reaching the Red River, and the contractors were straining every nerve to accomplish that distance, when the recent snow storm set in. They have now about sixteen inches of snow, on a level, while the cuts are drifted full; water tanks along the line are frozen up, and several locomotives are also frozen up and standing upon the tracks at various points. There seems to be little prospect of striking another blow until next spring.

Source: Saint Paul Pioneer, *November 25, 1871.*

---

[17]The "informant" was Alvred Bayard Nettleton (1838–8/10/1911). An Ohio cavalry officer, brevetted brigadier general, and Oberlin College graduate, Nettleton became a trusted assistant to Cooke, frequently acting as Cooke's "eyes." He handled delicate situations, including tracking down Gregory Smith and forcing him to sign a letter of resignation. See Hunt, *Brevet Generals in Blue*; Malone et al., *Dictionary of American Biography*; *National Cyclopedia of American Biography,* 6:532; and *New York Times* obituary.

[18]The likely location Nettleton was referring to is between the hamlets of Tamarack and Wright, almost on the Aitkin–Carlton County line, some 35–40 miles west of Thomson Junction.

R.R. Accident on the Northern Pacific

Geo. A. Brackett and D. C. Shepard Seriously Injured
Special to the Tribune.

BRAINERD, Dec. 11.—Last night a party of gentlemen connected with the N.P.R.R. and [the] Northwestern Construction Company were returning east from the end of the track [near Moorhead] to Detroit Lake, when the box car in which they were ran off the track and turned bottom side up, some twenty miles west of Detroit Lake, injuring some of the party seriously.

D. C. Shepard had his arm dislocated at the shoulder;[19] Geo. A. Brackett had his leg broken above the knee, and A. O. Canfield received severe injuries on the head and face.[20] As soon as the accident was known here, an engine with Dr. Thayer on board was dispatched to the scene.[21] The wounded were cared for as well as circumstances would permit, and were brought to the construction's company's coach [mobile office], which was at Detroit Lake, and thence to Brainerd. . . . General Spaulding, R. L. Harris, and several other gentlemen were on board the car, but none except those mentioned were injured.[22] No blame is attached to any one on account of the accident. The train was backing [up] and the car for some reason ran off the tracks.

Source: Minneapolis Daily Tribune, *December 12, 1871.*

[19]David Chauncey Shepard (1828–1920) was a civil engineer and longtime Minnesota construction executive. In 1871 he was general manager of the Northwestern Construction Company, which held the NP's lead Minnesota contract. Later in his career Shepard would partner with Fendall "Jack" Winston (1849–1928), Tom Rosser's brother-in-law. For Winston see *National Cyclopedia of American Biography,* 36:130.

[20]Earlier reports had erroneously indicated that it was Canfield's father, Northern Pacific Board member Thomas H. Canfield, who had been injured.

[21]Most likely Dr. Charles P. Thayer (1842–ca. 1915) or his father, Dr. Samuel W. Thayer (1817–82). Another paper, the *Minneapolis Daily Tribune* of December 14, specifically states both father and son were involved in treating the injured. Malone et al., *Dictionary of American Biography* for father; both mentioned at 1906 Surveyors Reunion and in *Jay Cooke's Gamble,* 290–91.

[22]Robert Harris (1830–94) was with Northern Pacific for five years. He replaced Henry Villard, who had resigned following two and a half years of fiscal mismanagement that bankrupted the Northern Pacific in its race to become the second transcontinental railroad. While there is no *L* in Harris's name, one cannot help but wonder if Robert and Robert L. are the same person. Northern Pacific histories and Wikipedia.

Accident on the NPRR

The train to which the accident occurred was composed of thirty-nine flat cars, one box car, and two locomotives. They had been out to the end of the track to carry materials needed in the construction of the road and were backing into Oak Lake. The box car was attached to the locomotives, and in it were fifteen to twenty gentlemen. Mr. Brackett says that the accident was caused by the rails spreading (*owing to the scarcity of spikes, they had not been fully secured* [emphasis added]) under the locomotives, and as soon as the ponderous engines were thrown from the track, the box car was also thrown off, and a general smash up followed in which the caboose was thrown down an embankment of ten feet, totally wrecked and left bottom side up.[23]

Mr. Brackett's injuries consist of a compound fracture of the left thigh, involving somewhat the knee joint. His face was also seriously bruised. Mr. Shepard suffered dislocation of the right arm and shoulder, and was otherwise injured, though to what extent cannot yet be fully determined, owing to its swollen condition. It is possible that the shoulder is fractured. Both the gentlemen sustained severe bruises in addition to the injuries given. Their injured limbs were properly set and the wounds dressed, as were those of Mr. Canfield, which were of a serious and painful nature. His nose was terribly cut and his face and hands badly bruised.

Source: St. Paul Pioneer *(undated), cited in* Helena Daily Herald, *December 30, 1871.*

Beheading by a Railroad

A horrible accident occurred at Hinckley [Minnesota] on the L.S. & M.R.R. [Lake Shore & Mississippi Railroad] on Tuesday night last, at about midnight. We would premise that when Conductor Crawford's freight train passed there in the afternoon, an Indian known as "Horace," and also as "Greeley," from his putative white father, and said to be the principal man of the Kettle River band of Chippewa, was noticed by Mr. Crawford to be badly intoxicated. Conductor Bond's up-freight train, heavily loaded, which came along at midnight, found some difficulty at

---

[23]A "scarcity of spikes" reflected both the contractor's and the Northern Pacific's desperation to build regardless of the consequences. It is unclear whether the writer is using "caboose" and "box car" interchangeably.

first in making the ascending grade north of Hinckley and had, after starting, to back down again; when more steam being raised it put out and passed successfully northward.

After it had gone awhile, one of the employees at Pulle's Dining House was attracted by a squaw's excited motions to where an Indian apparently laid across the tracks: he caught hold of him by the heels and drew him on one side: when he was astonished and horrified to find that he *had no head!* Investigation showed the man's head to be lying on the other side of the rail; and on reviewing all the circumstances the conclusion was reached that the Indian had laid down on the track just after Bond's train had made its first venture northward, and when it backed down, his head and shoulders being on each side of the rail, he was instantaneously beheaded by the car wheels. In the darkness of the night the train hands had not observed him and were his innocent executioners.

Source: Duluth Minnesotian, *November 4, 1871.*

CHAPTER 10

Conclusions

For a company that was in the first phases of serious financial trouble and could no longer afford to make strategic errors, the eastern and western Yellowstone surveys were manna from heaven. "You see," Jay Cooke or Governor Smith could say in late 1871, "the Indian issue is concluded once and for all. We will not be bothered by them, and we now have a direct route across Dakota to the Yellowstone. The Bozeman Pass is now surveyed, and we can put the finishing engineering touches on a 'line of survey' from Lake Superior to Puget Sound next year."

Equally important, other than bruised feelings and frostbite, there had been no significant injuries or a single death on the two surveys. For early 1872 the Northern Pacific would almost always have clear sailing. At the height of his congressional and public relations and with his bank still seemingly impregnable, Cooke retained his clout. Amazingly far-sighted in some respects, Cooke had instantly recognized Yellowstone Park's tourist potential. His relationship with Nathanial P. Langford, a Montana vigilante, went back to at least 1869, for Langford's name appears on the list of those who participated in the "survey" that left St. Paul that summer. Cooke and Langford were to work closely together in the following two years.[1]

Cooke had also lent his political weight to the congressional financing of Frederick V. Hayden's explorations and personally paid for the artist Thomas Moran's joining Hayden. In the winter of 1871–72 he arranged for Moran's gigantic painting of Yellowstone Falls to be hung, on short notice, in the Capitol's Rotunda, then rammed the creation of Yellowstone National Park through Congress.

---

[1] *St. Paul Weekly* Press, July 15, 1869; Oberholtzer, *Cooke,* 2:316; Haines, *Yellowstone,* 1:105.

Later that same winter, when Senator Henry Wilson of Massachusetts (selected as Grant's vice president months later) commented on the worthlessness of Northern Pacific land, Cooke stated, "We will smash him flatter than a pancake," and he soon received a groveling public apology.[2] When the colorful but militarily incompetent Massachusetts congressman Nathanial P. Banks, chairman of the House Pacific Railroads Committee, called for an investigation into shoddy Northern Pacific construction, the Cooke brothers chewed him up as rapidly as Stonewall Jackson had in the Shenandoah Valley in 1862.[3] Ultimately Banks let his committee's report be written by Cooke business associate and friend "Uncle Samuel" Wilkeson.[4]

Cooke's bond sales were never enough to meet Northern Pacific costs. After the 1871 surveys, they reached their peak, occasionally exceeding $1 million a month, decreasing after news of the Banks investigation, and rising again to near $1 million in mid-1872.

On December 31, a telegram from D. C. Linsley told Cooke that Moorhead had been reached, but only the sound of a railroad whistle went as far as the Red River. Predictably, Cooke soon learned that completed track was 1.5 miles away.[5] As to trusting Smith, this was the straw that broke Cooke's back. By mid-June Cooke had forced Smith's resignation. Nevertheless, the success of both Yellowstone surveys gave the Northern Pacific ample momentum to continue construction and engineering surveys while its financial problems remained hidden.

Yet, had the eastern survey failed to find a route through the Badlands to the Yellowstone, had the entire expedition reached the Yellowstone near the Powder River, or had Sitting Bull attacked either survey and caused significant casualties, one can only speculate on how long the Northern Pacific could have survived. After all, 1872 was an election year and Grant was running scared, two campaign issues being the treatment

---

[2]Larson, *Jay Cooke,* 362.

[3]Banks (1816–94) had been a popular Massachusetts governor. For his military achievements, or lack thereof, see *Generals in Blue* among other Civil War sources. Also *Dictionary of American Biography,* most encyclopedias covering that period, and Wikipedia.

[4]Oberholtzer, *Cooke,* 2: 322–23. Henry D. Cooke (1821–81) was a card-playing crony of the president, and Grant had appointed him the District of Columbia's first governor (mayor). See numerous references in Oberholtzer, *Cooke*; Larson, *Dictionary of American Biography*; *National Cyclopedia of American Biography* (10:510); and the *Philadelphia Inquirer* obituary and editorial on February 25, 1881.

[5]Oberholtzer, *Cooke,* 2:262; *Railroad Gazette,* January 6, 1872.

of Indians and his support for the privately owned Northern Pacific. It seems unlikely that Grant would have taken the position he did *after* his reelection and committed more than 10 percent of the army's infantry. With the Northern Pacific fighting off financial collapse, it probably would have halted temporarily at Fargo-Moorhead.

And if no eastern path had been found in 1871, would another survey have been sent looking for an alternative route through the Badlands? There had always been a second strategic option from Fargo-Moorhead, with track angling northwest to reach the Missouri River above Fort Buford (the Yellowstone-Missouri confluence). This approach stayed north of the Missouri until central Montana (Fort Benton), the route that the Great Northern was to take twenty years later. Would Grant then have supported Cooke and the Northern Pacific? Considering how rapidly he ditched Cooke and the Northern Pacific in 1873, Grant's most favorable 1872 decision likely would have been something of a face-saving nature.

Ironically, Northern Pacific failure in western Dakota and eastern Montana would likely have prevented Jay Cooke & Company's bankruptcy in 1873 and the worst of that year's Panic. The lack of falling financial dominos might have prevented the 1880s emergence of both J. Pierpont Morgan and James J. Hill. Whether Sioux independence would have ended with a whimper or a Custer/Little Big Horn–like bang can only be speculated upon, but one can rest assured that the end was near.

With all these *What Ifs* of American expansionism, one logical answer is as good as another. What we know is that the Yellowstone surveying expeditions *did* find a route through the Badlands, the absence of hostile Indians was misunderstood, and the Northern Pacific had been given another year to move forward.

APPENDIX A

Early Railroads

Early Locomotives (by 1846)

The greatest speed of [British inventor Richard] Trevithick's engine (ca. 1801) was five miles an hour.[1] The ordinary speed of George Stephenson's Killingwood engine, in 1814, was four miles an hour. In 1825 Mr. Nicholas Wood, in his work on railways, takes the standard [to] six miles an hour, drawing forty tons on a level, and so confident that he has gauged the power of the locomotive, that he thinks it right to say "that nothing could do more harm towards the adoption of railways than the adoption of such nonsense as that we shall see locomotive engines traveling at the rate of twelve, sixteen, eighteen, and twenty mph."[2]

The promulgator of such nonsense was George Stevenson.[3] . . . Before the end of [1829] Stephenson got with his *Rocket* [weighing 4½ tons] reached a speed of 29½ mph, carrying a net load of 9½ tons. In 1831 his engines were able to draw 90 tons on a level of 20 mph. [Today, i.e., 1846, the top speed is 75 MPH and the working speed 55 MPH.][4]

---

[1]Richard Trevithick (1771–1833), British engineer, inventor, and developer of the first high-pressure steam engine. *Encyclopedia of North American Railroads,* 1064–65.

[2]Until the time of this 1871 article, there was a general consensus that British railroad engines were superior in design. However, American engineers had surpassed the British in far more rapid production with simpler, less expensive designs. In 1871, for example, Baldwin alone had produced slightly more than one locomotive a day (Sundays excluded), a remarkable number. See Brown, *The Baldwin Locomotive Works.*

[3]George Stephenson (1781–1848), father of the British locomotive and railroad industry, began as an engineer for a large colliery, attempting to develop better ways to ship coal. *Encyclopedia of North American Railroads,* 1031–33.

[4]Although not stated, the 1846 weight was in the 25-ton range, a number that U.S. locomotives wouldn't reach until just before the Civil War. Excluding the tender, the average weight of the standard Baldwin engine used by the Northern Pacific in the early 1870s was 32½ tons. See Brown, *The Baldwin Locomotive Works.*

. . . Within the last seven years the London and Birmingham directors considered that 20 miles an hour was enough, and had they been free from competition and supported by public opinion they no doubt would have adhered to that rate from the conscientious conviction that a higher speed was incompatible with economy and safety. [However,] the enterprise of directors and the ingenuity of engineers . . . has tripled the working power of the locomotive and given us 60 miles an hour. . . .

Trevithick's greatest net load was 10 tons, that of Stevenson's first engine 30 . . . in 1831 90 tons, and now [1846] 1,200 tons. . . . Before 1829 the consumption of fuel was about 5 lbs. to carry one ton a mile and now can be ¼ lb. per ton mile.

Source: "Early Railroads," Railroad Gazette, *February 18, 1871, quoting an 1846 British article.*

Early Railroading: The First Conductor on the Pennsylvania Central

William Hambright, an old conductor on the Pennsylvania Central Road, who we are told is familiarly known throughout the State as "Cap," . . . has given to the Columbia (Pa.) Courant *some account of his experience.*[5]

Mr. Hambright commenced his career as conductor by taking the first train (horse cars) out of Lancaster in 1833, after which time he ran regularly, and has been employed nearly all the time since as passenger conductor on the Pennsylvania Central Railroad. He then acted as conductor, brakeman, and greaser, his compensation being $18 per month, which was considered good wages at that time. His train of horse cars would leave Lancaster at 5 o'clock P.M., and arrive in Philadelphia [some 75 miles] at 5 o'clock the next morning, making twelve hours for the journey, and the fare charged was $3.50.[6] Stoppages were frequent, fresh horses being employed every 15 or 20 miles.[7] At times they would be greatly detained by the severity of the weather, the winters in those times being much colder than at present.

[5]While I could not get a positive identification, William Henry Hambright was born in 1813 and appears to have lived until the mid-1880s.

[6]Since my 2014 *Rand McNally Atlas* (78 miles) and 2014 *AAA Tour Book* (71 miles) disagree, I have taken a middle number.

[7]One horse could easily pull multiple stagecoachlike passenger cars. When and for what type of passenger cars multiple horses were required is not known, horses lasting for only the first few years of railroad travel between cities. However, horse-drawn municipal travel (trolleys) lasted into the twentieth century.

There was no fire in the cars, and when a stop was made to change horses, the conductor would make for the nearest haystack or barn for the purpose of procuring straw or hay to strew upon the floor of the cars in order to make his passengers more comfortable, himself riding outside, the cars generally being packed so full that he could scarcely gain admission. Down grade the horses were generally kept at a full run. Horseflesh was very cheap then—sometimes five good animals could be purchased for one hundred dollars.

In the year 1835, a locomotive built by Norris was brought from Philadelphia to Lancaster, in wagons.[8] The wonderful machine was put upon the track, and fired up in the presence of an immense assemblage of spectators. It appears that the enterprise was not very successful, as it would run a short distance and then halt; then a number of muscular young men would lend their assistance by pushing. Every device was resorted to make the critter go, but to no purpose. Sometime after this three small engines were purchased in England and sent over, which answered all the purposes for which they were intended, one of which is [still] in use at the present time in York, Pennsylvania, sawing wood.

For the Harrisburg and Portsmouth Railroad, as it was then called, being laid upon strong pieces of wood, using flat bar iron, fastened down with spikes, it was necessary to carry a hammer and [spare] spikes on the engine. Very often spikes would come out at the end of the bar, causing the end of the same to stick up, which was termed "snake-heads," and the engineer would be obliged to stop and spike down before attempting to pass over. Before starting, information had to be given to the engineer where stops were to be made. To Mr. Hambright belongs the credit of inventing the bell and rope system for signaling engineers. He got permission from his "boss" to put his idea of the thing into practical shape. Procuring a rope and common door bell, he attached the latter near the engineer, no house [roof] being over the locomotive at the time, then stretching the rope over the top of the cars. Ever after that and

[8]The Norris Locomotive Works was located in Philadelphia. At one time it was the largest American manufacturer of steam locomotives, producing over a thousand between 1832 and 1866. For whatever reason its owners seem to have lost interest in the business or its best engineering people left to join Philadelphia's Baldwin Locomotive Works before the Civil War. In any event, following the Panic of 1857—which may have weakened the company—its design changes were minimal, and its business shrank once the war ended. See *Encyclopedia of North American Railroads*, Frey, *Encyclopedia of American Business History and Biography*, and Wikipedia.

up to the present time, bell ropes have been in vogue, though in more improved style than the one just described.

Conductors were not required to make reports at the end of each trip, as is now the practice; they would hand over the gold and silver—perhaps $200 or $300 or more—to the clerk, who would enter it in a book provided for the purpose somewhat in this [way]: "Conductor Hambright, so many dollars," and that was all the formality about it.[9]

Checks for baggage were not used, but when the cars arrived at Columbia[10] or Philadelphia, the conductor would open the car door for delivery of baggage, etc., to the passengers who crowded around, and secured their parcels by answering "Mine" to the conductor's interrogatory "Whose trunk is this?" which was kept up until all had disappeared. . . . Strange to say, there was not as much baggage lost then as now.

Very often the conductors would help the proprietors [along] the lines during harvest and assist at other labor when off duty.

Source: St. Paul Weekly Press, *April 27, 1871.*

Railroads Thirty-Two Years Ago

A correspondent of the *Springfield* [*Mass.*] *Republican says:*—

In 1839 it was a great achievement for Springfield to dispatch and receive from Boston [90 miles] a train each day: at present seven [passenger] trains pass daily over the road each way and five between Springfield and Albany. . . . The increase in the number of freight trains is equally noticeable. There is in every department of the road a discernible difference between the present and the past, when . . . old style tickets [were] white for first class passengers and colored for second class "double-decker" cars . . . the shell roofs of the cars that did run were hardly high enough to admit the tall men without stooping.

As the conductors never wore tall hats, they got along very well. The cars were heated with wood burning stoves, often only one to a car, and located in a break in a row of seats on one side of the passage way, midway from end to end. The cars were not heated by steam, and ventilators were then unknown.[11] There were no drawing room cars; Pullman's palace

[9] If $3.50 was charged and $245.00 was brought in, there would be seventy passengers.

[10] Did the article mean Lancaster?

[11] The necessity for effective ventilation would have been magnified by the early use of "dry" bathrooms in each passenger car.

[cars] might have been dreamed of [but hadn't been introduced]. Sleeping cars didn't ply between Springfield and Albany, not until some years later, between Boston and New York. In fact the "Owl" trains were not yet invented, and the idea of an express train from Boston to Albany in 6½ hours would have been set down as preposterous. The lightning train, which now makes that line, was put on at the beginning of the summer arrangement for 1871, and is becoming known to, and quite popular with, businessmen and tourists.

[There was] a night train or two over each section of the route[s]. "Bill" Dennison, in the days of yore, head freight conductor on the Springfield-Pittsfield [51 miles] rode in the "passenger car attached" to the last train: the boys used to call it the "buggy."[12] Bill was a good conductor, and the "buggy" convenient for passengers who didn't catch the passenger trains. In those halcyon days there was no double track, and the trains had appointments to meet [and] there were no telegraph lines to inform conductors of every train's departure from regular running time.

[Russian roulette, anyone?]

Source: "Railroads Thirty-Two Years Ago," Philadelphia Inquirer, *September 4, 1871.*

[12]The original reads "Pittsburg," but in the context of the story, Pitts*field,* Massachusetts, would be correct.

APPENDIX B

Management's Misfeasance and Malfeasance

Some Secondary Sources

In numerous sections of this book, I have alluded to the graft and corruption that permeated the Northern Pacific from J. Gregory Smith on down. However, researchers and readers searching for the proverbial "smoking gun" will not find it, as neither recordkeeping nor accounting were close to today's lowest minimal standards. In fact, the one historian who appears to have had the time and requisite financial understanding, Henrietta Larson, could not make heads or tails of what financially occurred. Although we follow the "innocent until proved guilty" philosophy for criminal activities, perhaps for Smith the most objective approach 145 years later is to assume he was ethically guilty, the burden of moral proof on his defenders. Needless to say, if someone pores through the ancient records and suggests my assumptions have been wrong, I shall be the first to apologize.

Lorenz P. Schrenk & Robert L. Frey (2010)

Unfortunately, there is good reason to believe that Smith's actions were sometimes unethical. They apparently included such things as over-charges, excessive reimbursements, and double leasing—all buried in complicated, intertwined deals. Although there were a number of efforts by aggrieved parties to bring legal action against him, none succeeded until 1875. Then an attorney named Charles Davenport was able to document numerous instances of fraud and abuse. In retrospect it seems clear that Smith was overcommitted with running and manipulating his Vermont companies and was too remote to be an effective manager of the Northern Pacific. He was too slow in making important decisions, allowed shoddy work, and grossly overspent the firm's resources.

. . . [Cooke] came to see Smith as a reckless spender who bought rail, locomotives and rolling stock long before they were needed and extended branch lines where they were unnecessary.[1] In addition, Cooke believed Smith was an incompetent and perhaps unethical manager.[2] Cooke was a proven financial manager of unquestioned ethics.

Source: Schrenk and Frey, Northern Pacific Pioneer Steam Era, *57.*

Kevin Graffagnino (1988)

After several years of delays and false starts, [Smith] also got construction of the [Northern Pacific] with some 500 miles of track laid during his years as president. Meanwhile, he soon came under attack for the same sort of financial tactics he had perfected in Vermont, as a growing number of observers charged him with extravagance and misuse of NP funds to enrich himself and his associates.[3]

Source: Graffagnino, Encyclopedia of American Business, History and Biography: Railroads in the Nineteenth Century, *364 (1988).*

Louis Tuck Renz (1980)

During the summer of 1871, the result of haste and poor judgment in the previous winter showed up[4] Between the [Thomson] Junction and Brainerd the grade [that] had been built on frozen ground began to

[1]In 1872, U.S. commissioners inspecting the Northern Pacific inventoried 68 locomotives in service, 18 passenger cars, and 1,500 freight cars. Even if these numbers included Dakota construction operations, the number was excessive for perhaps 400 miles of operational track in Minnesota and Dakota. See *Before Custer.*

[2]I would respectfully disagree with the word *perhaps*. By the end of 1871, Cooke was certain that Smith lying to him.

[3]As for the Vermont Central, Graffagnino writes of the same period, "While his administration continued to attract charges of corruption, nepotism, and mismanagement, Smith weathered every storm and retained control."

[4]Actually this occurred in April.

disappear into the marsh. Much reballasting and piling work had to be completed before a solid roadbed was available. The [rebuilding] work was completed by mid-August when the road east of Brainerd was accepted by the NP from the contractor.

Source: Renz, History of the Northern Pacific Railroad, *39–40.*

John L. Harnsberger (1956)

[As early as 1870] Ex-Governor [William R.] Marshall, who was being paid by Cooke to keep him informed . . . believed that the affairs of the Northern Pacific were not being managed either wisely or economically. He did not blame only General Spaulding but [also] the high officials of the company. He wrote Cooke that "I am afraid that your resources will not prove adequate to the scale of expenditures and costs that seem to prevail. I think an interested, responsible and thoroughly incorruptible officer of the company ought to be here constantly.[5]

[In 1871] A. B. Nettleton inspected a portion of the completed line and reported that much of it would have to be done over within a short time. The contractors used inadequate materials while at the same time charging the full price for doing the job properly. Moorhead believed that "the ambition is to construct many miles of the road within a given period, rather than build a good and sufficient business road. If such is the fact it will prove the downfall of the Enterprise."

Source: Harnsberger, Jay Cooke and Minnesota: The Formative Years of the Northern Pacific Railroad, *78–79.*

Henrietta M. Larson (1936)

One reason for Smith's neglect of the [NP] was that he was very heavily involved as the president . . . of the Vermont Central, which was still

[5]William Rainy Marshall (1825–96) was a highly popular governor of Minnesota, 1866–70. Cofounder of Minnesota Republican Party and wartime regimental commander. He fought numerous actions in the Dakota Wars (1862–63). His regiment was later sent south where he commanded a brigade at the battle of Nashville (December 1864), and later was brevetted a brigadier general. Wiped out by the Panic of 1893, he died in Pasadena, California. *Brevet Generals in Blue, Encyclopedia of Frontier Biography, National Cyclopedia of American Biography,* 10:64, and Wikipedia.

having an extremely difficult [financial] time. But this is not a sufficient explanation. Many executives have handled two heavy jobs. They have been able to do this by having an organization which could be entrusted with details. It is not impossible that Smith neglected the Northern Pacific for the reason that under Jay Cooke's scrutiny the road did not yield such great opportunities for irregular profits.

That the Northern Pacific was badly managed was obvious to all. . . . [Milnor Roberts] was an able and fair-minded man who was in the best position to observe how things were done. He held that the road could not be properly located or planned or economically and honestly built "until the total absence of sound system or under the curious spasmodic system now prevailing."

An accurate financial statement of the Northern Pacific at this time would throw some light on the question of irresponsibility of management—whether it grew out of incompetence, neglect or dishonesty [or all three]—but such a statement does not exist and could probably not be constructed from existing material. . . . [T]he road's accounting was very bad. It is impossible to derive from the information given even an approximate idea of the cost per mile of road built.

Source: Larson, Jay Cooke: Private Banker, *375–77.*

Ellis P. Oberholtzer (1906)

The early history of the construction of the Northern Pacific Railroad was marked by a good deal of scandal. While much of the trouble arose from local rivalries and jealousies, and flourished in rumors, the actual condition of affairs occasioned Mr. Cooke great anxiety. . . . That there was some actual dishonesty in the awards of contracts and the execution of them on the line of the Northern Pacific Railroad, both in Minnesota and on the Pacific Coast, is certain, but the jobbery was magnified and it was promptly and summarily brought to an end by Jay Cooke.[6]

William G. Moorhead was in Minnesota at this time [late 1870]. . . . He knew there was corrupt speculation in the building of the road and wished to wash his hands of the Northern and the firm which was constructing it.

---

[6]It was never brought to an end; rather, it was simply hidden better.

Despite this appearance of vigor [the fall of 1871] the charges of corruption and mismanagement continued. W. D. Washburn wrote from Minneapolis on December 9, 1871: "I will only say that if the Northern Pacific has the vitality and prestige to go along while being constructed under the auspices of a corrupt ring, and under its present management, it is strong indeed."[7]

That the Smith party [or the Vermont clique] was not competent to manage such an enterprise is very clear. It had no time to devote to the business of the road. It gave offices which should have been filled by men of tried scientific [technical] ability to politicians and paper generals. The president [Smith] and his associates were connected with the enterprise for [personal] gain and had the capacity to ruin it, as they did.

Source: Oberholtzer, Jay Cooke: Financier of the Civil War, *2:242–43, 244–45, 262–63, 265.*

Eugene V. Smalley (1883)

In reviewing [1870–73] . . . credit must be given to President Smith and directors for the zeal, enterprise, and far sighted sagacity.[8] [However,] the faults of their management were a too lavish use of money and a too hopeful view of the future. They acted as if their treasury would never run dry. The thirty million they expended, if carefully employed, even in that day of high prices, would have produced a better result than the 600 miles of road burdened with a floating debt of nearly five millions. They floated with the confident and extravagant times, without hearing the roar of the breakers ahead.

Source: Smalley, History of the Northern Pacific Railroad, *189.*

---

[7]William Drew Washburn (1831–1912), appointed chief government surveyor in Minnesota by Lincoln, leading entrepreneurial Minneapolis businessman, later four-term congressman and U.S. senator. Became millionaire with an eighty-room mansion. Wikipedia.

[8]By the time Smalley wrote this, he was economically dependent on the Northern Pacific and had long since distanced himself from Cooke, whom he blamed—naively, I think—for many of the railroad's problems. See *Dictionary of American Biography.*

APPENDIX C

Jay Cooke and the Great Chicago Fire

What Jay Cooke Thinks about the [October 8–10] Fire and Its Circumstances

Reaching the banking house of the well-known firm of Jay Cooke & Co., corner of Wall and Nassau streets, the reporter entered, presented the *Herald*'s compliments to Mr. Jay Cooke, and asked for a few moments conversation, which Mr. Cooke most willingly granted.

Reporter—Do you think, Mr. Cooke, that this news from Chicago will have a very serious effect on the financial and commercial affairs of this city [New York]?

Mr. Cooke—Oh, it must have some, sir; it must have some; but nothing very serious, I think. I do not anticipate any great calamities as far as we are concerned here, or as far as the business interests of the country at large are concerned.

Reporter—What do you think the immediate results will be?

Mr. Cooke—Well, you see, some of the insurance companies will undoubtedly have to go under. Many others will not, but they will be looking for money to pay up their liabilities. Then some of

The Banks and Bears

will hold tight and make money as tight as possible; of course you know the effect of that. An attempt may be made—I shouldn't wonder if it would—to create a panic; but I don't think that it will be very successful. The fire will stop the decline in the grain market. Grain has been steady on the decline for some time past.[1] This will stop that; in fact, grain has gone right up again today.

Reporter—How about the banks, Mr. Cooke?

Mr. Cooke—The banks will certainly feel panicky for a few days perhaps; but it will be nothing—nothing. The banks always anticipate a panic. They, to be sure of being on the safe side, always prepare for a panic but when they find—as they will find—that there is no cause for alarm they will resume their old aspect and all will go on smoothly again. During the brief season it lasts, the ripple will touch everything.

It is like a small fire in a building; the fire itself may do much harm, but the water, in endeavoring to extinguish it, will slightly damage everything in the house.

Reporter—What do you think of the prospects of poor Chicago, Mr. Cooke?

Mr. Cooke—Oh, you know, it would be strange if the fortunes of that city were not seriously impaired by this terrible disaster; but I feel certain that all is not lost to her. I think she will do a good business still, even in her crippled position. Have you heard [if] many of the [grain] elevators have been spared?

Reporter—It is so stated, sir.

Mr. Cooke—Well, if so, Chicago will continue to do a large business in grain, even now, with the elevators that remain.

Reporter—What about the chance of Chicago being rebuilt?

Mr. Cooke—The chance is certainly, sir. Her situation is most advantageous, and, therefore, the base, untenanted real estate is too valuable to let lie idle. Why, the greater part of the real estate of Chicago is owned by men whom I know in New York, Boston, London and Liverpool. Those cities are more deeply interested in Chicago than in any other American city. The prosperity of New York is dependent in a great measure on the grain trade of Chicago; and while this is the case, and while the real estate of the burned city is so valuable in itself, there is no doubt of it being rebuilt. The rebuilding, I feel certain, will in point of rapidity and completeness surpass anything that this country has witnessed.[2] Chicago has been a great overgrown boy. Every boy must have his eye teeth cut. Every American city must have its eye teeth cut

[1]A particularly interesting comment, seeing that farms growing grain were a key to Northern Pacific immigration efforts.

[2]Cooke could not have been more accurate.

by fire. And the operation does the city good. You remember when our own dilapidated old New York was burned off all around here and away clear down to the Battery? Think of what New York looked like before that burning, and see what it is now. Same way with old wooden San Francisco. Same way now with Chicago. It has just had its eye teeth cut by fire. And the process will be of service to it. When it is rebuilt—which it will be in an astonishingly short space of time—it will be improved to a vast extent every way.

Reporter—Meanwhile, Mr. Cooke, while Chicago is being rebuilt, the grain-trade of the West must necessarily have an outlet somewhere. I should think some of the other Western cities already in proper trim will have a chance now to improve themselves by taking a share of the work Chicago has monopolized?

Mr. Cooke—That is true, sir; Milwaukee will be apt to receive the trade of Southern Wisconsin and Northern Illinois. The trade of Eastern Illinois and all that section will go to Toledo.

Reporter—What about Northern Iowa and the surrounding section? That trade, I suppose, will fall to Duluth?

Mr. Cooke—Precisely, sir. A splendid trade it is, and growing every day; and Duluth has so many natural advantages that it must necessarily retain the trade of that section once it has it.

Reporter—I heard a gentleman remark before now that little Duluth would one day become one of the most thriving and prosperous towns in the West. Perhaps its day has come sooner than its friends expected.

Mr. Cooke—Yes, perhaps so; but I don't think anybody, even in Duluth, will rejoice over the immediate cause of its good fortune.

Reporter—Oh, I hope not, sir; but, then, you know the old adage: "it's a bad wind that blows nobody any good"—even when it blows a fire.

Mr. Cooke smiled and pointed to the patent indicator, saying:—"At work already, you see."[3] The indicator indicated that while the reporter and Mr. Cooke were chatting, the price of gold had fallen one percent [clearly indicating that public confidence was rising].

Source: Duluth Minnesotian, *October 21, 1871.*

---

[3]A "patent indicator" likely was an early form of a stock market ticker.

Bibliography

Primary Sources

Ball, Edward. Report concerning the 1871 Yellowstone Surveying Expedition from Fort Ellis, Montana, December 10, 1871. MF-339, reel #1, Montana Historical Society, Helena.

Brackett, George Augustus. Miscellaneous papers, catalog # P1547, Minnesota Historical Society, St. Paul. Correspondence, "Remembrances," etc., relating to 1906 surveyors' reunion.

Campbell, Lafayette E. 1871 Diary. American Heritage Center, Collection #10435, University of Wyoming, Laramie.

Canfield, Thomas Hawley. *The Life of Thomas Hawley Canfield . . . and His Connection with the Early History of the Northern Pacific Railroad.* Burlington, Vt.: privately printed, 1889.

———. *Reads Like a Fairy Tale: The Early History of the Northern Pacific Railroad.* Fargo: North Dakota Institute for Regional Studies, North Dakota State University.

Coffin, Charles Carlton. *The Seat of Empire.* New York: John W. Lovell, 1870.

Cooke, Jay. "Jay Cooke's Memoir." 1894. Unpublished and unedited; microfilm, Minnesota Historical Society, St. Paul.

Cooke, Jay & Co. *The Northern Pacific Railroad's Land Grant and the Future Business of the Road.* Philadelphia: privately printed, 1870.

———. *The Northern Pacific Railroad: Its Route, Resources, Progress, and Business.* Philadelphia: privately printed, ca. 1871.

De Trobriand, Philippe Regis. *Military Life in Dakota: The Journal of Philippe Regis De Trobriand.* Trans. Lucille M. Kane. St. Paul: Alvord Memorial Commission, 1951.

Hone, Philip. *The Diary of Philip Hone.* Ed. Bayard Tuckerman. 2 vols. New York: Dodd, Mead, 1889).

Irvine, Javan Bradley. Correspondence, diaries, press clippings, obituaries, and miscellaneous, South Dakota State Archives, Cultural Heritage Center, Pierre.

Jordan, Edward C. *Account of Edward C. Jordan's Experiences in the West during the Construction of the Central Pacific and the Northern Pacific Railroad,* ca. 1906. Courtesy Mark Jordan, Gorham, Me.

———. Diary, May 1870–May 1871, P-2245, Minnesota Historical Society, St. Paul.

———. Miscellaneous Letters, 1870–73. Courtesy of Mark Jordan.

Latrobe, Benjamin H. "Engineering: The Introduction of Railways." *Railroad Gazette*, April 30, 1870.

McClernand, Lt. Edward J. *On Time for Disaster: The Rescue of Custer's Command.* 1926; reprint, Lincoln: University of Nebraska Press, 1989.

———. *With the Indian and the Buffalo in Montana, 1870–1878.* Glendale, Calif.: A. H. Clark, 1969.

"The Northern Pacific Railroad System." *Harper's Weekly*, January 21, 1871.

Northern Pacific Railroad. Annual Reports, 1869–1876. Minnesota Historical Society, St. Paul, microfilm 369.

———. Clippings and Scrapbooks, 1866–1904, Office of the Secretary of the Northern Pacific. Minnesota Historical Society, M-522.

———. Secretary's Department. Unregistered letters received and related records, undated and 1864–1876. M-459, Minnesota Historical Society, St. Paul.

Poole, DeWitt Clinton. *Among the Sioux in Dakota: Eighteen Months' Experience as an Indian Agent.* St. Paul: Minnesota Historical Society Press, 1881.

Relf, Richard. *Narrative of Richard Relf.* George A. Brackett Miscellaneous Papers, catalog no. P-1547, Minnesota Historical Society, St. Paul.

Roberts, William Milnor. Autobiography, two drafts, 1874. Collection 783 (Roberts Papers), series 1, box 1, files 4 and 5. Burlingame Library, Montana State University, Bozeman.

———. Correspondence, 1871–74. Roberts Papers, series 2, box 2, folders 4–5.

———. *Down the Valley of the Yellowstone: Extracts from the [1871] Letters of. . .*, Roberts Papers, series 6, box 10.

———. Field Diary of 1871 Reconnaissance, October 30–November 20, 1871. Roberts Papers, series 3, box 4, folders 1–4.

———. Journal, August 18–September 1, 1871. Roberts Papers, series 3, box 3, folders 18–19.

———. *Special Report of a Reconnaissance of the Route for the Northern Pacific Railroad between Lake Superior and Puget Sound via the Columbia River . . .* Philadelphia: McLaughlin Brothers, 1869.

Rosser, Thomas Lafayette. *Across Dakota and up the Yellowstone, General Rosser's Report* [1871]. Roberts Papers (see above), series 6, box 10.

———. Diary for 1871, Alderman Library, 1171-g-h-j, box 16.

Smalley, Eugene Virgil. *The Great Northwest: A Guide Book and Itinerary for the Use of Tourists and Travelers over the Lines of the Northern Pacific Railroad . . .* St. Paul: Riley Brothers, 1886.

———. *History of the Northern Pacific Railroad.* 1883; New York: Arno Press, 1975.

Surgeon General's Office. *A Report on Barracks and Hospitals with Descriptions of Military Posts.* Circular no. 4, December 5, 1870.

Topping, E. S. *Chronicles of the Yellowstone.* 1884; reprint, Minneapolis: Ross & Haines, 1968.

U.S. Department of the Interior. *Annual Report of the Commissioner of [the U.S. Office] of Indian Affairs for the Year* . . . Washington: Government Printing Office, 1867–74.

U.S. Department of War. *Annual Report for* . . . Washington: Government Printing Office, 1866–74.

———. Department of the Dakota. *Outline Descriptions [and Detailed Maps] of the Posts in the Military Division of the Missouri Commanded by Lt. Gen. P. H. Sheridan* . . . Chicago, 1876.

———. *Official Army Register for January* . . . Washington: Government Printing Office, 1869–74.

Whistler, Joseph Nelson Garland. *Report of the Expedition Accompanying the Engineers of the Northern Pacific Railroad* . . . Microfilm 751, MMDM 1871, Montana Historical Society.

Winser, Henry J. *The Great Northwest: A Guide-Book and Itinerary for the Use of Tourists and Travelers over the Lines of the Northern Pacific Railroad.* New York: G. P. Putnam's Sons, 1883.

Secondary Sources

Books

Bain, David Haward. *Empire Express: Building the First Transcontinental Railroad.* New York: Viking Press, 1999.

Brown, John K. *The Baldwin Locomotive Works, 1831–1915: A Study in American Industrial Practice.* 1995; reprint, Baltimore: Johns Hopkins University Press, 2001.

Brown, Mark H. *The Plainsmen of the Yellowstone.* New York: G. P. Putnam's Sons, 1961.

Burlingame, Merrill G. *The Montana Frontier.* 1941; reprint, Bozeman: Montana State University Press, 1980.

Bursack, William W., with Jerry R. Masters. "The Northern Pacific before the Last Spike: Locating the Route." 2004, unpublished.

Bushong, Millard K., and Dean M. *Fightin' Tom Rosser, C.S.A.* Shippensburg, Pa.: Beidel Printing House, 1983.

Chittenden, Hiram Martin. *History of Early Steamboat Navigation on the Missouri River: [The] Life and Adventures of Joseph La Barge.* 2 vols. New York: Francis P. Harper, 1903.

Clodfelter, Michael. *The Dakota War: The United States Army vs. the Sioux, 1862–1865.* Jefferson, N.C.: McFarland, 1998.

Cooper, Bruce C., ed. *The Classic Western American Railroad Routes.* New York: Chartwell Books, 2010.

Crutchfield, James A., ed. *The Settlement of America: Encyclopedia of Westward Expansion from Jamestown to the Closing of the Frontier.* Armonk, N.Y.: M. E. Sharpe, 2011.

Cullum, George W. *Biographical Register of the Officers and Graduates of the United States Military Academy.* Boston: Houghton Mifflin, 1891.

DeBarthe, Joe. *Life and Adventures of Frank Grouard.* Ed. Edgar I. Stewart. Norman: University of Oklahoma Press, 1958.

Denig, Edwin Thompson. *Five Indian Tribes of the Upper Missouri: Sioux, Arickara, Crees, Assiniboines, Crows.* Ed. John C. Ewers. 1961; reprint, Norman: University of Oklahoma Press, 1989.

Ege, Robert J. *"Tell Baker to Strike Them Hard": Incident on the Marias, 23 Jan. 1870.* Bellevue, Neb.: Old Army Press, 1970.

Engelhardt, Carroll. *Gateway to the Northern Plains: Railroads and the Birth of Fargo and Moorhead.* Minneapolis: University of Minnesota Press, 2007.

Ewers, John C. *Indian Life on the Upper Missouri.* 1968; reprint, Norman: University of Oklahoma Press, 1988.

Flynn, John T. *Men of Wealth.* New York: Simon and Schuster, 1941.

Fox, William F. *Regimental Losses in the Civil War: A Treatise on the Extent and Nature of the Mortuary Losses in the Union Regiments.* 1898; reprint, Dayton: Morningside Press, 1985.

Frey, Robert Lovell, ed. *Encyclopedia of American Business History and Biography: Railroads in the Nineteenth Century.* New York: Facts on File, 1998.

Gray, John S. *Custer's Last Campaign: Mitch Boyer and the Little Big Horn Reconstructed.* Lincoln: University of Nebraska Press, 1991.

Greene, Jerome A. *Fort Randall on the Missouri, 1856–1892.* Pierre: South Dakota State Historical Society Press, 2005.

Haines, Aubrey L. *The Yellowstone Story: A History of Our First National Park.* 2 vols. Niwot, Colo.: Yellowstone Association for Natural Science, History and Education, 1996.

Hanson, Joseph Mills. *The Conquest of the Missouri: Being the Story of the Life and Exploits of Captain Grant Marsh.* 1916; reprint, Mechanicsburg, Penn.: Stackpole Books, 2003.

Harnsberger, John L. *Jay Cooke and Minnesota: The Formative Years of the Northern Pacific Railroad, 1868–1873.* 1956; reprint, New York: Arno Press, 1981.

Hassrick, Royal B. *The Sioux.* 1964; reprint, Norman: University of Oklahoma Press, 1989.

Hedren, Paul L. *Traveler's Guide to the Great Sioux War.* Helena: Montana Historic Society Press, 1996.

Heitman, Francis B. *Historical Register and Dictionary of the United States Army . . . , from September 29, 1789, to March 2, 1903.* 1903; reprint, Urbana: University of Illinois Press, 1965.

Houston, E. Lina. *Early History of Gallatin County.* Bozeman: privately printed, 1933.

Howard, Joseph Kinsey. *Strange Empire: A Narrative of the Northwest.* 1952; reprint, St. Paul: Minnesota Historical Society, 1994.

Hoxie, Fredrick E. *Parading through History: The Making of the Crow Nation in America, 1805–1935.* Cambridge: Cambridge University Press, 1995.

Hunt, Roger D. *Brevet Generals in Blue.* Gaithersburg, Md.: Olde Soldier Books, 1990.

Hutton, Paul Andrew. *Phil Sheridan and His Army.* 1985; reprint, Lincoln: University of Nebraska Press, 1989.

Innis, Ben. *A Chronological Record of Events at the Missouri-Yellowstone Confluence Area from 1805 to 1895.* Williston, N.D.: Fort Buford Sixth Infantry Regiment Association, 1971.

Jones, Robert C. *The Central Vermont Railway: A Yankee Tradition,* vol. 1, "*The Early Years, 1830–1886.*" Silverton, Colo.: Sundance Books, 1981.

Josephson, Matthew. *The Robber Barons: The Great American Capitalists, 1861–1901.* 1934; reprint, Norwalk, Conn.: Easton Press, 1987.

Kirby, Richard Shelton, and Philip Gustave Laurson. *The Early Years of Modern Civil Engineering.* New Haven: Yale University Press, 1932.

Krech, Shepard, III. *The Ecological Indian: Myth and History.* New York: W. W. Norton, 1999.

Lamar, Howard. *New Encyclopedia of the American West.* New Haven: Yale University Press, 1998.

Larson, Henrietta M. *Jay Cooke: Private Banker.* Cambridge: Harvard University Press, 1936.

Larson, Robert W. *Red Cloud: Warrior-Statesman of the Lakota Sioux.* Norman: University of Oklahoma Press, 1997.

Lass, William E. *A History of Steamboating on the Upper Missouri River.* Lincoln: University of Nebraska Press, 1962.

———. *Navigating the Missouri: Steamboating on Nature's Highway.* Norman: Arthur H. Clark, 2008.

Linklater, Andro. *Measuring America: How an Untamed Wilderness Shaped the United States and Fulfilled the Promise of Democracy.* New York: Walker, 2002.

Lubetkin, M. John. *Before Custer: The 1872 Yellowstone Surveys.* Norman: University of Oklahoma Press, 2015.

———. *Custer and the 1873 Yellowstone Survey.* Norman: University of Oklahoma Press, 2013.

———. *Jay Cooke's Gamble: The Northern Pacific Railroad, the Sioux, and the Panic of 1873.* Norman: University of Oklahoma Press, 2006.

MacDonald, John G. "History of Navigation on the Yellowstone River." Master's thesis, Montana State University, Bozeman, 1950.

Malles, Ed. *Bridge Building in Wartime: Colonel Wesley Brainerd's Memoir of the 50th New York Volunteer Engineers.* Knoxville: University of Tennessee Press, 1997.

Malone, Dumas, et al. *Dictionary of American Biography.* 24 vols. Includes 2 supplements. New York: Charles Scribner's Sons, 1928–44.

McNeill, William H. *Plagues and Peoples.* Garden City, N.Y.: Doubleday, 1976.

Meigs, Cornelia Lynde. *Railroad West: A Novel.* Boston: Little, Brown, 1937.

Middletown, William D., George M. Smerk, and Roberta L. Diehl, eds. *Encyclopedia of North American Railroads.* Bloomington: Indiana University Press, 2007.

The National Cyclopedia of American Biography. 61 vols. New York: James T. White, 1898–1982.

Nelson, Ann M. *The Northern Pacific Railroad in Brainerd.* Crow Wing Historical Society [Brainerd], Minnesota, ca. 2002.

Oberholtzer, Ellis Paxson. *Jay Cooke, Financier of the Civil War.* 2 vols. 1907; reprint, New York: Augustus M. Kelley, 1968.

Powell, William H. *List of Officers of the Army of the United States from 1799 to 1900.* 1900; reprint, Detroit: Gale Research, 1967.

Prucha, Francis Paul. *The Great Father: The United States Government and the American Indians.* Lincoln: University of Nebraska Press, 1984.

Renz, Louis Tuck. *The Construction of the Northern Pacific Railroad.* Walla Walla, Wash.: privately printed, 1973.

———. *The History of the Northern Pacific Railroad.* Fairfield, Wash.: Ye Galleon Press, 1980.

Riegel, Robert E. *The Story of the Western Railroads.* New York: Macmillan, 1926.

Robinson, Doane. *A History of the Dakota or Sioux Indians from Their Earliest Traditions and First Contact with White Men to the Final Settlement of the Last of Them upon Reservations and Consequent Abandonment of the Old Tribal Life.* 1904; reprint, Minneapolis: Ross and Hayes, 1956.

Robinson, Elwyn B. *History of North Dakota.* Lincoln: University of Nebraska Press, 1966.

Sandburg, Carl. *Abraham Lincoln: The War Years.* 4 vols. New York: Harcourt, Brace, 1939.

Schneider, Bill. *Montana's Yellowstone River.* Helena: Montana Magazine, 1985.

Schrenk, Lorenz P., and Robert L. Frey. *The Northern Pacific Pioneer Steam Era, 1870–1905.* Minneapolis: Monad, 2010.

Sharp, Paul F. *Whoop-Up Country: The Canadian-American West, 1865–1885.* 1955; reprint, Norman: University of Oklahoma Press, 1973.

Sheridan, Lt. Gen. Philip H. *Record of Engagements with Hostile Indians within the Military Division of the Missouri from 1868 to 1882.* Chicago: Military Division of the Missouri, 1882.

Sinclair, Angus. *Development of the Railroad Engine: A History of the Growth of the Locomotive.* 1907; reprint, Cambridge: MIT Press, 1970.

Smith, Phyllis. *Bozeman and the Gallatin Valley, a History.* Helena, Mont.: Falcon Press, 1996.

Somsen, Chelle. "Dakota Resources: The Javan Bradley Irvine Papers at the South Dakota State Historical Society." *South Dakota History* 37, no. 2 (Summer 2007).

Stearns, Harold Joseph. *A History of the Upper Musselshell Valley of Montana [to 1920].* Harlowton, Mont.: Times-Clarion, 1966.

Stewart, Edgar I. *Penny-an-Acre Empire in the West.* Norman: University of Nebraska Press, 2004.

Sully, Langdon. *No Tears for the General: The Life of Alfred Sully, 1821–1879.* Palo Alto, Calif.: American West, 1974.

Thornton, Russell. *American Indian Holocaust and Survival: A Population History since 1492.* Norman: University of Oklahoma Press, 1987.

Thrapp, Dan L. *Encyclopedia of Frontier Biography.* 3 vols. 1988; reprint, Lincoln: University of Nebraska Press, 1991.

Topping, E. *Chronicles of the Yellowstone.* 1884; reprint, Minneapolis: Ross and Haines, 1968.

Tucker, Glen Edgar. *Hancock the Superb.* 1960; reprint, Dayton: Morningside Press, 1980.

U.S. Department of Commerce, U.S. Bureau of the Census. *Historical Statistics of the United States: Colonial Times to 1970*. Washington: Government Printing Office, 1975.

U.S. Department of Interior. *Biographical and Historical Index of American Indians and Persons Involved in Indian Affairs*. Boston: G. K. Hall, 1966.

U.S. Military Academy. *Annual Reunion of the Association of the Graduates of the United States Military Academy*. West Point, N.Y., annual publication.

U.S. Works Projects Administration (WPA), Federal Writers Project. *Minnesota: A State Guide*. 1938; reprint, New York: Hastings House, 1954.

———. *WPA Guide to 1930s Montana*. 1939; reprint, Tucson: University of Arizona Press, 1994.

———. *WPA Guide to 1930s North Dakota*. 1938; reprint, Bismarck: State Historical Society of North Dakota, 1990.

Utley, Robert M. *Frontier Regulars: The United States Army and the Indian, 1866–1891*. New York: Macmillan, 1973.

———. *The Indian Frontier of the American West*. 1984; reprint, Albuquerque: University of New Mexico Press, 1993.

———. *The Lance and the Shield: The Life and Times of Sitting Bull*. New York: Henry Holt, 1993.

Veenendaal, Augustus J., Jr. *The Saint Paul & Pacific Railroad: An Empire in the Making*. DeKalb: Northern Illinois University Press, 1999.

Vestel, Stanley. *Sitting Bull: Champion of the Sioux*. 1932; reprint, Norman: University of Oklahoma Press, 1989.

Warner, Ezra J. *Generals in Blue: Lives of the Union Commanders*. Baton Rouge: Louisiana State University Press, 1964.

White, John H. *A History of the American Locomotive, Its Development: 1830–1880*. 1968; reprint, New York: Dover, 1979.

White, Richard. *Railroaded: The Transcontinentals and the Making of Modern America*. New York: W. W. Norton, 2011.

Wishart, David J., ed. *Encyclopedia of the Great Plains*. Lincoln: University of Nebraska Press, 2004.

Withington, Sidney, Arthur B. Darling, and Frederick G. Kilgour. *Engineering in History*. 1956; reprint, New York: Dover Publications, 1990.

Articles

Bray, Kingsley M. "Teton Sioux Population History, 1655–1881." *Nebraska History* 75 (Summer 1994): 165–88.

DeLand, Charles E. "Basil Clement (Claymore): The Mountain Trappers." *South Dakota Historical Collections* 11 (1922): 245–389.

Farr, William E. "Going to Buffalo: Indian Hunting Migrations across the Rocky Mountains." *Montana* 53–54, nos. 4 and 2 (Winter and Spring 2003–2004): 2–21, 26–43.

Hamilton, James M. "History of Fort Ellis." Speech, May 12, 1933, Burlingame Library, Montana State University, Bozeman.

Hammer, Kenneth M. "Railroads and the Frontier Garrisons of Dakota Territory." *North Dakota History* 46, no. 3 (Summer 1979): 24–34.

Harnsberger, John L. "Railroads to the Northern Plains, 1870–1872." *North Dakota Quarterly* 27 (Summer 1959): 53–61.

Hutton, Paul. "Phil Sheridan's Pyrrhic Victory: The Piegan Massacre, Army Politics, and the Transfer Debate." *Montana* 32, no. 2 (Spring 1982): 32–43.

Lubetkin, M. John. "Captain Javan B. Irvine and the 1871 Eastern Yellowstone Survey." *South Dakota History* 37, no. 3 (Summer 2007). 125–62.

———. "The Forgotten Yellowstone Surveying Expeditions of 1871: W. Milnor Roberts and the Northern Pacific Railroad in Montana." *Montana* 52, no. 4 (Winter 2002): 32–47.

Masters, Jerry R. "Routes across the Rockies." *Mainstreeter* 21, no. 3 (Summer 2002): 4–9, 25.

Mattison, Ray H. "Fort Rice: North Dakota's First Missouri River Military Post." *North Dakota History* 20, no. 20 (April 1963): 87–108.

Sibbald, John R. "Frontier Inebriates with Epaulets." *Montana* 19 (Summer 1969): 50–57.

Newspapers and Other Periodicals

Army and Navy Journal, weekly, May 1869–July 1874

Bozeman Avant-Courier, weekly, September 1871–January 1872

Duluth Minnesotian, weekly, January 1870–December 1871

Frank Leslie's Illustrated Newspaper, weekly, September 1870–February 1872

Greasy Grass, Custer Battlefield Historical & Museum Association, annual, 1985 to current

Harper's Weekly, January 1871–December 1873

Helena Herald, daily and weekly, January 1869–January 1872

Journal of the Little Big Horn Associates, biannual, June 1987 to current

Mainstreeter, quarterly, 1995 to current, Northern Pacific Railway Historical Association

Minneapolis Tribune, daily, selected dates 1871–72

New York Herald, daily, June 1871–January 1872

New York Times, daily, Spring 1869–Winter 1871

Northwest Magazine, monthly, January 1883–December 1889

Philadelphia Evening Bulletin, daily, July 1871 and January 1872

Philadelphia Inquirer, daily, July 1871–January 1872

Railroad Gazette, weekly, January 1870–December 1873

Sioux City Journal, daily, May 1871–January 1872

St. Paul Pioneer, daily and weekly, January 1870–January 1872

St. Paul Press, daily and weekly, 1869–71

Acknowledgments

This book is part of a trilogy about the Northern Pacific Railroad's efforts to build the nation's second transcontinental railroad. Much of this volume's research was completed in the winter of 2008–2009 when the nasty recession came along and shelved everything. Three years later, Bob Clark, the editor-in-chief of the Arthur H. Clark Company, a University of Oklahoma imprint, reignited the project, but then left for a publishing position in the Northwest.

Since then Chuck Rankin has overseen *Custer and the 1873 Yellowstone Survey* (2103), *Before Custer: Surveying the Yellowstone* (2015), and now *Road to War: The 1871 Yellowstone Surveys.* His common sense, diverse historical interests and knowledge, and his sense of humor have made these three volumes and *Jay Cooke's Gamble* (2006) possible. Equally important is that art of producing a good read.

For all three books, I have tried to follow the example of Japanese film director Akira Kurosawa who, in his classic *Rashomon,* has four people tell the story of a rape-murder. To tell this story, I have let the participants describe the Northern Pacific's efforts to explore, design, and build the technically difficult route from Duluth, Minnesota, across the Dakota Territory and present-day Bismarck and on to Bozeman, Montana.

This latter leg, some 585 railroad miles, represented the remaining ecological heart of "intransigent" Sioux and Northern Cheyenne under Sitting Bull. The Hunkpapa Sioux leader faced two equally unpleasant options: fight and be destroyed or voluntarily live on reservations and watch the Northern Pacific operate in the Yellowstone Valley and thereby let buffalo hunters "harvest" the remaining northern buffalo herds.

Today, some 1870–71 newspapers are available online. However, when I began my research (1995), all period newspapers, magazines, military documents, and business correspondence could be read only on microfilm. Contemporary letters and diaries invariably required manually searching through indexes and files, photocopying them, and then reading them with a magnifying glass and taking notes and highlighting with fluorescent markers.

Difficult as this often proved, without the help of invariably friendly personnel (over two hundred) at university libraries, state historical societies, museums, historical associations, and government institutions, I never would have reached first base. Thank you all, particularly the Fairfax and Arlington County, Virginia, public library systems. Also Alderman Special Collections Library, University of Virginia–Charlottesville; Burlingame Special Collections Library, Montana State University–Bozeman; Harvard University's Houghton Reading Room, Cambridge; the Library of Congress and National Archives in Washington, D.C., and Silver Spring, Md.; Minnesota Historical Society, St. Paul; Montana State Historic Society, Helena; North Dakota State Historic Society, Bismarck; South Dakota State Historic Society, Pierre; U.S. Army Military Academy, Archives and Special Collections Department, West Point, N.Y.; and the U.S. Army Military History Institute, Carlisle, Penn.

To those I have inadvertently skipped, my apologies. Additionally, my thanks to members of the Custer Battlefield Historical and Museum Association, the Little Big Horn Associates, and the Northern Pacific Railway Historical Association. Each organization holds annual conferences, publishes quality magazines, and involves intelligent, well-informed, and supportive individuals.

As a reader often frustrated by good books with bad maps (or none), I am particularly appreciative of the work of Vicki Trego Hill of El Paso, who took maps (all from 1871–72 and 1883) and my rough directions and turned them into something first rate.

Again, hats off to my son, William Andrew Lubetkin, who has painstakingly brought this "old man" into the electronic world of the 1990s—perhaps even the twenty-first century. I especially wish to thank my wife, Linda, a retired high school English teacher, who spent hundreds of hours making critical suggestions and comments and deciphering the 1871 hieroglyphic-like writing of Capt. Javan Irvine. Without her skills, patience, and good humor, this book couldn't have been completed.

Index

References to illustrations appear in italic type; references to maps appear in bold type.